Isamb rd

A Ra

Young Isambard, Volume 1

Written and illustrated by

Mr. Robert Guidi

ISAMBARD
& the
AMULETS OF RA

Written and illustrated by Robert Guidi.

ISBN: 978-0-9955968-4-9 (paperback)
ISBN: 978-0-9955968-5-6 (eBook)
ISBN: 978-0-9955968-6-3 (audiobook)
Buy all formats at robertguidi.com/shop

Thanks to:

Cover design: TwinArt (trifbookdesign)
Editor: Andrew Noakes (History Quill)
ARC readers: Nic and Lynda

1812 – Borodino, Russia

In the sudden calm, Grant became aware of a familiar, intoxicating fear. She was about to move into the most dangerous part of the mission and had no idea what to expect.

Though she had watched and memorised the process up to this point, she had never seen inside Napoleon's tent. She followed The Keeper in through the drapes and paused in a kind of ante-chamber designed to keep the cold out – behind her the tent-flaps had closed and in front of her a heavy curtain blocked the way. This was Grant's moment. With hardly a break in her step, she deftly swapped the box on the tray for the replica she had hidden in her belt and continued through the heavy drapes, adjusting the stolen uniform as she went.

Grant was entering the lion's den.

Inside, the tent was alive with candlelight. The assembled crowd of generals continued to discuss the maps and charts that covered a large table in the centre. Only Napoleon looked up at the newcomers, staring directly at Grant with burning eyes. Finally, the Emperor spoke.

"Gentlemen, I approve of General Sorbier's proposal to advance towards the Western pass, beginning at sunrise," the Emperor said, looking at each of the assembled generals in turn. "Make it so."

The group broke up and left the room in twos and threes, talking in low voices as they went. After a few moments there were only three people left in the room – Grant, the mysterious Keeper and the most powerful man in Europe.

Napoleon stood at the head of the table, leaning forward onto his fists, his undivided attention now focused on the Keeper.

"Maximilien, thank you for coming."

The Keeper replied with an attempted smile, his jaw stiff and unnatural.

"This is the most important campaign so far, Maximilien," Napoleon said as he approached. "Russia holds the key to our defeat of the English and the completion of our European Empire. But I could not have got this far without you. Or this little box." The Emperor stared at the object on Grant's tray, reaching and taking it with a look of wonder in his eyes.

The Keeper produced his key and placed it on the silver tray. Grant did the same, taking the stolen key from around her neck. Napoleon twisted his own into place on the front face of the small, plain box, then twisted the other two keys on its side faces. The lock popped and the lid jolted open a fraction.

Napoleon narrowed his eyes and lifted the lid. Grant stared ahead unflinching, as the world came to a standstill.

"What is the meaning of this?" Bonaparte hissed.

The Keeper stiffened, his eyes flashing down to the box.

"Your Excellency?"

"Where is the amulet?" Bonaparte asked, spinning the box around on the tray.

The Keeper reached out, his hand moving slowly, as if trying to catch a butterfly.

The box was empty.

Bonaparte knocked the tray to the ground, where it clattered for a moment before coming to a rest. He approached, rage burning across his face, his gaze moving first to the Keeper then to Grant.

"Well Corporal. You were the last one to hold the amulet. Perhaps you can tell us where it is."

"With all due respect, your Excellency," Grant began, making no effort to hide the terror in her voice. "Although I was the last to hold the box, I regret that I was not able to check its contents when I received it."

The sound of a drawn blade cut the air and Grant saw the flash of a knife.

"So if I cut you in half, you're saying I wouldn't find my amulet inside?" Bonaparte asked, pressing the blade into Grant's right cheek - she felt hot blood trickle down her face like a thick tear.

"Need I check?" he asked.

Grant didn't answer, instead allowing the beads of sweat which glistened on her forehead to tell Napoleon all he needed to know. Napoleon moved the tip of the dagger to the dry blood at her shoulder. Grant thought back to the soldier she had shot for this uniform.

"Recent wound?" the Emperor asked.

"Yes sir, sniper fire, sir, your Excellency," she said with a sharp nod of the head.

The Emperor paused and stepped back. A crooked smile flashed across his face.

"What do you think, Maximilien? Traitor, or honest gun?"

"Your Excellency, I..."

"Yes, I agree, honest gun. But then that only leaves you. After all, you are called the Keeper for a reason. Because you 'keep' the amulet. That's your job - to keep. Where are you keeping the amulet now, Maximilien?" Bonaparte asked, hitching himself up to rest on the edge of the map table. He plucked an apple from the bowl on the table and cracked it in half with the knife.

"Your Excellency, I'm sure there is a perfectly reasonable explanation for this..."

"Yes. Yes I'm sure, perfectly. I just can't imagine what it is."

Napoleon bit a segment of apple in half and chomped on it with an amused smile. "Unfortunately, I'm rather attached to that amulet as you know. Bit of a lucky charm if you will – seems to help me win all these battles," he continued, waving the knife. "Not sure how we'll get along without it." He flashed a smile at the Keeper. "What to do? You already owe me your life, so I can't take that from you again."

There was a pause. Suddenly Napoleon punched the point of the dagger into the table. The Keeper jolted visibly. Napoleon approached and put his face against the Keeper's.

"You will leave here and not return until you have recovered the amulet," Napoleon spat. "In the meantime, I will kill one member of your god-forsaken family every month until you do. Now find it," he said, turning and walking back towards the table.

"Go!"

The Keeper stood in stunned silence. Grant saluted stiffly and left the room. Outside, night had fallen. By the time The Keeper had pulled himself together and found the strength to exit the tent, Grant and the amulet had already melted into the Russian countryside and disappeared.

1. http://www.robertguidi.com/isambard2

Map of Isambard's London

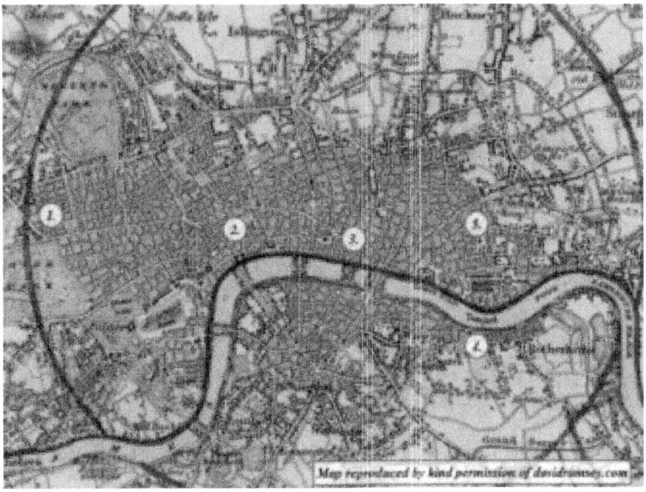

1. No. 20 Cato Street
2. Bow Street Magistrates' Court
3. Brunel's workshop on Poultry Street
4. Site of the Thames Tunnel dig
5. Worshipful Company of Gunmakers

Chapter 1

Isambard tiptoed past the door to his father's study, willing the floorboards not to creak. The kit in his battered satchel rattled and squeaked despite his best efforts to keep it quiet. He could see the light up ahead, his window to freedom. If he could just make it to the ladder that led up to his room, he would be able to escape. But it was not to be – behind his right shoulder, a French-accented voice called his name, sending a chill down his spine.

"Isambard."

He froze, eyes squeezed shut, hoping against hope that somehow the calling of his name had been a coincidence and that he hadn't been discovered.

"Isambard," came the voice again.

"Yes father?" Isambard answered, with as much innocence in his voice as he could muster.

"Come into my study please."

Isambard's shoulders dropped and he sighed.

"Father," Isambard said, presenting himself, head bowed.

"Listen I... what's this? Where do you think you are going?"

"Father, it's Saturday. I've been studying every day and working every evening with you in the workshop. You promised that I would be able to get over and see William today."

Marc looked confused for a moment, before raising his eyebrows

"Really? Well, I'm sorry but I simply can't let you go. In a matter of days we have the investor presentation and we cannot afford to leave anything to chance. We have much testing to complete." Marc began searching through a pile of drawings rolled up on a shelf behind him.

"But father, I promised William that I would go over there today. I haven't seen him since I got back from France. I gave him my word." Isambard looked up at his father, trying to catch his eye. Marc grabbed the drawing that he had been searching for and turned to meet his son's gaze.

"I'm afraid you do not have the authority to promise anything to anyone. Here," he said, taking a coin from the overflowing desk and flicking it for his son to catch.

"What's this?"

"A coin for a messenger – send a note to your friend apologising."

Isambard looked at the French Franc in his hand.

"Father, I'm not working today. I won't. It's not fair."

"I tell you what," Marc said, making for the door. Isambard's heart leapt momentarily, before crashing again when he saw the insincere smile on his father's face. "I'll come down and help get you started. Perhaps you will finish before it gets dark."

Isambard watched his father striding out of the room studying the blueprint.

"We'll be finished sooner than that," Isambard said to himself.

Isambard dropped his satchel and followed his father along the corridor and down the narrow staircase that led to the workshop, the familiar smell of cart-grease and leather filling his nostrils. As he looked across the spotless floor and ranks of neatly arranged tools, a faint smile spread across his face – his father's obsession was making him predictable.

"Reach over and engage the drive belt, would you?"

Isambard knelt down and squeezed himself into the gap between the two machines and, in the dark cramped space, expertly stretched the long loop of leather over the drive wheels of the machine.

Suddenly, he froze - from the shadows, a pair of yellow eyes stared back at him.

"Father, that cat has got back in the machine – I think he likes the warmth in there."

"Well get rid of it will you – we have work to do."

"Go on," Isambard whispered, shooing the cat away, "get out of it."

With the cat gone, Isambard carefully drew the sturdy hunting knife from its sheath at his waist and pressed its sharp teeth against the belt.

For a moment, he held his breath, unsure whether to go through with it. But before he could change his mind he began cutting into the fleshy belt with rapid strokes of the knife. Once he'd got halfway through the belt, he stopped, sheathed the knife and backed out of the tight space on his hands and knees.

"There," Isambard called to his father. "Drive connected."

"Very good," Marc replied with his hand on the drive release lever. "Thank you master Brunel. Stand back, ready to engage... Engaging."

Marc gave the lever a firm push, sliding the transfer bar forward and releasing the brake. The vast water tank above them shuddered and began to descend, driving the flywheel into motion as it did so. The drive wheel began to rotate, tightening the belt, pulling for a moment and transmitting the tension to the circular sawblade. Isambard could see the cut he had made in the belt momentarily opening like a V before it sheared in two with a whip's crack. The two ends of the belt leapt apart from each other like duelling snakes, knocking themselves out on the surrounding machinery before coming to a rest on the floor.

Marc yanked the lever to stop the descent of the water tank and cut the power. The machinery groaned to a halt, except the circular saw, which continued to spin lazily for a moment or two.

"What's happened?" Isambard asked, feigning surprise. His father was already burrowing between the two machines and soon re-appeared holding one end of the torn belt.

"Drive-belt. Snapped."

"Oh... Dear," Isambard said, with simulated disappointment. "Shall I run and get the spare?"

"We don't have a spare. We had it specially made over in Bermondsey, don't you remember? Five inch, double-seamed, 13-foot loop," Marc said, cradling the broken belt as if it were a deceased pet.

"Well it's only a few miles. If I set off now I can be there by lunchtime and back by tea," Isambard said.

Marc placed both hands on the cast iron body of the machine and gripped it until his knuckles turned white.

"Very well," Marc sighed. "But be quick."

Isambard bounded up the stairs and into his father's study where he recovered his tattered bag, propped up against the desk, just as he had left it. He couldn't leave without double-checking its contents – there, amongst the new surveillance gear that he was going to show William, he found the spare belt that he had picked up a few days before: five inch, double-seamed, 13-foot loop. He allowed himself a triumphant smile, pulled the bag shut and ran up the ladder to his loft-bedroom and freedom.

ISAMBARD CLAMBERED out of his bedroom window onto the familiar rooves of Poultry Street and gazed out over the stormy sea of rooftops which stretched to Saint Paul's Cathedral in one direction and the Bank of England in the other. The image of his father's anguish at losing the belt crossed Isambard's mind, but after a lungful of clear, cold air it was gone.

Despite the bulky gear in his satchel he made rapid progress across the uneven rooftops, sticking to the familiar route, avoiding slippery tiles, rotten planks and loose ropes as he went. Apart from the occasional flash of an escaping cat or pigeon, and one or two washer-women draping wet laundry over their long clothes-lines hanging between chimneys, he had the rooves to himself.

When he finally clambered back down to ground level, it was into a chaotic backyard where Mrs Woodington was drying laundry in a mangle between the chicken coop and a stack of bricks. Isambard had to leap the last bit, jumping off a decrepit shed and landing roughly in the middle of the yard.

"Ooh, Sam, it's you!" Mrs Woodington gasped, pressing a hand to her chest. "You'll be the death of me giving me a fright like that."

"Sorry Mrs Woodington. I didn't mean to...."

"No matter!" she said with a laugh. "How ever have you been? We've missed you so. You haven't written to me and you promised that you would," she said, reaching out and wrapping him up in a hug that involved a bit too much of the cold wet sheet that she'd been mangling.

"I'm very well Mrs Woodington and yes, I'm sorry I haven't written to you. I've been ever so busy with my studies. And the workshop."

"Studies I'm sure," she said with a knowing smile before calling over her shoulder, "William! Sam is here to see you. Oh Sam it's so nice to see you. I've just taken some ginger cake out of the oven - you'll stay for a slice won't you?"

"I have been dreaming of it ever since November 28th, when I finished the last crumb of the cake you gave me to take to France," Isambard beamed. He was expecting William to appear at any moment, so was surprised when William's older sister Millie was first to appear in the doorway in front of him.

"Good day, Sam," she said, leaning on the door frame. Isambard was struck by how much she had changed since he'd seen her last - her long red hair was tied back and she wore the smart uniform of a housemaid.

"Ahoy there, Millie," Isambard blurted.

"*Ca va?*" she ventured in French.

"*Très bien merci, très bien. Et toi? J'espère que tout va bien?*" Isambard asked, noticing her face growing more and more uncertain. There was a pause as a quizzical look came over her face, but mercifully the awkward silence was shattered by the sound of William opening a window above them.

"What ho Isambard! There you are, you blasted Frenchman. What's taken you so long? Don't move. I'm coming down," William yelled before disappearing back inside the house.

"You'd better come inside, you'll catch your death of cold out here," Millie said. "I'll make some camomile tea."

They bundled into the somewhat gloomy kitchen, pulling the heavy curtain across the back door to keep the cold out. Isambard sat on one of the plain wooden chairs and put his hands up to the stove to take the chill off his fingers.

"So I hear you have a new job, Millie. At the Bow Street Magistrates' Court isn't it? Congratulations," Isambard said with a big grin on his face.

"Yes. It's just Housekeeping but I'm hoping to be able to move into something a bit more... rewarding. Something like the Bow Street Runners."

"You want to get a job with the Bow Street Runners? Tracking down criminals and bringing them to justice?"

"Yes, why not?"

"Well, they don't generally employ... girls... do they?"

"No," Millie said defiantly, "Not generally. I'll just have to be the first. I'm bored, Sam, bored of folding napkins and carrying tea-trays."

Isambard paused to consider this, before the sound of someone tumbling down the stairs came to a crescendo and William threw himself against the door frame.

"Good morrow, Sam!" William said striding over and shaking Isambard vigorously by the hand. "Should we kiss, like the French do? I can tell that you want to. My painting teacher's a Frenchman and he's forever kissing other chaps about the place. Not me, fortunately. Ha. Now tell me about Paris. You must have seen some beautiful things. What is the most wonderful thing you've seen? And don't say the Austerlitz Bridge or some engineering monstrosity like that," he said with a knowing grin at Millie. "Tell us about the art."

Millie brought the teapot over whilst William slid three plates onto the table. Moments later there were steaming cups of tea and chunks of ginger cake in front of each of them as they took their seats around the kitchen table.

"I'm not in Paris, I'm in Caen and I haven't seen anything that you'd call art. Just lots of buildings. Here, I've got a sketchbook."

"Buildings? Pah!" William said, throwing himself back in his chair with mock contempt.

"Oh William, pipe down, will you? He's just a bit overexcited to see you Sam. Let's see these drawings," Millie said, edging round for a closer look. William soon joined as, in truth, he also loved Isambard's sketches. Isambard flicked through the pages which showed details of the boats, buildings and bridges of Caen and the surrounding countryside. Isambard even had a map of the area upon which he had marked the site of each drawing.

"Oh you are so lucky to be in Paris. Imagine what I could learn if I were studying my art in Paris."

"Will, Sam's not been in Paris," Millie said. "He's not listening."

"Well then," Isambard said, closing his sketchbook, "as you are so keen to talk about yourself, tell us, how is William Woodington the artist's apprentice?"

"Amazing. Preternatural. Prodigious!"

"Idiot," Millie said, sipping her tea.

"Hold on Millie, hold on. Mr Sievier says I have the makings of a fine engraver."

Just then a distant bell tolled quarter-past the hour.

"Oh crumbs!" Millie cried. "Is that the time? I'm on duty at ten. I've got to go. Sam, will you come and see us again?" she asked, hurrying towards the door.

"Yes, I'm here for a few weeks, all the way through to Easter."

"Splendid. See you again. 'Bye mother!" Millie called, leaving with a slam of the front door.

"She seems well," Isambard said. "Excited about her new job."

"She's glad to be out of the house and earning some money."

"She's the lucky one – my father has me locked up, working like a slave," Isambard grumbled. But William had heard it all before.

"She's got it into her head that she wants to work with the Runners and be a thief-taker for the King. But they won't give her a try until she proves herself and she can't prove herself until they give her a try. So what's she to do?"

"Sounds like she needs a new source of information," Isambard said, an arch smile spreading across his face.

William had seen that look before. "What are you on about?"

"You remember at the end of last summer I built those gadgets for listening in to people's conversations? Well I've been refining my designs and have a couple of things that I thought that you might like to see."

"Go on..." William said tentatively, watching as Isambard produced his threadbare satchel and began emptying its contents onto the table between them.

"A giant leather belt?" William asked, unconvinced.

"No, that's for one of father's machines," Isambard said, still rummaging. "This."

"What is it?" William asked, peering at a long tube as it emerged from the bag.

"This is the new Telephonic Magnifier. Conducts sound along its length so you can hear things at a distance."

"And this?" William asked, prodding what looked like a very chewy chocolate roll.

"That is my very own Flexible Periscope. Similar sort of thing but with light – when you look in at the top end, you can see what's happening at the bottom."

William tried to look into the eyepiece, but Isambard snatched it out of his hand.

"It has to be carefully unravelled to work properly."

"And this?" William asked.

"This," Isambard said, "is my sandwich tin. As you can see, there is nothing in it, so it is perfectly suited to carrying a few slices of this magnificent ginger cake," he said, collecting a handful of cake, jamming it into the tin and pressing the lid shut.

"So how's all this gear going to help Millie?"

"Follow me and I'll tell you."

UP ON THE ROOFTOPS, the weak sun brought little warmth to the cold air as Isambard led the way West, past St Paul's and above Fleet Street towards Bow Street and the Magistrates' Courts where Millie worked. They positioned themselves above the East windows where the roof was flat apart from a small raised brick perimeter. Isambard took off his satchel and carefully unravelled the surveillance gear.

"This is capital, Isambard," William said, grinning excitedly.

"Quiet," Isambard hissed. "Here, lower one end of this will you."

William began uncoiling the hose and feeding it down the outside of the building. Isambard made a start on the Flexible Periscope, which was, in effect, a long leather sock with a box attached at either end. Mirrors were mounted inside these purpose-built wooden boxes, making them quite heavy. Which is why, when one end tipped over the edge of the rooftop, it took the entire length of leather sock with it.

Isambard and William looked on in horror as it unspooled and disappeared over the parapet. Thinking fast, Isambard slammed a hand down on the other end of the periscope, stopping the whole thing slithering over the edge. However, this had the unintended effect of pulling on the loose end, just as it dropped past the window of the room where a meeting of the Bow Street Runners was underway. The leather sock went taut, snapped tight and sent the mirror-box swinging sideways into a large window, with a loud bang. Isambard and William froze, staring at each other for a moment, before Isambard spoke.

"We'd better get out of here."

Isambard began coiling up the Periscope as quickly as he could whilst William pulled up the hose and fed it back into Isambard's satchel. But the Periscope was stuck and Isambard was leaning over, trying to free it up.

"Leave it, Sam. Come on, we've got to go," William said, looking around nervously.

But Isambard was intent on recovering the Periscope and crouched down to try and release it.

It was then that things in Isambard's head began to go very slowly.

From the corner of his eye, Isambard became aware of a large booted foot arriving, followed by the sound of William shouting. Isambard sprang to his feet to see a large man grappling with William. But a brick at the edge of the roof had cracked and crumbled under his weight - Isambard began to rock backwards and overbalance. William and his captor turned and looked on with mounting anguish, both reaching out towards Isambard's windmilling arms. Terrified, Isambard looked from William to the large bearded man who was now holding William by the scruff of the neck.

William's captor reached out as Isambard took the instinctive step back, out of reach. There was now nothing left to stop him falling over the edge of the roof.

They watched as Isambard disappeared, fully reclined, as if at any moment expecting to slump into an armchair made of clouds.

Twisting in the air, Isambard had just enough time to confirm that there was nothing between him and the unyielding surface of flagstones far below, before he passed out.

On the roof, time had not slowed down for William and his assailant. As Isambard had slipped away from them, an unspoken truce had emerged.

William ran to the roof's edge in a couple of short strides, fearing the worst. But instead of seeing Isambard in a mangled mess on the pavement below, William saw Isambard's star-shaped body lying in a horse-drawn cart of straw standing outside the Courthouse. William watched as the horse began slowly walking away, taking Isambard and the cart with it.

"Isambard. You okay?" William called over the parapet. No answer.

William looked round to tell the bearded man but saw he was already well on his way to the door which led back into the Courthouse.

William finished stuffing the kit into the satchel and followed through the weather-beaten door into the Courthouse. A wrought iron spiral staircase took him to a rough-walled corridor which led through a door into the main staircase, lined with marble pillars, where lawyers, officers, criminals and their families churned past each other. Suddenly disorientated, William was only able to make out which direction to go by following the trail of chaos caused by the big man who was obviously quite accustomed to giving chase through crowded buildings.

Apologising all the while, William picked his way through the crowd in the man's wake and stopped at the side door of the Courthouse. From behind a pillar, William watched as the bearded man's disbelieving gaze moved between the rooftop to Isambard's estimated landing point and back again.

But, of course, Isambard was nowhere to be seen.

---

1. http://www.robertguidi.com/more

Chapter 2

Isambard was still coming to his senses when the horse and cart stopped at the end of an alley, deep in the shade of the surrounding buildings. He propped himself up on an elbow and looked back the way he had come, towards the sunlight in the main street. Seeing the bearded man from the rooftops, Isambard quickly burrowed back into the cart until the man gave up and moved on.

Isambard was just beginning to emerge from the straw when he heard a voice at his shoulder.

"Master Brunel."

Isambard turned quickly and peered through the straw to see a tall man in a black cape.

"Forgive me if I startled you – please don't be alarmed," the newcomer continued with a smile. "That was quite a fall you just had – you must be feeling a little light-headed."

Isambard looked up and realised that his vision was a bit fuzzy.

"No, I'm fine I...."

"What a stroke of luck that this cart was there to break your fall, hmm?" the man said, tapping a hand on the cart's edge.

"Is this... is this your cart?" Isambard asked, brushing the straw from his arms.

"Save your questions for later. There is something that I'd like to talk to you about first - come and get some fresh air with me up on the roof. You don't mind, do you?"

Blinking and shaking his head clear one more time, Isambard clambered out of the cart and followed the man onto the roof as quickly as he could.

Breathing hard from the climb, Isambard stood up carefully, scanning the roof-scape as he went. The air was perfectly still and there wasn't a sound to be heard.

"Thank you for following me up here," the man said from a nearby chimney stack. Isambard turned sharply to look at him properly in the light but became transfixed by the man's cape – it now looked more purple than black and, bizarrely, it seemed to be moving, as if covered in worms writhing over each other.

"We require some privacy for this conversation, and I know that you are a keen amateur of the rooftops. Allow me to introduce myself - my name is Mr Hardleygrieve," the man said, coming forward and proffering a hand.

"Isambard Brunel. But it sounds like you know that already," Isambard said, shaking Hardleygrieve's hand.

"You're probably wondering why I saved your life back there, with the hay-cart."

"I hadn't got as far as 'why' – I'm still stuck on the 'how'."

"Of course. Always the engineer, looking for the rational explanation," Hardleygrieve said with a stiff smile. "Shall we walk?"

He turned and began making his way between the chimney stacks. After a slight hesitation, Isambard followed.

"I don't suppose that during your attempts at spying on the Bow Street Runners you learnt anything about the Cato Street Conspiracy?" the man asked, looking back over his shoulder.

"Never heard of it."

"It seems that a small group of Radicals have come up with a plan to assassinate several senior members of his Majesty's Government."

"Assassinate? What for?"

"Oh you know, the usual – start a revolution, destroy the aristocracy, share out the wealth, that sort of thing. Standard fayre in this day and age, but what the Bow Street Runners don't know is that the attack is merely a smokescreen. It is in fact being masterminded by a secretive sponsor called Cato to achieve a much more sinister end."

"What could be more sinister than killing off key members of the government?" Isambard asked.

"Let me give you a little bit of a history lesson which I'm sure will not have been included in your education to date."

"Try me," Isambard retorted.

"According to the Roman historian Flavius, during Ptolemy's dynasty, the three amulets of Ra were cut from a single billet of Alexandrian gold. One of these amulets was assigned to each of the great Egyptian Pharaohs. The amulets became the driving force behind the expansion of the Ptolemaic Kingdom and every great civilisation since then. The Romans? Genghis Khan? They all owed their dominance to the amulets. Have you ever wondered why Napoleon was so difficult to stop?"

"Don't tell me - Napoleon had an amulet?" Isambard asked sardonically.

"From the moment he acquired it on his Egyptian campaign of 1798 he began to dominate Europe. Right up until his disastrous Russian campaign of 1812 when the balance of power mysteriously swung England's way. Any idea why that might have happened?"

"The English stole Napoleon's amulet?"

Hardleygrieve nodded. "Exactly."

"Well that makes for a nice bedtime story, but what do you want me to do about it?"

"I need you to find out who is secretly trying to acquire the Prime Minister's amulet. Who is this Cato character?"

"Me?" Isambard laughed. "Why me?"

"Because I cannot. I shouldn't even be here. But you are one of the few who can help me. You are intelligent, capable and, of course, you owe me your life."

Isambard couldn't help giving a derisive snort at this. "Listen Mister..."

"Mister Hardleygrieve."

"Mister Hardleygrieve. I don't know why you think I would be interested in this cock-and-bull magic story, but it's not for me, do you hear? Thanks for saving my life and all that – maybe I'll return the favour one day, but right now I'm needed back at the workshop," Isambard said before moving away.

"Ah yes, the workshop that you love so much. Your father's workshop. Isambard, I know a thing or two about your father, the pressure he is under. I'm not sure how he would manage if anything were to happen to you."

Isambard stopped walking and half-turned his head. "What do you mean?"

"I'm just not sure that he could cope if you were to be convicted of spying - I'm sure Officer Ruthven of the Bow Street Runners would be very grateful to me for passing him the names of the boys who made a fool of him on the Courthouse roof this morning. Oh yes, it is not just your own future that you are dicing with. Your father. William. Maybe even Ms Woodington."

"Millie? You set this whole thing up," Isambard said in a moment of realisation, "the collapsing roof, the hay-cart. But how..."

Hardleygrieve's eyebrows flickered momentarily. "As I said, there isn't necessarily a rational explanation for everything."

Isambard took a sharp breath and looked out across the rooftops – the sky was clear blue, the air crisp and windless. He turned and squinted into the low sun which hovered above Hardleygrieve's head.

"What is it you want me to do?"

"At six pm tonight, the leader of the gang of conspirators has a meeting with this mysterious sponsor called Cato – I want you to listen in and find out everything you can about him and his plans. They meet at number 20 Cato Street."

"And just exactly how am I supposed to get inside number 20 Cato Street?"

"As I said, you're an intelligent, capable lad – I have every confidence in you. Perhaps you could use your surveillance equipment," Hardleygrieve said with a sickly smile. "But to help you on your way, you will find a useful little something in that bag on your back."

Isambard looked down to find a smart leather case across his shoulder.

"What kind of something?" Isambard asked, slowly lifting the flap of the case.

"In that bag you will find a jar containing a talking gas. His name is Trafalgar and he does an excellent job as anti-fire, should you need him."

"Anti-fire? What's that supposed to mean?"

A pigeon flapped over Isambard's head and the sound of sheep being driven to market drifted up from the street below. But when Isambard looked back, Hardleygrieve was gone.

Chapter 3

AT LAST CAME THE CODED knock at the roof-hatch that Isambard had been waiting for. He jumped up and hastily threw down his quill-pen, sending a spray of ink across his unfinished maths homework. Undeterred, he navigated carefully around the piles of books and half-finished models that littered the floor of his cramped bedroom. He wound hard on a wheel which slowly cranked open the roof-hatch letting air rush in from the freezing rooftops outside. Before long it was open wide enough for William to slide in.

"What ho, Isambard, how are we feeling after your death-defying fall?" William said, dropping deftly to the floor. "And, more importantly, what is that?" William was pointing at the heavy object lying on the bed.

"It's father's prototype diving helmet. He's trying to work out how to make it waterproof so we can explore the site of his Tunnel under the Thames. Whatever you do, don't put it on – it's a bit tight," Isambard warned.

"Good afternoon Isambard," Millie said, clambering through the same hatch in the roof that William had used.

"Millie! I didn't know... William didn't say that you were coming," Isambard said, straightening his neck-tie with one hand and flattening his mop of brown hair with the other.

"Sorry, Sam, didn't have a chance to..." William grinned fiendishly.

"No matter," Isambard said, glaring back at William, "Millie, please do come in, take a seat on the, erm, bed, here," Isambard said, patting down the threadbare blanket that hung untidily across his unmade bed.

"No, thank you Master Brunel, I don't think that would be the proper thing for a lady to do," Millie replied.

"Oh come on Mill, what would you know about being a lady?" William teased, pushing her towards the bed with a shove. And, as if to prove her brother right, she deftly grabbed the diving helmet from the bed next to her and propelled it into William's abdomen with a positively unladylike force.

"Thank you, William," she retorted, watching William double over with the helmet clutched against his chest, "but I really would prefer to stand. So, William tells me that it was you making all that commotion at the Courthouse this morning."

Isambard flashed a stormy look at William.

"Oops," William said.

"We were trying to be helpful," Isambard explained. "We thought that we could find out something that would improve your standing with the Bow Street Runners."

"Well it didn't work out like that. Quite the opposite in fact."

"Obviously, falling off the roof was not part of the original plan," Isambard muttered, self-consciously.

"Oh, it was capital, Isambard, absolutely capital," William chortled as best he could through the pain in his gut, lowering himself carefully into the spindly chair that stood against Isambard's overflowing desk.

"That big fellow, the chief, gave us a bit of a fright," Isambard continued.

"That big fellow is Officer Ruthven, my future boss," Millie said with a defiant look on her face. "Probably best if you keep away from him from now on."

"Ok, but what would you say if I told you that I now have some information that really will impress this Officer Ruthven?" Isambard replied.

"What do you mean? What kind of information could you possibly have that would be of interest to him?" Millie asked, pretending not to be intrigued.

"A little bird has told me that there is a conspiracy being planned."

"If you're talking about the Cato Street gang, you're wasting your time," Millie said.

"What's all this about?" William asked excitedly, keen to get in on the action. Isambard and Millie took turns to explain.

"Well, there's a group of radical revolutionaries..."

"...led by a bloke called Thistlewood..."

"...who are plotting to assassinate Members of Parliament."

"What?" William shrieked, before clapping his hand over his mouth - this was supposed to be a secret meeting, after all. "Assassination attempts?" he continued in a strained whisper.

"But Isambard, none of this helps – the Bow Street Runners are already onto that one. They're going to catch them in the act."

"Aha but," Isambard said theatrically holding up his hand. "What Ruthven and the Bow Street Runners don't know is there is another side to this story."

"Go on," Millie said with undisguised suspicion in her voice.

"The gang leader, Thistlewood, is actually taking orders from someone else. Someone called Cato."

"What do you mean?"

"Cato is using this assassination plan as a smokescreen – to get close to the Prime Minister and steal something valuable."

"What could be that valuable?" William blurted.

Isambard hesitated momentarily.

"I don't know. But according to my source it has the potential to shift the balance of power across Europe."

Millie and William looked at each other with raised eyebrows.

"So who is this Cato?" Millie asked.

"That's what we're going to find out."

"Ooh, Isambard's got a plan. I love it when Isambard gets a plan," William fizzed.

"The Cato Street gang are due to meet tonight to discuss plans for the assassination attempt. Before that, their leader, Thistlewood, is going to meet with Cato, the true ringleader. So we are going to use the surveillance equipment to listen in. William can sketch a portrait of Cato through the periscope," Isambard explained.

William was wide-eyed and grinning. But Millie was not convinced.

"Not sure I like the sound of this."

"Look Millie, you said you wanted to show the Runners what you can do – this is your chance."

Just then, Isambard's father, Marc, called from downstairs.

"Isambard!"

All three froze and looked at each other.

"He's coming - you two need to hide," Isambard hissed at Millie and William.

"What about this?" William asked, realising that he was still holding the helmet.

"No, William...!" But it was too late, William's blond curls had disappeared into the helmet.

"...don't put that on," Isambard said anyway.

"Wumf mot?" William asked with his head deep within the copper plated globe.

"Because it has a nasty habit of getting stuck,"

"WAAH? Yum gumf gen din onf, Inabarn!" William cried, tugging at the bauble which now encased his head.

"Here, stand still, I think I know how to get it off," Isambard whispered.

The two of them wrestled with the helmet, knocking over several piles of books as they did so.

"Isambard," came Marc's voice again from downstairs, this time much closer. Gambling that his father would not look around too much, Isambard gave up and guided William towards the back wall, behind the hatch in the floor where Marc would undoubtedly appear in a few moments.

Isambard turned to see Millie standing with a haughty look on her face and her arms crossed.

"I'm not moving until you promise to tell me what it is that Cato's trying to steal," Millie whispered.

"Millie you've got to hide – if father sees you he'll...."

There was a creaking sound at the base of the steps which Isambard knew to be his father taking the first step on the ladder up to Isambard's loft room. But Millie wasn't budging.

"Okay Millie, I'll tell you on the way there. Now get..."

The hatch swung open and Marc's top hat emerged, followed by his head and shoulders.

"Isambard. Do you know where that diving helmet is?"

"Well sir, I..." Isambard said, a wave of nausea crashing inside him as he casually gazed around the room. But the uneasy feeling ebbed away as he realised that William, Millie and the helmet had somehow disappeared from the scene.

"No, sir, I... haven't seen it," Isambard said, seeing Millie and William squatting in the shadows behind his father's head.

"Very well. I have to go out now but I will collect some blank retaining plates on my way back - I would very much appreciate it if you would join me in the workshop at eight o'clock this evening to assist, no?"

"Of course, father," Isambard said with a forced smile.

There was a pause. But instead of descending, Marc began to haul himself up through the trap door. "Another thing - may I show you an idea I had for the tunnelling shield excavation mechanism? Matthews and I have been...."

"Oh no, no, no, Father," Isambard said, panicking that his father would spot the hiding visitors if he came much closer. "No I am... I'm right in the middle of my homework and I would really rather not... break my concentration if it is all the same to you. I would very much like to see it, perhaps at eight o'clock when we meet downstairs," Isambard beamed. Marc stopped half way up the ladder, looked at Isambard for a moment, and smiled politely.

"Of course. Until eight o'clock."

And with that, Isambard's father disappeared back down through the hatch and creaked down the ladder.

Once they were sure he had gone, Millie and William emerged from their hiding place.

"C'n oo hump me gen nis hing aawf?" William said from within the helmet.

"Better be quick," Millie grinned, "Isambard's got to be back here by eight."

Chapter 4

The three of them clambered out of the hatch in Isambard's roof and climbed up to the familiar roofline of Poultry Street. They were able to navigate the closely packed rooves of the area thanks to years of practice and exploration together. They crossed paths with the occasional like-minded roof-walker, countless cats, pigeons and vermin, and a fair number of indifferent householders and washer-women of the neighbourhood.

"So, what's the story?" Millie asked when William was out of earshot. "What is it that Cato is trying to steal?"

"It's a long story..." Isambard mumbled.

"It's a long way to Cato Street - we've got plenty of time."

"Ok but... you've got to promise not to tell a soul about it, promise?"

"Promise."

"There are these amulets – ancient Egyptian amulets. They've got some kind of incredible power. There are three and one of them has ended up in the hands of our Prime Minister. Cato is using this Conspiracy as a way of getting to this Amulet."

"What do you mean ancient amulets? Sam where have you been getting this nonsense from?"

"You know I fell off the Courthouse roof? By rights I should be dead – they should have been scraping me off the paving stones. But between the time I fell off the edge and the time I should have hit the ground, a haycart had magically appeared to catch me. And not only did it appear, it then drove me off down a dark alley so I wouldn't get caught. Then out of the shadows comes this fella – Hardleygrieve his name was. I knew there was something strange about him as soon as I saw his coat."

"His coat?"

"It was alive, covered in crawling beasties – most disconcerting. Anyway, he went on to tell me all about these amulets and made me promise to find out the identity of this Cato character. And then, when I turned around, he was gone."

"Gone?"

"Gone. Disappeared. Evaporated."

"Ok Sam, there's no need to worry – I think I know exactly what's going on here."

"Really. What?"

"Well, I know you're not the gullible type, so it's not you being stupid. And you're much too in love with science to believe in any kind of magic. So the only possible explanation is that you took a nasty bump to the head and had some sort of a waking dream. I had the same thing when I was little and fell out of my papa's apple tree. Convinced I could see little fairies for hours afterwards."

"No, Millie, no. It wasn't a dream or a vision or an apparition."

"How do you know?"

"Because… because he gave me this bag," Isambard said, indicating the new satchel around his neck.

"Nice bag."

"Yeah, it is…"

"Did he say it was magic too?" Millie teased.

"No but," Isambard said, about to explain about the jar of anti-fire, when William called back from ahead of them.

"Building's collapsed so we can't go on – we'll have to climb back down to street level for a while."

WITH THE PALE EVENING sun hanging low in the sky, the three of them stood on the roof of number 20 Cato Street, watching a steady stream of smoke emerging from the chimney.

"So this could be a problem," Isambard said.

"What do you mean?" William asked.

"Well we can't get the scope down there if they've got a fire blazing, can we," Millie replied.

"Hmmm. Perhaps we could pour some water down and put the flames out," William suggested half-heartedly.

Millie turned to Isambard with a pitying smile on her face. "I suppose that means we'll have to give up this insane idea of yours."

"Of course not," Isambard said, taking the jar from his new case. "We've got this."

"What's that?" Millie asked, eying the jar with suspicion.

"Hardleygrieve gave it to me - it's called anti-fire."

"Who's Hardleygrieve?" William asked, but was roundly ignored.

"What's anti-fire?" Millie asked.

"I'm not exactly sure, but he said it might be useful," Isambard said, setting the jar down and taking a step back.

The three of them looked at it.

"How's a big sweetie jar going to help?" William asked looking at Isambard. A frown flashed across Isambard's face and he shrugged.

"Not sure - let's open it and find out."

The other two watched as Isambard picked up the jar, held it at arm's length and slowly took the lid off. The air inside it turned a kind of greeny-grey and emerged slowly to form a small cloud.

"Sweet Lord, Isambard, put it back," Millie whispered urgently. But it was too late.

"Hullo," it said, in a low, monotone voice. Millie looked at Isambard with one eyebrow raised quizzically. William looked on, dumbstruck and horrified.

"Good day. My name is Isambard. Isambard Brunel. And these are my friends, Millie and William."

"I know that already. I can hear everything that goes on outside my jar you know. Unless I'm asleep. Which, admittedly, is quite a lot of the time. My name is Trafalgar. I'm a talking gas."

"Yes, Mister Trafalgar, I've heard all about you and your magnificent smothering skills."

"Really? I must have been asleep for that bit. Anyway, haven't we got some sort of meeting to attend?"

"Yes, yes of course. We were wondering if you wouldn't mind heading down this chimney and putting the fire out so we can lower our scope. If that's... the kind of work you do."

"Yes that sounds like just my kind of thing. I can hang around down there and listen in. Take some notes if you'd like. They'll only be mental notes, of course. I can't hold a pen, you see."

"No of course, of course. Mental notes would be... most useful," Isambard said, looking at Millie for confirmation.

"Very well. I'll slide down there, put the fire out and make sure the way is clear for your scope thingy. Would that be alright?" Trafalgar hung in the air as a blob, wobbling gently in the breeze.

"That would be... marvellous. Thank you very much."

"Right-ho. See you in a jiffy."

And with that, Trafalgar oozed snake-like down the chimney.

"Does... that answer your question?" Isambard asked.

"It answers one question. And asks about a thousand more."

"Where did you get that jar from again?" William said, still staring at the jar still standing on the roof.

"I don't like the sound of this," Millie said.

"Don't worry about it. Just think what Ruthven is going to say when we come back with news from inside the very heart of the Conspiracy – talk about making a name for yourself," Isambard grinned.

"That's what I'm worried about," Millie replied.

"It's working – look, the smoke's stopping. I'll get my sketchbook, you get the scope ready," William said as Isambard began to unravel the long leather periscope.

AFTER TWENTY MINUTES of uninterrupted sketching, William broke the silence. "Looks like the meeting's coming to an end," he said, eyes still glued to the top half of the scope.

"Did you manage to get what you needed, Will?" Millie asked, peering at the sketchbook on her brother's lap.

"I've managed to get one of the chaps but haven't been able to get a look at the other one."

"Okay well that will have to do, Will. Let's get the scope out and wait for Trafalgar."

With the utmost caution they reeled in the scope. Just as they were easing the optical box out of the chimney, Trafalgar slithered out and re-formed as a cloud in front of them.

"Hmmm, that was interesting," he said in an extremely uninteresting voice.

"What did they talk about?" Millie asked excitedly.

"Well there were two of them: one Englishman,"

"Thistlewood, the gang leader," Millie said.

"And one Frenchman. Charismatic. Persuasive. Slightly gurgly voice."

"Gurgly?" William echoed.

"What did they talk about?" asked Millie.

"This conspiracy they're planning. Killing members of parliament, that sort of thing."

"So nothing new then," Millie said, casting a stern look at Isambard.

"There was one rather important thing."

"Well come on then, what was it?" Millie asked.

"They want to destabilise the whole situation. Decapitate the ruling classes. Pave the way for revolution. This is not just about the conspiracy to attack Members of Parliament."

"Well what is it?" Millie demanded, unable to hide her impatience.

"It's the King. They're going to kill the King."

Chapter 5

Isambard slid back into his bedroom through the roof-hatch and rested his hands on his knees, chest heaving. He'd run most of the way home and had heard St Paul's ringing half-past-eight on the way, so he knew he was late. And someone was climbing the ladder into his room.

"Oh there you are," Isambard's mother said, emerging from the trap-door. "Where have you been? Your father's been looking for you. He wants to see you in his study," she said with a raised eyebrow. "And before you ask, I'm afraid we've nothing for supper," she added as she disappeared back down the ladder.

Isambard hammered down the stairs and came to a stop in front of the study door, trying to smarten up his jacket which was two sizes too big for him. Being short was another thing Isambard had to thank his father for.

Remembering that his lank brown hair needed some urgent maintenance, Isambard did his best to slick it down. He had a nasty feeling that this conversation with his father was not going to be a good one. Distracted, he failed to notice the new satchel which was still slung across his shoulder, took a deep breath and knocked on the study door.

"Ah, at last," Marc said with a sardonic smile, standing over a large mechanical drawing which lay draped across the desk. Behind him the bookshelves groaned with engineering reference books and odd shaped metal objects from projects long past, some of which Isambard recognised as the toys he had played with as a boy.

"Sir, I'm sorry..."

"Tell me, what is the hour?" Marc asked, removing his wire-frame spectacles.

"A quarter to nine, sir."

"And what hour did I ask you to present yourself in the workshop?"

"Eight o'clock, sir," Isambard replied with his eyes downcast.

"So how do you explain your late arrival?"

"Well, sir, just after you and I spoke, Millie and William came over with something of an emergency. I had to go along and help out."

"Isambard, as you know, we are in the middle of an emergency of our own. If we do not complete the prototype before the investor presentation, we will not get the funding to continue the project. The family is... already running out of money," Marc said, his voice losing power.

"Sir, I sincerely apologise. I will make it up to you, I promise."

"Yes, you will. I am sure you did not go out without having completed your entire calculus workbook, so I shall be inspecting that at seven am. You will then begin work on those new retaining plates."

"Yes sir," Isambard said with a heavy heart.

"One more thing - what is this new... bag? Where did you get it from?"

Isambard's mind raced as he attempted to explain away the expensive looking leather bag that Hardleygrieve had given to him.

"It was a gift, from the... Geometry master at school. A prize," Isambard lied. Isambard's father came around the desk and held out a hand.

"Give it to me," Marc said, taking the case.

Isambard cursed his father's ability to spot a weakness. His heart began to gallop as he remembered that the sketch that William had made at number 20 Cato Street was still in the bag.

Marc put the bag down on top of the blueprint and opened it.

But when he saw William's sketch, the expression on his face suddenly changed from irritated to deeply troubled. Marc took the sketch, let go of the bag and held the portrait in both hands, arms outstretched, staring into the eyes of the man in the picture, attention undivided.

"*Mon Dieu*," Marc said, finally. "*C'est lui*."

"You know this man?" Isambard asked. For a long while, Marc gave no answer. He finally managed to pull his gaze away from the magnetic eyes in the portrait and turned to Isambard with a fearful expression on his face.

"Father, do you know this man?"

Isambard's father shook his head slowly, before finally speaking.

"This is Robespierre, France's Prince of Terror. Where did you get this picture?"

"William drew it today as part of a... study that he has to do for portrait class," Isambard found himself fibbing.

"No. This is not a copy of a portrait. How could William produce a picture like this?" Marc asked.

Isambard noted the gravity in his father's voice and decided to tell the truth this time. "We were on watch outside a house in Cato Street."

"Cato Street. There were some who used to refer to Robespierre as Cato," Marc recalled. "And what were you doing in Cato Street when you should have been here helping me?"

"Millie was sent there by the Bow Street Runners, to have a look. Like I said, it was an emergency. A gang of conspirators were meeting there. They're planning to assassinate senior members of the government."

"Of course, Cato is up to his revolutionary tricks again," Marc said, looking back at the portrait. "Listen to me," Marc hissed, taking a step closer to his son. "Isambard. This man has blood on his hands, the blood of thousands of innocent French men, women and children. He used the Revolution as an excuse to destroy his enemies, and murder thousands of ordinary people. Families, like ours. You will not go near this man, do you hear me? Promise me you will keep away."

Isambard was shocked by his father's sudden seriousness.

"Yes sir. I... I promise."

"*Mais.... mais c'est pas possible*," Marc continued, after a pause. "It is his face, his eyes, just as he would be today. But how can this be Cato? This is a picture of a ghost."

"What do you mean, father? Why do you say ghost?"

Marc looked from the picture to his son.

"Maximilien Robespierre was executed 25 years ago."

Chapter 6

THE FOLLOWING EVENING, even though it had been dark for several hours, Isambard was still hard at work, cutting threads into his father's metal plates. The light from a nearby lantern sent shadows dancing around the cavernous workshop and glinted off the oily surface of the plates in his hand.

But he was too hungry and exhausted to be angry at his father anymore – that sentiment had peaked mid-morning as the small bowl of porridge that passed as breakfast became a distant memory. Even the normal buzz of noise and energy was absent today as the whole crew were running a trial down at the tunnelling site.

An unusually cold blast of air washed over Isambard and crept up his sleeves towards his core. Isambard shivered and glared at the big wooden doors which fitted snugly in their frames. If there was an advantage to being the son of an obsessive engineer it was that everything in the workshop functioned perfectly. Even so, Isambard thought, maybe they needed a bit of a push.

Seeing this as a welcome distraction, Isambard put his tools down and ambled across the freshly swept floor which, as visitors never failed to point out, was clean enough to eat your dinner off. If only there was some dinner to eat, Isambard thought ruefully.

As he passed the lathe he gave one of the control wheels a spin and watched the headstock advance at a slow, precisely measured pace. He stood by the machine, as he had done for many hours in his long apprenticeship at his father's side. He spun the wheel again, this time the other direction. Perfectly weighted, it was almost frictionless. How obedient the machine was – ask, and the machine would respond.

The big doors shuddered in their frames again, this time more noisily. Isambard snapped out of his daydream and looked around, holding the lantern up and peering into the shadows. Something caught his eye - an unusual object on the otherwise pristine floor. He approached it cautiously and, as he did so, he could see that it was an envelope. With one hand on his knee and the other holding the lantern up above his head, he peered down – a pure white envelope with just a name – his name – written on it.

Isambard looked around, to check that there was no one about. He picked up the envelope, then stood and held it, looking at it for a moment, weighing it in his hands. Were his hands trembling? Isambard watched them for a moment, placed the lantern on the floor and pulled the envelope open.

Inside he found a sheet of paper with a single line written on it. He flipped the letter over but it was blank. Isambard read it, frowned and read it again. It meant nothing.

"The bird's eye sees not what the worm's eye sees," he read out loud.

The bird's eye, Isambard thought. Birds are known for their flight - that's sort of their distinguishing ability. A bird's eye view is usually from the top down. So a worm's eye view would normally be...

Isambard held the letter up and looked at it from below. Words began to appear. The more he raised the letter, the darker the ink became, so that, when he viewed it from directly underneath, he was able to make them out. He lay on his back and read by the light of the lantern on the floor beside him.

'For your own good, tell no one about Cato. Hg'

Tell no one about Cato, Isambard thought to himself – but nobody knew about Cato, except Isambard himself and, well, his father who, for all his eccentricities, would never have sent such a note. Perhaps Millie or William had worked it out. But who would sign it 'Hg'? Who else knew about the trip to Cato Street? The mysterious man on the roof – what was his name? Hardleygrieve. Hg.

Just then there was a hammering at the door – Isambard had time to stuff the note into his breast pocket before the door swung open and Millie and William appeared.

"What ho, Isambard. What are you doing on the floor? Not sleeping on the job are you?" William said with a smile.

"I should be so lucky. Father's had me at it since first light because of our late finish last night. And there's not a scrap of food in the house," Isambard said, getting to his feet and brushing himself down.

"Here, I thought you'd be hungry so I brought some cake from the kitchen at work," Millie said, opening a crumb-filled handkerchief and laying it out on a nearby workbench. "Maybe it's time you got out and started earning some money for yourself, like I do," she teased.

"If only – it doesn't look like Father is ever going to let me out of this workshop."

"Look I'm... I'm sorry about last night," Millie said. "Us finishing late and you getting into trouble."

"Wouldn't have missed it for the world," Isambard grinned, grabbing at the cake. "Anyway, I know how you can make it up to me."

"How?" Millie asked tentatively.

"Take Trafalgar back to... to wherever he came from."

"Where's that then?"

"I don't know – you'll have to ask him."

"Why don't you do it?"

"I'm stuck in here aren't I – come on Millie. It'll be a good bit of detective work for you – good practice." It was obvious that Isambard wasn't taking no for an answer and pressed the satchel with the jar in it into Millie's hands. Reluctantly, she accepted.

"Pretty successful surveillance operation though wouldn't you say? Some meaty new intelligence for Officer Ruthven eh?" William said. But all of Isambard's attention was on the cake.

"I tried to find out a bit more about this Thistlewood character," Millie said. "I had a peek at his file in the Magistrates' Court. The Bow Street Runners have got him down as a 'Dangerous Character' and have been tracking him since 1816. He's quite a serious player on the revolutionary scene. But that Frenchman that he was with didn't match the description of any of Thistlewood's known associates."

Isambard could feel Hardleygrieve's letter burning in his breast pocket. Millie looked at Isambard and raised an eyebrow.

"What are you not telling us?" she asked.

"The man in the picture – his name's Robespierre," Isambard said.

"Robespierre? What kind of a name is that?" William asked.

"Robespierre was one of the leaders of the French Revolution. He was in charge of the government for a while. Murdered thousands of innocent people"

"I could tell he was a nasty piece of work just looking at him," William said.

"But here's the spooky part. In July 1794, he lost the trust of The Revolutionary Committee and they had him executed."

"Executed? So it can't have been him," Millie said.

"It was him," Isambard said grimly.

"What makes you so sure?" William demanded whilst picking at the cake crumbs.

"My father was still living with his family in France back then. He was in Paris in 1794. He met Robespierre face to face. When my father saw the drawing, it was like he'd seen a ghost."

"You showed him the drawing?"

"I couldn't stop him," Isambard said, taking the cake back. "He was grilling me about being late back and he opened the case and found it."

"Well Millie – you wanted to make an impression on the Bow Street Runners. This is just what you need," William said.

"I'm not sure this is the kind of impression that I want to be making. Too risky. You two should do it. Go and tell Officer Ruthven first thing in the morning," Millie said.

"The last time he saw us he was trying to arrest me for spying," William complained.

"Well you'll just have to hope that he doesn't recognise you then won't you."

"Hang on, hang on," Isambard said. "We are not getting involved with Robespierre. It's too dangerous."

"Too dangerous?" William said with a look of disbelief on his face.

"It's a bit late to think of that Isambard," Millie said, the shock still visible on her face. "We're already involved. The King is in danger - you have to go see Ruthven. Tomorrow."

Chapter 7

William had a still-life session at his master's studio the following morning, so Isambard used the time to make some progress with his French and Mathematics studies. But he could barely concentrate, with thoughts of the recent events continually turning over in his mind: How had Cato escaped execution back in 1794? Who was Hardleygrieve and why did he want to keep Cato's identity secret?

Time slid by and suddenly the church bell was tolling quarter to 11. He would be late meeting William.

Isambard arrived at Bow Street breathless and soon spotted William up in the eaves of the roof. Isambard sat on the steps opposite, as planned, putting his cap on to signal that he had seen William. Within a couple of minutes William had clambered down, dodged the carriages to cross the busy street and sat down next to Isambard.

"Where you been?"

"I was doing some research. On Robespierre."

"Right. Well, whilst you've been tucked up nice and warm, I've been out here watching the lay of the land, freezing my schnoz off."

"Sorry about that. Seen anything interesting?"

"No."

William sniffed, shuffled on the cold flagstones and sat on the back of his hands.

"No sign of Ruthven?" Isambard asked.

"Not a sniff."

"Who's that then?" Isambard asked, nodding at the Courthouse steps.

"Gadzooks. It's him. Quick!" William jumped up, closely followed by Isambard. Officer Ruthven bounded down the Courthouse steps and began striding purposefully along Bow Street. Without breaking into a run they struggled to catch up with him through the crowds. At last, they drew up next to him, each trotting to keep up with his vigorous pace.

"Officer Ruthven," Isambard said in the most authoritative voice he could muster between gasps of air. Ruthven looked down at Isambard without breaking his stride.

"Who's asking?"

"Isambard Brunel, if you please sir."

"And if it don't please?"

"Sir, it's about Thistlewood. Of Cato Street," Isambard persevered.

Ruthven stopped dead in his tracks, scanned the crowded street ahead and paused.

"Follow me," he said, making off down a side-alley, away from the crowds. There was an eerie quiet in the alley which ran between two windowless buildings. Ruthven stopped where there was no chance of being overheard. He was a mountain of a man, looming over them, piercing blue eyes below a shock of black hair.

"Now then, what d'you know about Thistlewood and Cato Street?" he growled.

"We know the plan to assassinate members of the Cabinet. We know that they are now including the Prime Minister in their list of targets."

Ruthven narrowed his eyes and looked at William - a look of recognition passed across his face.

"Hang on a minute. You're the one I chased off the Courthouse roof the other day. I should've shopped you on the spot." He grabbed each of them by the collar with his enormous hands and pulled their faces up close to his own, until they could nearly feel the bristles of his beard.

"Who you working for?" he growled. Isambard was now choking like a fish on a line, so William answered on his behalf.

"Officer Ruthven, if we are working for anyone, it is you. We've come to you because we have found out something that you need to know about Thistlewood."

Ruthven grunted and relaxed his strangling grip slightly. Isambard took a deep, gasping breath.

"Go on then. Surprise me."

"Thistlewood is a puppet. It's not him who's behind this treason," Isambard croaked.

Ruthven loosened his grip again and paused.

"So who is?"

"Robespierre," Isambard said.

"Robespierre? What kind of a name is that?"

"That's just what I said. Isn't it Isambard, that's just what I said," William babbled.

"Robespierre. 'The Butcher of Paris' The tyrant of the French Revolution? Some call him Cato – we can call him Cato for short. For code," Isambard said.

"Never 'eard of him," Ruthven said, loosening his grip and glancing up and down the alley furtively.

"Robespierre...Cato. He erm. So, in 1793...." Isambard began.

"Look, he's bad news," William interrupted. "His paw-prints are all over countless executions of innocent people during the French Revolution. He terrorised the whole country until he was executed by his own side in 1794."

"Executed. So he's... dead?" Ruthven asked, cocking his head to one side.

"No. That's the thing. He's not dead. He's here in London trying to destabilise the government and cause a revolution."

"Oh, I get it. He's come back from the dead?" Ruthven said, a wicked smile forming on his lips.

"Officer Ruthven. Robespierre is alive and he's planning to kill the King. In the next few days."

"Kill the King? What, really kill him or just pretend kill him?"

"Really kill him."

"Oh well. Why didn't you say? I shall just nip over to the Palace and warn his Royal Highness myself. Perhaps we should even put a few guards around the place to stop your would-be assassins from wandering in and knocking him off." Ruthven was enjoying himself now, relaxing after the initial shock. "Yes, I shall call in and let the King know directly. He'll appreciate it, I'm sure," he said, fixing them with a broad smile. But as suddenly as it had appeared, the smile evaporated. He jabbed both arms out, pinning each of them to the wall by their throats.

"In the meantime," he said, his face turning hard and peering closely at each of them, "if I ever see either of you young gentlemen again, I shall personally procure a warrant for your transportation to the colonies. For life. Now get out of here and don't even so much as think about Cato Street again." Ruthven let go of them roughly and, with a few long strides, disappeared into the flow of human traffic on Russell Street, leaving the two boys gasping and rubbing their necks.

"I thought that went well," William ventured in a strained voice. "I think we can safely say that our medals are in the post on that one."

"Do you think?" Isambard croaked in reply, stretching his neck. "I'm not convinced that he really bought it. Something about the way he nearly squeezed the life out of us with his bare hands suggests that he didn't really like what he was hearing."

There was a pause as they caught their breath.

"So. What do we do now?" William asked, bent over with his hands on his knees.

"Wait for the King to die?" Isambard replied, only half joking.

Chapter 8

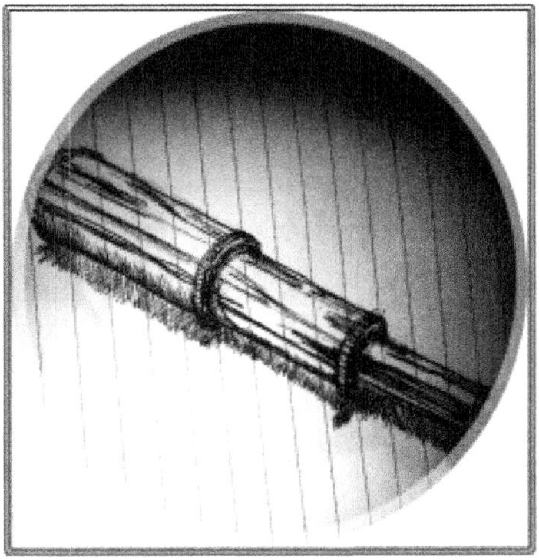

THE MAN FROM THE WAR Office stood at the rail, following the horses' progress through a stubby telescope. In another corner of the hippodrome, crowds roared and cheered as the horses crossed the finish line. A second man arrived and leaned on the paddock rail, as horses from the next race paraded by and the crowd pressed in around them.

"Feeling lucky?" Special Intelligence Directorate asked.

"You know I don't gamble," War Office said. Special Intelligence Directorate smiled but didn't lift his eyes from the programme in his hand.

"So. To what do I owe the pleasure?"

"This? A pleasure? You're too kind. I just thought you might like to know."

"Know what?"

"About The Emperor."

"Napoleon?" War Office said in a strained whisper. Special Intelligence Directorate winced at the indiscretion.

"Sorry. It's been a few years..."

"For us all, my dear, for us all. But suddenly he's right at the top of the bill at Abchurch Lane. All anyone is talking about."

"How so?"

Special Intelligence Directorate allowed himself a meaningful glance in War Office's direction.

"Good heavens..."

"Not a trace. We all thought he was on his last legs - seems he can add acting to his list of talents. Murdered his doctor, swapped clothes and wandered out of the lock-house into the doctor's cab. Didn't stop until he'd boarded a coffee ship nominally bound for Marseille. Evidently he hasn't lost his touch for theatre. Not a trace."

The two men stared into the middle distance at the flurry of activity before the next race began. Itinerant barmaids served gin by the tumbler even though it was barely past mid-day.

"Is he making a move for the amulets?"

"We think so."

"We need to get hold of that scroll."

"I've got someone on it."

Secret Intelligence Directorate squinted across the racetrack.

"And Lord Liverpool?" War Office asked.

"There's to be a Prime Minister's Extraordinary Cabinet meeting at 6-o'clock tonight. I just thought you might appreciate the racing tip," Special Intelligence Directorate said before leaving the rail and melting back into the crowds.

Chapter 9

"ARE WE NEARLY THERE yet?" Millie asked after what seemed like hours of aimlessly wandering across the empty rooftops. Isambard had asked her to take the talking gas back to wherever he'd come from, but it was proving difficult to get anything resembling directions from the strange green glow in a jar.

"Have you any idea where you are?" Trafalgar asked.

Millie looked around for a landmark she recognised. "No," she said, giving up.

"Good."

"Why good?"

"Well, you can only find the Candlewicks' shop once you have become entirely lost. And even then..."

"And even then what?" Millie snapped – she was beginning to run out of patience with the featureless voice.

"You might not even know it when you see it."

But Millie had stopped in her tracks.

"I think I will," she said in a dream-like voice.

From the rooftops, the yard below looked pristine - a few well-kept pot plants, a white-painted corner bench, a hutch for live animals. The high walls formed by the surrounding buildings kept the sounds of the city out. The yard's quiet tidiness made Millie subconsciously climb with extra care. Her stealth, however, was redundant - a tall lady watched her descent from the roof into the yard with a severe look on her pinched face.

"Um, good day. My name is... my name is Millicent Woodington. I have come to return a jar. Um... a talking gas, called Trafalgar."

Madagascar Candlewick stood unimpressed, her plain black frock acting as a perfect mirror of her mood. She reached down into a white-painted bird coop, from which she pulled a collared dove. Cradling it she turned back to Millie and flashed a sour smile. "Have you come to see my sister?"

"Um, yes I suppose so."

"Well. Won't you come in?" she said, more as a threat than an invitation.

The back door of the house opened onto a narrow corridor leading through to a room bathed in sunlight at the front of the building – the bright light was a stark contrast to the cold shade of the yard and dazzled Millie momentarily. All around them, order and tidiness persisted. The surfaces were hard, white and polished, in places decorated with simple black lines. On the wall of the hallway hung two plain-looking framed certificates, one for each of the Candlewick sisters, from the Middlesex Chapter of the ParaChemical Society, both made out for something called 'Architectural Telekinesis'.

She moved through to the shop at the front of the building, dazzling in the sunshine that poured in through the large bay windows opposite.

"Ah, hullo! A visitor!" someone said from behind Millie. She turned to find a shorter, rounder version of the first Miss Candlewick, this one wearing a white coat and an unusual pair of specially thickened spectacles.

"How did you get in?" she asked, wide-eyed.

"I came down from the roof."

"Well, well. That is most... unusual. Madagascar!" she called without taking her eyes off Millie. "Are you responsible for this young thing?"

"No I am not - she said she was here to see you."

The taller Candlewick was carefully placing a stuffed collared dove, amongst the handful of objects which decorated the shop window - a theodolite, a bowl of fruit made of wax, a line of lead soldiers depicting the Norman invasion of 1066 and a model of an Egyptian cat. Suddenly the cat began to make uncannily life-like movements.

"The cat," Millie murmured. "That cat. It's... it's moving."

The cat's ear twitched, its head lifted and its paws stretched out.

"It's a cat, Miss Woodington. Cats tend to move," Madagascar said, turning and giving Millie a reproachful look.

The cat stood up and stretched, as if to confirm that he wasn't part of the window display at all.

"I'm sorry, I..."

"Don't fret dear," Esmerelda said with a gentle smile. "Now tell us, what brought you here?"

"I was told that I would be able to return Trafalgar. He's a talking..."

"Talking gas, yes, yes we know," Madagascar grumbled.

"Trafalgar?" Esmerelda repeated with a guarded look to her sister. "And you found us yourself. I mean, you didn't have any... help?"

"Trafalgar gave me directions. But to be honest we got completely lost."

"Yes. Yes. You would need to."

"I'm sorry, I shouldn't have bothered you," Millie said, turning back the way she came.

"No no, not at all. It's an absolute... pleasure to have a visitor to our shop," Esmerelda soothed. "No, no, you are really most welcome. We were half expecting you... or someone like you, to turn up. Madagascar had a feeling in her waters."

"Oh for goodness sake, Esmerelda, don't be ridiculous. This girl..."

"What did you say your name was again?"

"Millie. Millicent Woodington."

"This girl needs to have the truth."

"Yes. Well yes, I suppose she does."

"The truth? What do you mean? What's going on?"

"Millicent, how did you come across Trafalgar?"

"Well, Isambard was given it. By a man. A man called... called. Oh curses, Isambard told me on the way to Cato Street. Was it Hartley..."

"Hardleygrieve."

"Yes Hardleygrieve. Do you know him?"

"Yes, we... know him," Esmerelda said with a tight-lipped smile.

"Here," Madagascar said, dropping a kind of book onto the counter in front of Esmerelda.

"We can't show her this."

"We can."

"No."

"Yes."

"No."

Madagascar slid the book in front of Esmerelda and held it there. Esmerelda glared at her sister, who simply glared back with more intensity.

"Very well," Esmerelda conceded, opening the book. Instantly a light rose from it and formed a glowing ball in front of Millie, so brightly and suddenly that it caused her to take a step back. But then, it disappeared.

"What's wrong? What happened?" Madagascar asked.

"I don't know,"

Madagascar leaned forward and slid a finger across the blank pages of the book.

"Did you initiate the Voice o' the Wind?"

"No. You're the one who opened the book..."

"Alright, alright," Madagascar said, tilting the book towards herself, resting a hand on the page and muttering.

"Sorry about this," Esmerelda whispered to Millie. "Won't be a moment."

"There."

"Ready now?"

Madagascar touched the corner of the page and closed her eyes briefly. "Ready."

"Right." Esmerelda smiled and opened the book. The same white ball formed in the air between them. It swirled like smoke caught in a glass bauble then exploded into colour.

"How do you make it...?"

"What?"

"How do you make it do the talking...?"

"You just have to... make sure that the... here pass it to me."

Esmerelda slid the book back to Madagascar and gave Millie a cheeky smile.

"Perhaps we should continue the old-fashioned way, whilst we wait for..."

The glowing ball flashed and disappeared.

"So, Millicent, Good news and bad news. The good news is that it would appear that you are one of The Few."

The book flashed and produced a loud pop which made Esmerelda yelp in surprise. "Can you just put that thing to one side and fix it later?" Esmerelda hissed.

"Nearly there."

"What do you mean 'The Few?'" Millie asked, ignoring the light-show.

"The Few are... People like you, and Isambard who can be called upon in times of need."

"Like this business with the amulets?"

"Exactly. Which brings us to the principal of Magical Symmetry."

"Magical Symmetry?"

"Hmmm," Esmerelda said with a grimace, "I'd forgotten how complicated it all is."

"We can't do it without the..."

"But it's not working."

"I know it's not working!"

There was a stony silence and the two sisters glared at each other.

"We shall just have to invite Miss Woodington back another time," Madagascar said through gritted teeth.

"Quite," her sister replied, turning to face Millie with what she hoped was a sweet smile. "We'll have to do it another time. So, what can we do for you today? Oh, I know, I've got just the thing," Esmerelda said, scuttling behind one of the three glass counters that stood about the floor.

"This is for you," she said, plucking a small box from the display under one of the counters and handing it to Millie.

"What is it?" Millie whispered, peering at the beautiful white stone which was blue and almost entirely covered with a liquid pale green. She picked it up, box and all, transfixed as it swirled from colour to colour.

"It's beautiful," she said, looking up at Esmerelda.

"We hoped you would like it," Madagascar replied evenly, a rare look of warmth in her eyes.

The sisters looked on for a moment like proud grandparents as Millie gazed at the stone. Millie noticed an inscription on the inside of the box and read it out in a low voice.

"'*Place me where you want to be, and by my motherstone you shall see.*' What does it mean?"

"This is an Eyestone. We can see everything that it sees when we look into the motherstone."

Millie didn't understand but was quite lost just watching the kaleidoscopic flow of colours.

"Oh," Millie said with a start, as if emerging from a trance. "I've remembered what I came for – I'm here to return Trafalgar."

"Trafalgar?" Esmerelda said with a note of alarm in her voice.

"Yes, he's just here," Millie said, presenting the jar.

Esmerelda turned the jar upside down and inspected its base.

"Careful, he'll... he'll bang his head," Millie said.

Esmerelda raised an eyebrow at Millie before turning the jar the right way up and slowly unscrewing it. "May I?"

"Hullo Esmerelda," Trafalgar said from deep within the jar. Esmerelda screwed the top shut with a quick twist of her hand and glared long and hard at her sister.

"Best keep the lid closed..." Madagascar said in a low voice.

Esmerelda fluttered her eyelids and smiled. Millie placed the jar on the nearest of the glass counters.

"What... what are you doing?" Madagascar asked indignantly. "We can't possibly take him today - haven't you heard?"

"Heard what?"

"We have been told that we cannot execute any transactions today, as a mark of respect," Madagascar chided with an air of borrowed superiority.

"As a mark of respect to whom?" Esmerelda asked.

"To the king. It's a day of mourning," Madagascar said in disbelief. "Didn't you hear - the King is dead."

WHEN MILLIE FINALLY spied her house from the rooftops and clambered down breathlessly, she found that she was nearly crying – the King was dead, just like Cato said he would be. But as she set foot on the street, still a hundred yards from her house, a stationary carriage jerked into life and clattered towards her. It stopped just a few yards away and a door swung open. Inside the gloomy cab, Millie recognised her brother's distressed face. A voice came from within.

"Jump in."

Chapter 10

With the investor meeting fast approaching Isambard had forgotten his grievances and become drawn back into the excitement of it all. His father had hired in some extra labour and there was a buzz of energy about the place – machines constantly whirring, always someone refilling the gravity-tank to provide more hydraulic power. Isambard couldn't help smiling as he watched his father move from machine to machine, discussing the work with the operators, checking it against the drawings, coaching when things didn't quite work out, and constantly updating a large chalk-board on one wall with the status of the current jobs against the target for the day.

On this morning, Isambard was pedalling at one of his father's lathes when everyone and everything around him fell silent. Isambard held himself still, trying to hear or see movement or signs of life. But none came. He cocked his head to one side and scanned the vast workshop – the operators stood in suspended animation, wood-chips hung in the air in a perfect arc, beginning at the drill where the blade met the wood and ending in a frozen shower over the floor. Marc stood motionless at the chalk-board. Matthews, the foreman, stood on the balcony, frozen, silently yelling at the operator responsible for a badly made component. Cautiously Isambard took a small step back and took a wider look around the workshop – it was the same everywhere he looked – motionless, soundless.

"Master Brunel."

Somehow, the sudden sound did not make Isambard jump – perhaps part of him was expecting to hear the voice of the mysterious man he'd first met on the roof near the Courthouse.

"What are you doing here?" Isambard asked, turning to face Hardleygrieve.

"And a very good morning to you."

"I'm not sure you should be here."

"You needn't worry. Only you can see me. They won't even notice."

"I don't understand."

"As you are beginning to find out, Master Brunel, not everything in this world can be understood. Suffice it to say, you are one of the special ones who can see me. One of the Few." Hardleygrieve paused for a moment. "But to answer your question about what I am doing here. It concerns the homework that you did for me. About Cato. I couldn't help noticing that you shared your findings with Officer Ruthven."

Isambard was not expecting this. How did Hardleygrieve know they'd been to see Ruthven?

"As you know, Officer Ruthven works for the judiciary which answers to the government which serves the King. So, instead of respecting my wish that you tell absolutely no-one about Cato, it would seem that you have done exactly the opposite."

"Listen Mr Hardleygrieve, I never wanted to play this game of yours – I just want to get out of this, do you see? I've done my bit for you and now it's over, so if you don't mind..."

"A game? Do you think that you can just hand this back to the grown-ups - get back to your school-books and be done with it? I'm afraid that is no longer an option. Perhaps before you shared our little secret, I could have let you go. But now?" Hardleygrieve paused and looked at Isambard with narrowing eyes before continuing. "Let's assume that, as you have warned, there is an attack on the King – whatever will they make of this young man who saw it coming? Will they pat him on the head and thank him for his clairvoyance?"

Hardleygrieve didn't wait for an answer, which is just as well, because Isambard didn't have one.

"Do you know why I asked you to keep quiet?"

"No."

"These Amulets are my concern – I could have contained the situation, controlled it. Now you've got the entire British establishment involved and I can no longer protect you."

"Protect me? From what?"

"From what's about to happen."

Suddenly the world started again – the sound of raised voices and machine-noise hit Isambard like a wall. Woodchips continued on their lazy arc through the air. The lathe behind him resumed its turning, cranking the pedal round as it went. Isambard found his senses and turned to ask Hardleygrieve what was about to happen. But, of course, Hardleygrieve wasn't there.

Over the din of the workshop, Isambard could hear an urgent banging on the great wooden doors – someone outside trying to get in. Marc emerged from the throng of activity around the broaching machine, turned down his sleeves as he walked and repositioned his stove-pipe hat before opening the door. From where he was standing, Isambard couldn't see the caller, but it wasn't long before Marc looked towards Isambard and nodded, an unreadable look on his face – part fear, part anger, part wonder. Father and son looked at one another for a moment, before Marc, wiping his hands with a grease-stained hanky, came over to Isambard.

"Isambard," he began, somewhat uncertainly. "There is a man here to see you. An Officer Ruthven, of the Bow Street Runners. He says that you have done something very special and that you are to go and see the Home Secretary."

Chapter 11

Isambard emerged from the dust and gloom of the workshop into the bright grey light of Poultry Street to see Ruthven standing next to a glossy black carriage, holding the door open. Isambard approached, but came to a stop when he saw the others in the gloomy cabin within.

"Come on, don't hang about. Get in," Ruthven grumbled.

Isambard pulled himself into the carriage and nodded at Millie and William. Millie responded with an uncertain smile whilst William just looked a bit terrified. Ruthven pushed in behind Isambard and found his seat just as the carriage lurched into motion.

Ruthven sat grim-faced, swaying with the motion of the carriage, legs planted out in front of him. William's slight frame and overwhelmed look made him look like a scrawny schoolboy next to Ruthven. The three of them exchanged nervous glances, but none of them dared speak until, finally, Ruthven unfolded his arms and pulled a pencil and notepad out of his coat pocket. He licked the tip of the stubby pencil and used his coat-cuff to swipe some of the beads of sweat which had emerged on his forehead. He coughed, thrust the pencilled hand through his hair and lifted his head to face them.

Nobody spoke for a good while, the others anxiously watching Ruthven as he clenched his jaw and stared at the pencil that he held poised over his notebook. Occasionally he would mutter to himself, apparently weighing his words and reworking them. Eventually he sighed and looked up. The others looked at him expectantly.

"I've a good mind to take you youngsters to the Courthouse and give you a good hiding. But, as it happens, the Home Secretary has asked to see you, no doubt to have that pleasure for himself. And I'll tell you for why – in passing I mentioned your prediction of the King's demise to my guvnor and he must have passed it right up the chain to Lord Sidmouth himself."

Ruthven stopped to check that they all understood the gravity of this and, seeing William's confused look, decided to elaborate.

"Lord Sidmouth is the Home Secretary."

William looked none-the-wiser

"Most powerful man in the country after the King and the Prime Minister."

"Sorry," Isambard interrupted, "has something happened to the King?"

"The King is dead Sam," Millie said.

"...and understandably," Ruthven restarted, "his Lordship has got some questions about where and how you got this little nugget of information about the King's death before it became reality. So, we have been called to the house of Lord Sidmouth, Home Secretary, ultimate superior for the magistrates' court and the Bow Street Runners, to explain. I have never met him before and he has never met me. So. It is very..." he paused mid-sentence and swiped his brow of sweat once more, "very important that you... behave yourselves in there, you got that?"

"Yes, yes," they all said, nodding vigorously at him and to each other.

"Because if he don't like what he hears, my future, and yours, very quickly goes up in smoke." Having said this, Ruthven put his outstretched hands on his knees and exhaled at length through puckered lips. For a while nobody spoke.

"Don't worry, Officer Ruthven, it'll be alright," Millie said, sensing Ruthven's nerves. He looked at her, grim-faced, and nodded.

"Let's hope so. For all our sakes."

ALTHOUGH BY LORD SIDMOUTH'S standards it was quite a modest town house, Spring Gardens was the grandest building Isambard had ever seen, let alone ever been in. From the gravel driveway where they dismounted the carriage, a butler led them down the polished marble hallways past statues on plinths, ornaments on stands and oil paintings on every square inch of the wall.

The butler brought them to a stop outside a pair of heavy wooden doors. A man's voice could be heard from the room beyond - although they couldn't make out the words, it was obvious that the man was angry. After several moments of sustained shouting, one of the doors opened and a maid slid out, her head bowed and tears gleaming on her cheeks as she pushed past Isambard. Ruthven looked straight ahead, even more grim-faced than before. Isambard turned and raised an eyebrow at Millie whilst William cringed momentarily.

A moment or two later, the butler knocked and the doors were opened. He led them across the breakfast room into a kind of conservatory which bristled with plants. In contrast to the chill outside, it was warm and humid here - fires burned in braziers at each corner of the room, some of them boiling pans of water causing steam to waft and drift into the air. What seemed to be all kinds of coloured leaves flickered and fluttered through the air and clung to the walls of the room. They were momentarily hypnotised by the aerial display, but, having remembered his place, Isambard tugged at the others' sleeves to make them focus their attention on the refined figure sitting behind the breakfast table buttering toast. The man wore a black jacket, a starched white shirt with a black satin neck-tie and was manipulating his toast with efficient precision. When he looked up, Isambard could see that his eyes were a piercing blue. A small dog began yapping energetically from below the table, but was soon silenced by a sharp tap from the man's cane.

"Ah, the four heroes of Cato Street I see! Welcome, on this most sad and lamentable day. The King is dead."

"Long live the King," William replied instinctively, instantly regretting it. The four of them froze as the words hung in the air. Lord Sidmouth blinked, then, with a sour smile forming at the corner of his mouth, concurred.

"Quite so. Just as Shakespeare's Bernardo would have said. Quite so."

A butterfly flapped across Millie's face.

"Ah, fret not at that Swallowtail, my dear. He is very inquisitive but prefers the leaf of a cactus every time."

"He is very beautiful," she said as cheerfully as she could.

"Yes, yes. I netted his great-grandfather when I was in Toulon at Naval negotiations for the treaty of Amiens. The Swallowtails have rather thrived here. We try to make it as Mediterranean as possible," Lord Sidmouth said gazing around the room in wonderment, joined by William who could not resist doing the same.

"But," he said, causing their attention to snap back to the breakfast table. "Back to this most important matter of the conspiracy at Cato Street. First of all, my sincere apologies for bringing you all the way here, by such a crude method and on such a doleful day. I'm sure you would all rather be with your families to mourn the passing of our much-loved King. However, as you know, dark forces threaten the very kingdom that his majesty King George devoted his life to, and we owe it to him to do everything in our power to defend ourselves. The officer here, officer...?"

"Officer, ahem," Ruthven began, his voice failing him. "Officer Ruthven, sir, of the Bow Street Runners sir, at your service."

"Ruthven? Scottish?"

"Yes sir. My grandfather was from the lowlands, sir."

"Officer Ruthven has told me of the intelligence that you supplied. Putting aside for one moment the regrettable nature of the event itself, your warning on the death of the King before the fact suggests that your intelligence is of the highest quality. I therefore made a request to hear the detail of it first hand, hence your presence here this morning."

Lord Sidmouth pushed his plate to one side, leaned forward, and steepled his lean hands on the table in front of him.

"So, tell me, how did a crowd of rough-shod scallywags such as yourselves manage to upstage the combined skills of his majesty's court at Bow Street?"

A butler appeared carrying a silver tray – Sidmouth raised a finger, stopping the waiter in his tracks.

Minds raced as Isambard, Millie and William attempted to put the events into an order that might be intelligible to a Lord of the Realm. To an adult. To anyone.

"My Lord," Isambard began, "my father, Marc Isambard Brunel built factories making ship's blocks and army boots for Lord Wellington so it is a great privilege to be of service in my own small way to His Majesty's Government."

"Yes quite. But how did you pick up on the plan to kill the King?"

William took up the charge. "My Lord, if I may be so bold, we have been informally assisting Officer Ruthven for some time now and..."

"Yes, yes, but this is mere procedure. I want action," Lord Sidmouth interrupted, obviously becoming impatient. Millie was their only remaining hope.

"My Lord, if I may. We located the premises on Cato Street and established the identity of the mysterious figure variously known as Robespierre and Cato from his time spent at the heart of the French Revolution."

"Robespierre. So the Frenchies are at the root of all this. I knew it!"

"We then positioned ourselves on the roof of the property to witness a conversation between this individual and Thistlewood who was heretofore believed to be the ultimate ring-leader, but who we now believe to be acting under the guidance of Cato."

Lord Sidmouth banged the table. "But how the devil did you know about the conversation and how did you access it?" Sidmouth demanded impatiently.

An icy silence filled the air. Millie held her breath and paused, her mind racing. "It all began when Isambard here had a visit from a man called Hardleygrieve."

"Hardleygrieve – you saw... you had a meeting with Hardleygrieve?" Sidmouth asked.

"Yes sir, I..."

"Well that is very unorthodox, but certainly explains a few things," Sidmouth mused, suddenly looking more relaxed. "Carry on,"

Millie tugged at her dress and took a sharp breath. Out of the corner of her eye she saw Sidmouth summon the butler, who arrived carrying a silver tray. Millie, still holding her breath, watched as Lord Sidmouth took the envelope with a languid sliding motion and waved impatiently at Millie to continue whilst he opened the letter. Millie took one last nervous look at Isambard who replied with a stiff nod. Millie began to explain. However, Lord Sidmouth didn't hear about Isambard's meeting with Hardleygrieve because he was reading the butler's note. He didn't listen to the bit about Trafalgar the talking gas because he was too busy writing a reply. And the flexible periscope didn't make any sense because he hadn't heard any of the rest of it. So, finding himself unable to make head or tail of the story, he allowed it to wash over him as he took a silver fob watch from his pocket and realised that he would soon be late for the emergency Cabinet meeting. With a start, he brushed his lapel and coat-front with a napkin and flattened his hands on the table, which Millie, quite rightly, took as a sign to stop.

"Well, well what an adventure and indeed what a fine piece of investigative work of which even you and your men, Officer Ruthven, would be proud," Lord Sidmouth said standing and looking squarely at the officer, whose brow was even more sweaty now than it had been in the carriage.

Ruthven paused, wondering if a trap was about to spring shut. "Quite so, sir. A very laudable piece of work and no mistake," Ruthven agreed.

But it wasn't a trap.

"Well," Lord Sidmouth said, fumbling a napkin briefly before tossing it onto his plate and manoeuvring himself out from behind the table.

"Credit to you, Officer Ruthven. Thanks to you, we have gone from viewing this crowd of conspirators as a troubling annoyance to a significant threat to the very fabric of society. I have a Cabinet meeting now, at which we will no doubt discuss the Cato Street conspirators and I am sure, Officer Ruthven, that as a result, you and your men will be receiving urgent direction in this regard. Until then however you will take no further action against this Cato character," the Home Secretary said, his voice suddenly becoming as cold as ice. “I trust I have made myself quite clear. No further action, do you understand?”

The words hung in the air for a second, but the Home Secretary was not expecting a response. He picked up the small dog from under the table, bid them good day and strode purposefully from the room.

THEY SAT IN SILENCE as their carriage pulled away, Ruthven's head once again bowed. After they had travelled for a few moments, he began to tremble and make a kind of sobbing noise. The other three exchanged worried glances, not daring to speak. But Ruthven wasn't crying. He looked up and his eyes were indeed gleaming, but with joy. His beard was split by a yellow-toothed smile and by now his whole body shook with the force of the laughter.

“You little beauties,” he chuckled, looking at the others and wiping a tear from his cheek. Isambard and the others felt an overwhelming sense of relief crash over them.

“I've got no clue what you was on about there, Missy, but whatever it was it worked. 'Credit to you' Lord Sidmouth said. 'Credit to you,'” Ruthven recalled, shaking his head in wonderment whilst mentally putting the Home Secretary's words in a frame and hanging them over the fireplace in his mind.

“And what about those butterflies? Weren't they ravishing!” William exclaimed. “And those paintings on the wall when we walked down the hall were as good as any at the Gallery."

But Isambard had other concerns.

"One thing I didn't understand. If we've done such a good job, why has he asked us to keep away?"

"Cato said that the conspiracy is happening tomorrow night. Surely we need to stop it," Millie added.

"This is a very delicate situation and the last thing we need is the three of you going off all over it like a sackful of fireworks," Ruthven said, looking at each of them in turn. "Best if you do as you're told and keep your noses out of it."

THE CARRIAGE CAME TO a stop and Ruthven parted the curtains with an outstretched finger, peering out across the empty streets. The carriage wobbled as the driver descended to open the door.

"This is where you get off. I shall send word if you are needed. Now get off home, and not a word of this to anyone."

Ruthven turned away as the three of them stepped off the coach onto the pavement below. William stumbled on the step and was helped back onto his feet by the driver. William couldn't help noticing the angry blister in the shape of a star, wet like a fresh burn, on the back of the man's hand. William looked up as the driver turned away and climbed back up to the driver's bench.

The carriage pulled away and once again the deserted street was silent.

"Well that clears up any doubt," William said. "A personal command from the highest authority in the land telling us to keep away from this Cato character. I'm certainly not going to have anything more to do with it. Looks like your dad was right, Sam. Come on Millie, they'll be wondering where we've got to at home."

William turned to walk away, but Millie wasn't quite ready to leave.

"Oh. Sam. Here's your bag back – I tried to get rid of Trafalgar, but I met the Candlewick sisters and they tried to teach me about magic and said the shop would have to shut so they couldn't... Okay so now I'm sounding like you."

"Millie, there's something very strange going on here, something that we don't have a hope of understanding on our own. But one thing I do know - tomorrow night there's a conspiracy planned and we need to be there to stop it."

Chapter 12

From the edge of the wood-panelled dining room of the Worshipful Company of Gunmakers, Isambard watched his father with a mix of pride and anxiety churning inside him. His queasiness was only made worse by the clouds of rich tobacco smoke that filled the room. Marc's talk about his plans for a tunnel under the Thames had been a great success and the audience of bankers, investors and government officials all seemed persuaded by the test-results of his patented Tunneling Shield. Isambard had never heard such a cacophony of polished accents, never seen such a collection of finely dressed gentlemen, or such a consumption of port, cigars and pudding. Marc now looked like a boy in a sweetshop, standing behind his lectern looking wide-eyed at the knot of investors that had formed around him to ask questions. Although the talk had started early, aiming to finish before nightfall, there had been so many questions that the chandeliers had been lit and more wine had been ordered.

But Isambard's nausea was not all related to the investors' meetings – it was the night of the Conspiracy, and his mind was racing with thoughts of Cato, Thistlewood and the conspirators readying themselves in a Cato Street hay-loft three miles across London. He looked again at the grandfather clock. Half-past six.

"Hey," came a voice from Isambard's side, making him jump.

"Millie! What are you doing here?" Isambard whispered, looking sideways at Millie who was clearing teacups and crystal glasses onto a tray next to him.

"I thought I'd come along in case you needed some help," she said without looking up.

"But you don't work here."

"They don't know that. Housemaids' uniforms are the same all over so I was able to slip in. Nobody is going to notice me as long as I'm keeping busy."

Isambard shook his head disapprovingly but couldn't help smiling at her audacity. From across the room, Marc caught Isambard's eye and beckoned him over. Isambard acknowledged with a nod.

"So what are you going to do?" Millie asked.

"What do you mean? Father needs me here."

"What about the conspiracy? It's tonight."

"I know, Millie, but I can't get away. Father will kill me if I disappear. And if he doesn't kill me, Ruthven and the Home Secretary will."

"If we don't do something about it, Sam, it'll be more than just you that gets killed."

There was a pause whilst Isambard agonised over the choice he had to make. "You're right. We need to get over to Cato Street," he said finally.

"I'll just sort this lot out and then I'll get changed. Meet me out the back in two ticks."

"I can't just walk out..." Isambard complained. But Millie was already bustling off with a tray full of used glasses, pushing her way through the crowded room, leaving Isambard clenching his teeth whilst he considered his excuses. Marc beckoned him over again, more urgently this time. Isambard took a deep breath and made his way over.

"Aha here he is, gentlemen, my son, Isambard," Marc said, placing his hands on Isambard's shoulders.

"Despite his height, or lack of it, he is already 16-years-old and a very accomplished engineer. He can respond to your questions as well as ever I could, in French or English!" Marc beamed, to a ripple of appreciative laughter.

"Well if he's anything like you, Mr Brunel, we shall all be offering him a job before the evening is done," one of the investors joked.

"I'm afraid he is not available for other engagements," Marc said, with a polite smile.

"Father," Isambard whispered once the conversations around him had resumed. "Father, I need to leave."

"What? What Isambard, what are you saying?" Marc said irritably, excusing himself.

"Father, I have to leave. I..." Isambard began, but he did not have time to finish his sentence as the room was rapidly quietening.

"Does anyone know how to deliver a baby?"

Silence. Isambard realised it was a voice he recognised.

"One of the maids has found herself to be in the family way and it seems that the moment has arrived."

Millie, Isambard thought. That's Millie's voice. All eyes were turned to her, standing in the service doorway across the room.

The men looked awkwardly at one another and at the floor.

"Well, don't look at me, it's not my fault!" one of the men joked, to gales of laughter.

Suddenly Isambard understood what Millie was doing – she was creating an escape path. "I helped with the forceps when Aunt Elizabeth was in trouble having Constance," Isambard said, looking up into his father's eyes.

"Oh, well look at that. A man for every occasion!" one of the lawyers opposite Isambard said.

"Step forward, Young Isambard," said another more portly man, moving to one side and opening a path all the way to Millie. Isambard looked at his father who gave a sharp nod of approval.

"My Lords and Gentlemen, I give you, the Young Isambard Brunel!" the portly lawyer announced, clapping energetically. Isambard made his way through the crowd, somewhat abashed, as the menfolk clapped half-heartedly and returned to their conversations.

"That was risky," Isambard said as he and Millie pushed through the doors and clattered down the back-stairs together.

"It worked didn't it?" she asked, grinning over her shoulder at him.

"So how are we going to get over to Cato Street? We'll need to move fast."

"Search me," Millie replied. "We could run."

Isambard scanned the dimly lit lobby at the bottom of the stairs and stopped when he saw a sign for the cloakroom.

"Wait here. I've got an idea," Isambard said. Moments later, he came back with a top-hat, a cloak, a cane and two wooden cigar boxes.

"The cloak and hat I get, but what are the boxes for?"

"Here, give me your laces..."

The two of them stepped out of the Worshipful Company's grand double doors at the top of a wide stone staircase which led down to a circular gravel driveway. Gas-lamps cast their yellowy light onto the shiny coats of black horses, and the even shinier bodywork of the black cabs that each of the horses pulled. Horse-tails swished while drivers and footmen broke up their conversations and stood to attention in front of their carriages, looking up at Isambard and Millie expectantly.

"Take it nice and slow, I'm a bit unsteady in this lot," Isambard whispered out of the side of his mouth to Millie. He had tied a wooden cigar box to the sole of each shoe, giving himself an extra 6 inches of height, a fact which he was able to obscure underneath the flowing cape. He had taken Millie's arm, not in the traditional gentlemanly manner, but more as a way of keeping his balance.

"They're never going to fall for this," Millie said, disguising her misgivings by smiling sweetly up at Isambard. He laughed, doing his best to emulate one of the investors that they had left behind in the room upstairs.

"Ah ha, my dear Millicent, bear a hand there would you?" Isambard said for the benefit of the onlookers, before adding in a lower voice, "we don't have any choice. We need to make this look convincing."

Millie thought for a moment as they walked clumsily down the last few steps, then, speaking loudly, said.

"Oh father, you've had too much of that port you silly old thing. Let's get you home."

She looked up at the footman who had been watching them with an increasingly perplexed look on his face.

"John Street please, near Cato Street, as quick as you can. My father is not well," Millie said, bustling past the footman and helping Isambard into the carriage.

The carriage pulled out of the Institute driveway but progress was frustratingly slow through the streets of Soho, whose crowds seemed to include all the hawkers, buskers, trained animals and common criminals of London. At times the horse and carriage had to literally push a path through the swirl of people whilst opportunistic vendors waved their wares at the cab window in the hope of a lucrative sale. On more than one occasion the driver had to flash his whip at the crowds to make them stand back. After what seemed like an age, the crowds thinned and the horse started trotting up Edgeware Road towards Cato Street. Isambard noticed a clock on the way.

"Nearly seven," he said grimly.

Fortunately for the penniless impostors, the cab had been pre-paid by the Company - the driver was about to pull away when Millie called up to him.

"It seems my father has had a terrible lapse and has picked up the wrong accoutrements – would you mind awfully returning these to the Gunmakers so that they might find their rightful owner," Millie asked. The driver took the hat, cape and cane, grunted and pulled away.

"Accoutrements?" Isambard asked "Millicent Woodington, we'll have you speaking French in no time," he grinned, releasing the cigar-box platforms from his shoes and handing Millie back her shoelaces.

A distant bell tolled seven times as they ran through the arch from John Street into Cato Street.

"There's the hay-loft - we should be able to get onto the roof if you give me a boost up onto that lean-to," Millie said. They raced to the wall, pushed and hauled each other onto the lower roof and then onto the roof of the barn. They could hear excited talk from within, even the occasional laugh or shout.

"It sounds like they are working each other up into a bit of a frenzy," Millie whispered.

"I bet they are. If they have their way, they'll change the course of history tonight."

"Here, there's a bit of a hole in the thatch - come and have a look."

Through the ragged layers of straw that covered the roof, Isambard and Millie were able to see down into the room where a long table lay covered in pikes, knives, a couple of pistols and what looked like some home-made explosives. Around the table 15 or 20 men waved weapons around in a grotesque rehearsal of the actions they were planning to take.

"They're armed to the teeth. What are we going to do?" Millie whispered.

"Well, we can't match them for firepower. But we can fight chaos with chaos."

"What do you mean?"

"We've got to set a fire..."

"A fire! Are you... are you mad?"

"They'll have plenty of time to get out, but not in an orderly fashion. They'll leave half the weapons behind and be scattered to the four winds. It's the only way to stop this happening."

Isambard produced a tinder-box and they stared at it.

"I don't suppose we really have any choice," Millie said.

Just then they heard the distinctive sound of a crowd of armed guards in the street below.

"Look, there's Ruthven, coming up the road with a load of soldiers," Isambard said.

"We should make ourselves scarce – he'll go mad if he sees us,"

"No let's just lie low – make sure he doesn't see us."

Isambard and Millie watched as, after a short exchange between Ruthven and the Captain of the guard, Ruthven led a line of Bow Street Runners towards the ground floor of the building. The conspirators had a lookout stationed below who now began crying out - he was quickly silenced, but he had made enough noise to alert his mates above, who now appeared to be in panic mode. Some were attempting to hide the armaments, others were readying for battle, a few simply froze in panic, not knowing what to do.

Through the holes in the roof, Millie and Isambard watched as Ruthven climbed up the ladder and emerged through the hatch into the hayloft, booming as he went. "I am an officer of the peace. I command you to lay down your arms in the name of the law." More officers arrived up the step-ladder, and a stand-off developed between the two ranks of men facing each other.

Suddenly a shape moved in the shadows, and Isambard could see the flash of a sabre heading towards Ruthven.

"Ruthven!" Isambard cried without thinking. At the sound of his name, Ruthven turned just in time to dodge Thistlewood's blade. But Thistlewood wasn't finished - the hay-loft was crowded and the next target was not far away. He lunged again, this time striking one of Ruthven's men, who crumpled to the ground. Like a shaken beehive, the hayloft erupted, officers shouting orders, conspirators pleading or threatening.

At the back of the room a candle was knocked over, then another, and another. In a few moments the hay loft was in darkness and Isambard could hardly see.

Suddenly, a blast as a grenade exploded in the corner of the room, blowing a hole in the back corner of the loft.

The shock of the explosion caused Millie to lose her balance and she found herself pitching forward onto the threadbare fibres of the roof. But of course it was not strong enough to hold her. Before Isambard could reach her, the roof collapsed and Millie was falling in a heap on the dusty floor between soldiers and conspirators.

Ears ringing from the blast and blinded by the smoke, Isambard looked on helplessly as Millie was swallowed up by the dark mass of shadows.

"Millie," Isambard cried as he scanned the scene helplessly for any sign of her. Gradually a certain kind of order was returning – the chaos of raised voices was resolving into a stream of barked commands from Ruthven and his men.

Lanterns were being re-lit and what remained of the conspirators were being rounded up into a small group in the corner of the loft.

But there was no sign of Millie

Isambard climbing through the hole in the roof and dropped down onto the wooden floor below, recovering his balance only to find himself face to face with a guard not much older than himself.

"Officer Ruthven," Isambard called out over the guard. The acrid smoke of burning straw caught in his throat. "It's me. Brunel. We've got to find Millie."

Ruthven squinted in Isambard's direction and turned.

"Brunel," he said through a crooked smile, whilst taking a step closer. And then, to the young soldier, "Chain this one up and put him in my carriage. Make sure you keep a hold of him - he's a slippery one."

Chapter 13

"Oh, I'd forgotten about you. Budge up will you," Ruthven said as he threw open the carriage door and hauled himself up into the cabin where Isambard had been roughly chained 20 minutes earlier by the young soldier. Making the carriage rock like a rowboat, Ruthven made himself comfortable on the seat opposite Isambard as they got under way.

Ruthven produced a handkerchief from his top pocket, placed it on his knee and unwrapped it. "My wife made these," he said, carefully taking one of the biscuits from the handkerchief. "Help yourself."

Isambard was famished but his hands were tightly bound behind his back and he was unable to move – he looked at Ruthven with as blank a face as he could muster.

"Suit yourself," Ruthven said with a shrug and a smirk, taking the remaining biscuit. "So then. Perhaps you can explain what you was doing dropping out of the sky on us like that. Just happened to be passing, did you? I've a good mind to drop in on the Home Secretary now and let him know that you've disobeyed his order to stay away."

"You should be grateful."

"How so?"

"Nobody else saw that blade coming."

Ruthven thought back to Thistlewood's first lunge and remembered how close he had been to taking a dagger in the chest.

"That was you?" Ruthven said, looking at Isambard as if for the first time.

There was a pause as they both thought of Smithers, the dead man, and how nearly it could have been Ruthven.

"You saved my life - here. Gimme them irons," Ruthven said, indicating Isambard to spin round so the manacles could be removed. Isambard stood unsteadily in the swaying carriage as Ruthven applied the key and released the irons.

Isambard rubbed his bruised wrists and sat down staring hard into Ruthven's eyes.

"So, seems like it's you that owes me a favour – you saw they made off with Millie?"

"The girl who fell from the roof – that was your friend, Millie? Of course."

"We need to get her back."

"Well I can see what you're thinking young Brunel, but I can't do nothing to help you. I got orders to break up the conspiracy, nothing more – I don't have any ways nor means of getting after her. They'll go straight to ground anyway."

"What do you mean?"

"The gang. They'll disappear – we won't get a sniff of them."

"How many of them got away? Did you get Cato?"

"Cato? No, no, he made it out the back with some of his heavies after that grenade went off."

"Cato doesn't even know we're onto him - he won't be as careful as the others."

"Maybe so, but how does that help us? We don't even have a working description of him."

"No," Isambard said, deep in thought. "But I've got something even better."

Chapter 14

Although it was late, Isambard persuaded Ruthven to drop him off near William's house. When the black carriage had pulled away, Isambard hauled himself onto the cottage roof next to William's window. With no moonlight it was impossible to see whether William was in there – Isambard gave three sharp knocks.

Nothing.

Isambard ran his hand along the windowsill and found what he was looking for – the free end of a piece of wire that led through a small hole in the windowsill. From there the wire ran through a couple of eyelets in the walls to a release mechanism suspending a heavy cushion above William's bed.

Isambard pulled the wire loop which activated the release mechanism which dropped the cushion onto the bed.

"Ooof. What the...?" Isambard heard William say from the other side of the thin pane of glass. Isambard knew how heavy the pillow was from the tests they had done at installation, and couldn't resist the smile that grew across his face. Isambard heard the sound of William's feet hitting the floorboards and leaned back as the window slid upwards.

"What d'you want?" William's blond hair looked like straw and his eyes were scrunched up against the dim light from the nearby gas-lamp.

"They've taken Millie."

"What? Who have? What's happened?"

"We went to the Conspiracy together. It was all about to happen when Ruthven arrived with a small army and swamped the place. But someone set off a grenade and some of the gang escaped out the back. Millie fell through the roof and next thing I knew she was gone."

"Gone?"

"They've taken her, Will. Cato and the gang have taken her – we need to find them."

"What... how are we supposed to find them?"

"Your sketch. Of Cato. Ruthven says he can get it to all his officers so they can seek him out. We need to make copies."

"Copies? How many?"

"Fifty."

"Fifty? You want me to make fifty copies of my sketch of Robespierre? That'll take forever."

"You've got until seven o'clock tonight when the mail coaches leave. And then we'll need another thirty for the towns and ports in the north."

"Eighty in total. It can't be done by hand. You'd need a printing press." There was a pause. William could see the thought forming in Isambard's mind and he didn't like it.

"Isambard, no. No way."

"Printing press, printing press, now there's an idea. How does a printing press work?"

"You have got to be joking."

"Millie has been kidnapped – of course I'm not joking," Isambard said. "Come on, tell me how this press works."

William gave a sigh and stared back at Isambard.

"Well, an engraving is done on copper plate. It's inked, then pressed onto the paper under pressure."

"We've got some copper plate in father's workshop. How much pressure?"

"Enormous pressure."

"In pounds per square inch?"

"...loads"

"Hmm. Not a quantity that I am familiar with. What kind of equipment do they normally use?"

"It's like a giant corkscrew: they put the plates in the jaws then spin the top round and round so it screws down and squashes the plates."

"A fly-press."

"Ok."

"We don't have one of those."

"Oh."

There was a pause.

"Don't worry about that bit. We'll think of something." Isambard said. "Get dressed."

"Isambard, it's gone midnight. Where we going?"

"My father's workshop. Come on."

WHEN THEY GOT TO THE workshop they found the package that Isambard had begged from Ruthven containing 100 sheets of paper and some ink.

"Right," Isambard said in a forced whisper, "we need to work quickly and quietly."

"If your dad catches us we'll be for the high-jump."

"Better not get caught then."

They lit a pair of lanterns and, whilst Isambard did his best to put a makeshift press together, William made a test engraving, both to practise the technique and to give Isambard something to use in trials. William then set about creating the finished copper-plate whilst Isambard found new and interesting ways to squash paper onto the ink-covered plate: under books (poor resolution, not heavy enough); under a precarious stack of iron castings (good, but too dangerous); and in Mr Isambard's largest vice (too much manual work and prone to smudging).

"It's no good," Isambard panted, exhausted from tightening the vice. "We need a couple of tons which we can move up and down without accidentally killing ourselves or dying of exhaustion."

"How much would those big bathtubs produce if we brought those to bear?"

Isambard looked over his shoulder at the gravity tanks which powered the band saw and all of his father's machinery. He looked back at William with a troubled expression on his face.

"Not sure we should use father's gravity power system. It drives everything he does in this workshop."

"But it would give us the pressure we need, wouldn't it?" William demanded. "Do you want to find Millie or not?"

Isambard sighed and began to mutter mathematical incantations.

"Four thousand gallons. Ten pounds per gallon. Forty thousand pounds. Twenty-four inches by fifteen... A couple of thousand pounds per square inch. It might just work."

"Great."

"We'll need a dummy plate the other side to make sure it doesn't skew to one side."

"Whatever you say, captain. Let's give it a try."

By three o'clock in the morning they had produced a sheet with very clear line reproduction from the test plate. William was finishing the shading and cross-hatching on the final engraving. By four, they had the first half-dozen prints laid out to dry and by six, having become well practised in rapidly setting and resetting their make-shift press, they had all fifty complete.

All was going well until William tripped over a pile of cast-iron bars – they slipped their bindings and tumbled over each other across the floor in a thunderous cacophony that could have woken the dead. When the last bar had finished clanging, Isambard and William found they were looking at each other with pained looks on their faces. Isambard motioned to the lantern and William blew it out, plunging the workshop into darkness. Outside the church bell rang once – quarter past six. They had been working all night. Suddenly there were noises upstairs.

"Sounds like father." Isambard whispered. William's eyes widened in panic. "Get the prints and hide yourself."

Isambard and William scrabbled around in the dark collecting the prints which were hung about the place to dry. A light appeared in the door on the mezzanine level above. William tucked himself into a dark corner with as much of their gear as he could manage.

"Who's there?" Marc asked, holding his lantern out in front of him, projecting a huge wavering shadow of himself onto the roof behind.

"Father, it's me. I woke up with an idea and wanted to come down and try it out. I thought maybe we could print our own pamphlets and save money on printing costs. Tell more people about the Tunnel. I've been doing some experiments."

"Oh Isambard, you... You are very kind but it will do us no good. We didn't make our investment target last night. The project is sunk. For now."

"Oh father, I'm so sorry to hear that," Isambard said, relighting the lantern and holding it up. "The man from the London Corporation seemed very keen..."

But Marc didn't answer - his attention had been wrenched away. "What is that?" he hissed, pointing to Isambard's left. Isambard scanned across the room, on the way briefly locking eyes with William's who looked up from his hiding place behind a milling machine. Isambard's gaze moved on to the thing that his father had spotted from high above them – a copy of Cato's portrait, drying on the back of a chair in the corner.

"Father, it's a test. I was just running some test prints..."

"Using that portrait? Of all the things? No Isambard, this was no test for the good of the Tunnel, nor for the good of this family. This was a test for your own selfish purposes."

"No Father, I..."

"You are pursuing your own fool's errand as I pursue mine. Well then, we shall continue to pursue our errands alone. You will have the freedom you obviously crave. You will leave this house, Isambard. Be gone. And do not let me see you or hear from you ever again."

THEY TIDIED UP, PACKED up the posters (53 in all) and made their way onto the rooves. William tried to lighten the mood, but every time he started a conversation Isambard shut it down or just ignored it. After a while William gave up and contented himself with observing the way the low sun picked out rich reds in the bricks, tiles and timbers of the rooftops.

"Here, you're welcome to use my bed," William said once they had climbed in through his bedroom window. "I've got to go to the studio - work at eight. You going to be alright?"

"Sure."

"There's bread downstairs if you're hungry – help yourself."

"No. I'm just gonna..." Isambard said sitting on the bed with his head in his hands.

"Long night?"

"Long week. Long life."

"Look Isambard I'm really sorry..."

"William, don't. It's my fault."

William's mind raced for something to say. "You did it for Millie, remember?"

"Yeah," Isambard said, collapsing sideways onto the bed.

"Hey, don't get your mucky boots all over my..." William said. Isambard unlashed his boots, tossed them to one side and got under the top blanket. "What time you meeting Ruthven with the posters?"

"Six thirty this evening at the post house. The mail coaches leave at seven."

"Ok. Well look I'd better get going. I'll be back at six to make sure you..."

"Sure. Thanks."

After William had got his stuff together and left, Isambard let the tears run down his cheeks before falling into a long deep sleep.

Chapter 15

It was raining hard that evening when Isambard met Ruthven standing in freezing puddles of rancid straw under the arches of the post office at Aldersgate.

"Here, I've got the posters," Isambard said, offering up the rolls that he and William had produced the night before. "How do we get them onto the coaches?"

"No need."

"What do you mean no need? We worked all night to get them ready. Not to mention the trouble it's got me into with my father."

"We don't need them because we already know where Cato is."

Isambard was stunned into silence for a moment.

"How?"

"A message."

"A message – a message from who?"

Ruthven looked out of one end of the tunnel into the grey sheet of rain.

"We've got a spy in the gang."

Isambard peered at Ruthven to check this wasn't some kind of bizarre joke.

"Okay. Well, we need to get over there and get Millie out."

"It i'nt that simple. I've got the Home Secretary, best mate of the Prime Minister, telling me to leave this Cato fella alone."

"But we need to find Millie...." Isambard objected.

"Gimme a minute, will you," Ruthven said, pressing on. "That's better. Now, let me tell you about the little voice in my 'ead telling me that Cato is about the biggest threat that England has faced since William the Conqueror. What do you suppose I should do about that?"

Isambard looked blank.

"I happen to know that you have the same little voice in your 'ead so I am going to cut you a deal. In recognition of your having saved my life in that barn on Cato Street, I am going to help you go against the Home Secretary's wishes."

"You mean go after Millie?"

Ruthven pressed down on Isambard's shoulders and looked around nervously.

"Go there. Get Millie. And get out. Nothing more. Don't let anyone see you."

"Okay, sure, of course. So where are they?"

Ruthven pulled out a well-thumbed notebook from his inside pocket and flicked through a few of its dog-eared pages. Finding what he needed he ripped out the page and handed it to Isambard.

"Number 7, Dowry Square, Bristol."

"Who lives there?"

"A certain man of science called Beddoes. We've got him on file as having radical tendencies but also as someone who knows a thing or two about these mighty amulets, so we're assuming he's helping Cato on his little endeavour. Here, take this," Ruthven said, looking hard into Isambard's eyes and pressing a five-pound note into Isambard's hand. "For expenses. Take William if you need company - you'll meet my man John McClavin in the Adam and Eve pub when you get to Bristol."

Ruthven gave Isambard's shoulder a squeeze before turning away to leave. "Oh, and by the way," he added over his shoulder, "if Lord Sidmouth finds out, or you get caught by Cato's mob, you're on your own. A couple of kids on a prank. I'll deny ever having met you. So look after yourselves."

Ruthven was about to disappear out of the arch and into the rain but stopped when he saw the forlorn look on Isambard's face.

"No need to look so glum. How about a pie? I reckon you deserve one. Come on, there's a place I know just round the corner where the pies slide out of the oven hot and sweet," Ruthven said, looking down at Isambard with a crooked smile. "Anyway, I think I might have found a use for you."

Ruthven's favourite pie shop was the kind of place that men would visit between a shift of work in the docks and a long night in the tavern, where fighting and singing were only ever moments away. As far as Isambard could see, it was a men only establishment, excepting of course the formidable Mrs Miggins who ran the place from behind the counter in the style of a battlefield general.

"Don't worry, son," Ruthven reassured Isambard as they walked in, watched with suspicion by the patrons. "Best pies in London and never any trouble. Isn't that right Mrs Miggins."

"As long as I live, Mr Ruthven. What'll you have?"

"Two pots of ale and two of your finest liver and bacon pies, if you please."

"They're all finest Mr Ruthven, you should know that."

"That's funny, I'm sure you said you always saves your best for me."

"I'll say anything if it'll sell more pies. That'll be six shillings," Mrs Miggins said, placing the pies directly onto the wooden table and switching on a well-practised smile.

"How's Seth?" Ruthven said, dropping the coins onto the counter.

The pie-seller's smile faded. "Still bad."

Ruthven nodded. "Tell him I want his cart when he's dead."

Mrs Miggins laughed and turned away.

"He knows. That's why he ain't dying any time soon."

They turned and made their way to a table, Ruthven nodding to a few of the other customers along the way.

"Get your laughing gear round that," Ruthven said as they sat down.

"Thanks."

"What's up with you anyway?" Ruthven asked through a mouthful of pie.

"Just worried about Millie I suppose."

"She'll be alright. We'll catch up with her soon enough."

"We should never have gone to Cato Street."

"If you hadn't of come, I would be a gonner. Six feet under. Making my way through the Pearly gates into heaven and taking a seat next to our recently deceased King. Thanks to you I'm still here. Everything for a reason, son, and a reason for everything. Come on," Ruthven said, pushing the last morsel of pie into his mouth, brushing his hands roughly across his jacket and gulping down the dregs of his ale.

"I've gotta get home. Off you trot – go and get some sleep. You'll need to be up early for the stage coach to Bristol"

Isambard thought of how he left his father at home and couldn't avoid some of his discomfort showing on his face.

"What's up? You look like a whipped dog. Trouble at home? Worried about that spot of bother with your old man?" Ruthven grinned. "What've you been up to?"

"My father caught me printing the posters of Cato. He wasn't pleased – he's thrown me out the house."

"Ha," Ruthven barked, planting a huge hand on Isambard's bony shoulder. "How old are you, son?"

"Sixteen sir."

"Thrown out at sixteen. I didn't last to fourteen under my old man's roof. Didn't do me no harm. Well, it's the doss-house for you then."

Isambard thought about spending the night in some squalid hostel and felt his eyes well up.

"I'm pulling your leg!" Ruthven said, giving Isambard's shoulder a gentle shove. "I'm sure Mrs Ruthven won't mind you kippin' on our floor."

Ruthven took one last look around the shop and nodded a goodbye to Mrs Miggins.

"Come on, we're not far. Ha, the look on your face..."

Chapter 16

A knock at the door and Cato looked up sharply. Near the fireplace the man tied to the chair writhed and moaned, his calls for help muted by the gag in his mouth. But the Frenchman wasn't listening – instead he straightened his coat with a few stiff tugs and made for the hallway.

By the time he reached the door he found that his palms were sweating – he felt like a young man meeting his sweetheart. He paused, straightened his coat again and opened the door.

Outside, in the pounding rain, a short man in a glistening oilskin cape stood in front of two heavy-set men who Cato recognised as hired bodyguards.

"Your.... your Excellency," Cato said in little more than a whisper.

"Robespierre. My dear old friend. Look at you. You haven't changed a bit," the visitor said, waving his cane vaguely in Cato's direction. Cato looked back at the careworn face and unsteady frame of the former Emperor of France and found that he couldn't truthfully return the compliment.

"Well," Napoleon said looking up into the rain-filled sky above him, "I've spent the last five years on an English prison-island and sailed these six weeks to get here. Aren't you at least going to invite me in?"

Cato apologised and Napoleon began to laugh, climbing the stairs unsteadily. Cato went to offer Napoleon a helping hand, but the Emperor shot him such a look that Cato instantly withdrew the offer.

"I take it our little conspiracy served its purpose?" Napoleon asked as he removed his dripping cape and one of the bodyguards closed the door behind them.

"Very much so. I have had news that the Prime Minister has moved the amulet into the Secretarium."

"Excellent. Ah, Doctor Beddoes," Napoleon said with a beneficent smile. The prisoner glared back at him through small dark eyes, deep set in flushed red cheeks and crowned by wisps of grey hair, mouth coarsely gagged by a scrap of cloth.

"It is a privilege to make your acquaintance. I was a keen follower of your work back when this place was operational – I remain convinced that there is untold potential for the use of poisonous gases on the battlefield. But perhaps the time for that has yet to come. In the meantime, allow me to introduce myself. My name is Napoleon Bonaparte. Your nation robbed me of my strength in Russia, humiliated me on the battlefields of Waterloo and sentenced me to live out the rest of my days on a wind-swept rock in the Atlantic Ocean. But I am not here for revenge," Napoleon said, leaning toward the prisoner. "I am here to bring light to the darkness."

Beddoes' breathing quickened and became laboured, his arms bound tightly behind his back and his chest lashed to the seat-back.

"And, as you are experiencing first-hand, I am unstoppable. Ultimately, I will triumph. But I cannot do it alone," Bonaparte said. "You, Doctor Beddoes, are going to help me."

Beddoes writhed and moaned in the chair, causing it to rock and tip.

"The amulet that your King stole from me has been in the possession of your Prime Minister these eight years. You have made no secret of the fact that you oppose the use of these amulets and that you have found a way to defeat them. To destroy them. Is this true?"

Beddoes shook his head vigorously.

"Because if you did," Napoleon said, resting both hands heavily on Beddoes shoulders, "we would need to know."

Beddoes stared back at Bonaparte, defiant. Napoleon nodded to one of the men in black who stepped forward and put a dagger to Beddoes' throat.

"It's quite simple, Doctor Beddoes, either you tell me the truth, or you die." Napoleon said.

A moment passed. Beddoes didn't flinch – if anything he became calm in the face of death.

"Well, if you won't do it to save your own skin, perhaps you will do it to protect someone that you love."

There was a yelp from outside in the hallway and Beddoes' eyes went from calm to terrified in an instant. He craned his neck to see his housekeeper being dragged into the room by the other bodyguard. Beddoes threw himself about like a fish trapped in a net, his gagged mouth emitting visceral noises of primaeval panic.

The bodyguard threw the housekeeper to the floor in front of Beddoes and the henchman with the dagger grabbed her by the hair and pressed the gleaming blade against her neck.

"Perhaps now you will consider helping us."

Beddoes could hardly acquiesce fast enough, nodding and begging for permission to co-operate through the gag in his mouth. Napoleon loosened the gag and words began to spill out.

"There is a scroll. The Scroll of Menhit. It describes how the amulets can be defeated."

"And where is the scroll now?"

"It was amongst the artefacts that you recovered in your Egyptian campaign twenty years ago – I believe it is now kept in the house of the French Ambassador in London."

"Is that so? Well then, perhaps we should pay the Ambassador a visit," Bonaparte said, turning to face Cato. Bonaparte made a silent gesture to the henchman with the dagger and, after a flurry of activity, the housemaid slipped to the floor, motionless.

Beddoes moaned and hung his head. But after a moment he looked up.

"If you... If you will allow me to look at my notes I can tell you more. I have done a large amount of research on the amulets and some of it will be of value to you."

Bonaparte narrowed his eyes and peered at Beddoes.

"You know of my sympathies for the Revolution, I'm sure," Beddoes continued. "Allow me the privilege of helping you."

Bonaparte stared at Beddoes for a moment. "Help Doctor Beddoes supply this information. Robespierre, a word."

Napoleon moved away from Beddoes and gazed around the room as if he were taking a summer stroll. Cato joined him at his side.

"Rather sad to see such a grand house gone to ruin like this, don't you think?" Napoleon said, reverting to French.

"Greatness can be rebuilt, your Excellency."

Napoleon smiled and turned slowly to his compatriot. They had left the dining room and now tarried in the hall by the front door. Napoleon looked around to confirm that there was no one within earshot. Cato felt the sudden thrill of Napoleon's confidence in him for the first time since Borodino, eight years before.

"Take this," Napoleon said, passing Cato a slip of paper. Cato looked down and opened it slowly – it was hardly legible in the lamplight which glowed from the next room, but he could see enough to make out that it was an address.

"As I told you in my letters, we have located the first amulet. This is the address - an antiquarian bookseller in Antwerp. You will stop at nothing to recover it. The first amulet will guide you to the second. And once we have two, the Prime Minister's Secretarium will prove no obstacle."

"Yes, your Excellency, I would be honoured. But how..."

The Emperor gripped Cato's hand, crushing the piece of paper with startling strength and causing him to gasp.

"You remember how we kept my amulet in the lead-lined box, to contain its influence? What fools we were. Through my research I have learnt that one Amulet will always seek its sisters. One will lead us to the other - if we would only follow, the others will surely be ours!"

"You mean all that time we could have simply followed its influence? Your excellency, this is..."

"But we must act quickly – you will leave for Antwerp first thing in the morning."

Upstairs the bodyguards had marched Beddoes to his study and were watching him as he muttered to himself and shuffled between his notebooks, technical drawings and reference books to give them what he had promised. Placing one small printed page in his top pocket, he handed a large pile of notes to the guard.

Whilst the guard puzzled what to do with the pile of papers, Beddoes moved to another cabinet and, with his back to the guard, slid a small glass vial into his jacket pocket. He then moved to a desk and began untangling a complex network of cables and blocks. But the guard didn't like what he saw and placed a menacing hand on Beddoes' shoulder.

"I need to use this old...calculating machine to re-run some of the calculations," Beddoes explained breathlessly.

The guard glanced over to his companion but, finding him slumped asleep in his chair, conceded and waved Beddoes on.

The Doctor cleared a space on his desk and set the equipment out. Bending over the device he squinted at each component with his one good eye, holding his wire-frame spectacles out of the way as he did so. After making some adjustments, he pulled down the code-book from the shelf above his head and began leafing through it.

The bodyguard who had returned to his seat had no reason to suspect that Beddoes was not simply looking at instructions for the use of a calculating machine. But when Beddoes completed the electrical connections and began repeatedly setting and pressing the switch, it was not calculations that he was performing. It was a transmittal – a message encrypted in a long dormant code. Beddoes worked on the message as quickly and accurately as his trembling hands would allow.

Once finished, Beddoes sat back for a moment, took the engraving from his top pocket and crushed it in his hand. With the other, he drank the contents of the glass vial and closed his eyes.

"Hey. What you doing?" the guard asked. But it was too late – the liquid was already seeping into his blood. As the guard pulled him to the ground and the poison began to overwhelm him, one question repeated itself in Beddoes' mind – would anyone still be alive at the other end to receive his message?

Chapter 17

CATERINA SAT ON A ROTTEN turnip, a cabbage leaf and several egg shells, surveying the Italian countryside of her childhood. As her breathing returned to normal, she fumbled in her knapsack and found her tobacco pouch. Over the next few moments she methodically massaged moist tobacco into a small clay pipe, whilst absent-mindedly singing one of her granddaughter's favourite lullabies. With the expert use of a tinder-box, she lit the tobacco which began smouldering in the pipe-bowl. After a generous puff on the pipe and several violent coughs, a stillness descended over Caterina, the jangling of a distant goat-bell the only sound.

The tobacco came as a gift from her son, who ran a small goods boat across the Mediterranean Sea, and would usually help himself to an "off-cut" when transporting bales of tobacco. The apple flavoured tobacco smoke which now wafted about her helped to mask the smell of the refuse tip upon which she sat, although she was somewhat hardened to the stench, having spent many happy years in its company. The tip was, to her, as the throne is to a King, or a desk is to a clerk: it was her place of work. She would come here every day, bringing refuse from each household in the village, learning their secrets: who was cooking for whom; which houses were celebrating; which were tightening their belts; who was buying from the butcher, the baker, the fishmonger. And from the other scraps: who was mending and making; who was courting; and who was mourning. All of these things gave her a view into the houses of the village which were invaluable in her role as wise-woman, village elder, maven, blackmailer. On occasion she would collect the more meaningful objects which she found, allowing her to connect more closely with each individual. Allowing her to cast her spells on them.

But despite spending large tracts of her day communing with the refuse, Caterina attempted to end each day smelling sweetly by standing under a waterfall, fully clothed. She would sometimes tarry in the tumbling flow for several minutes, enjoying the way that the cold water slapped at her head, the way it made a hollow hammering noise as it drummed on her clothes. She would dry herself in the sun, or, if there was no sun, in her simple cottage.

She tapped the now extinguished bowl of her pipe into the palm of her hand, held the resulting ash close to her face and peered at it. Raking through the ash with the pipe's mouthpiece, she muttered to herself about her future and that of the people in the village. None of it was very optimistic or pleasant, but her predictions were rarely correct so there was little to fear.

With a sharp puff she blew the ash from her hand, licked the remainder from her palm, and symbolically spat it out. She reclined, propped up on her elbows and ran her fingers through the putrid mulch which surrounded her.

Suddenly Caterina became aware of a warmth at her elbow which was rapidly becoming more of a burning sensation. She jerked her arm away, glaring at the offending patch of ground for a second or two, before her curiosity got the better of her and she began to dig, gingerly at first. But she soon grabbed her trowel and began to alternate between trowel-scraping with one hand and probing with the other.

The sensation which had begun as heat was now a more complex combination of a buzzing and a prickling all along her hand and up her wrist. It was neither pleasant nor unpleasant but was somehow irresistible and compelled Caterina to keep digging for some time. She reached for a shovel from the barrow where she kept her tools and treasures and began a more concerted attempt to find the source of the radiance. She checked each shovel-full with a touch of her fingers and, when there was no buzz, touched the pile to check it was still there. She continued in this way until she had dug a deep gouge in the composting heap. She was quite out of breath, but continued to hack into the muck with an almost manic vocation. By now she was bringing up soil having cut through the layers of village waste.

Suddenly, she lost it; wherever she hovered her hand, she couldn't pick up the prickly buzz that she had been hunting. Breathing hard through her nose, she ran her fingers over the newly exposed earth. Finding nothing, she discarded the shovel, stretched her cardigan which clung uncomfortably to her sweating neck and slumped to her knees.

She carefully picked over the soil from the centre of the hole to the pile where she'd been shovelling the earth. Suddenly a rush of energy tracked up her arm, sharp, like a bite. She resisted the urge to nurse her hand and instead picked up the spiky clod of earth that she had uncovered with the shovel. The clump of earth fizzed in her hand and, as she caressed the soil from it with a look of awe on her face, a tarnished metal surface became more and more visible.

Chapter 18

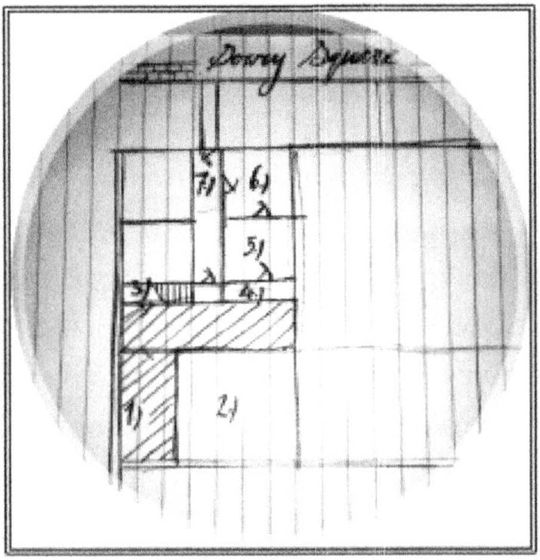

"NOW REMEMBER, THE BEST way to get noticed is to make a big fuss about lying low."

Ruthven's contact, John McClavin, was giving them the benefit of his experience as they walked through the streets towards Dowry Square.

"We're just taking a stroll, nice and easy round the square, having a nice chat. Maybe I'm your uncle. Your father even," McClavin chuckled.

"This is madness," William whispered to Isambard. "I thought Ruthven was going to give us an army of Bow Street

Runners. I'm not sure what we can do with just this chap on our side."

Isambard flashed William a stern stare telling him to keep his thoughts to himself.

"There it is, over there. Number seven Dowry Square. But we're just heading home after a lovely evening at the night-fayre. Come on, follow me, through the Square." They strolled through the overgrown garden which formed the centre of the gated Georgian square, McClavin chatting away with his singsong delivery, making very little sense, but keeping their minds off the fact that they were potentially a stone's throw away from the most dangerous criminal in the country.

"How about we take a little rest here and have a think?" McClavin said, easing himself onto a bench. On a bright summer's day, Isambard thought, this might be a nice spot for a picnic, but on this overcast night it was eerie and menacing. McClavin sat in the middle of the bench and the other two sat either side of him, facing McClavin but spending most of their time stealing glances over his shoulder at number seven.

"She's a bit of a fortress, granted. I haven't been able to get up close. Oh, I've walked past a few times: even saw the door open once. But these big houses are built to keep people like us on the outside."

"Have you tried the roof?" Isambard wondered, eyes still locked on number seven. McClavin sat stock still, with a slightly quizzical look in his eyes.

"Roof?" McClavin said eventually.

"Yes, you know. Get up on the rooves and see what you can see."

"What do you think, Sam - up off that stack of firewood?" William asked.

"Roof eh? You won't be able to get up on the roof, it's a sheer face and there's dogs in them yards," McClavin objected.

But he was talking to himself. The others were already crossing the street towards a long, dark alley between the towering town houses.

MCCLAVIN HEAVED HIMSELF up a freestanding wall but no matter how much he strained he couldn't get his leg up onto the ledge.

"It's these trousers," he grunted. "Too.... tight." With an explosive puff he gave up and dropped back down onto the tiled roof below. "You go on ahead, I'll stay here and... keep watch. Just don't get caught."

"Right-o," William whispered. They were now three storeys up, having climbed up an improvised staircase formed by the stable, the pantry, a washerwoman's balcony and the freestanding wall that had proved too much of a climb for McClavin.

Isambard edged along the top of a wall behind William, picking each step carefully – the wall was two bricks wide, with a 25-yard drop to the pavement on one side and a flat roof below on the other. Isambard was terrified, but thought better of mentioning it.

"Look at that?" Isambard gasped, pointing to a gas-lit room across the dark chasm. William looked up just in time to see a dark figure moving away from the window. "What was it?" he whispered sharply, before losing his balance and falling.

Isambard dived across the top of the wall, reaching desperately with an extended hand. But William had already disappeared into the blackness. Almost immediately, there was a terrific cacophony of cracking wood and smashing pottery.

"Will. You alright?" Isambard called urgently, still lying on the wall and peering into the blackness below. By shielding his face against the glow from the window opposite he could just make out his friend's prostrate body one storey below.

"Yes I.... I think I landed in the flowerpots..." came the shaky reply.

Just then, the scene was thrown into stark relief as a door opened hurriedly, and light flooded across the flat roof.

"Who's there?" came the harsh voice from the man standing in the doorway.

Isambard lay down and pressed himself flat as the man rested a heavy stick against the wall and hurried to William's side.

"What are you doing up here?"

"I was just clambering around and I... lost my way..."

"What's going on out there?" came another voice from the floor below.

As the man turned to answer, the light fell across his hand in such a way as to highlight a star-shaped welt - a connection was made in William's brain and, without having time to think why or why not, he spoke.

"Ruthven sent me."

The man froze, and although his head was turned away, William could tell his brow had become deeply furrowed, as he processed layers of information.

"George. What's going on?" came the other voice again, irritated this time.

"I.... It's nothing, I think," he replied uncertainly.

William and the man waited, motionless. But there was no response. George turned back to face William, his features returning to deep shadow.

"Who are you?" he whispered.

"My name's William. William Woodington. I'm working with Ruthven on Cato Street..."

Suddenly there was a crash as the door flew open again and a second man burst through it.

"What's going on? What's he doing here?"

"He's just... lost his way," George replied, without turning around.

"Lost his way? Three storeys up? Have you gone thick in the head, man?" the newcomer snarled. "He's seen too much. We'll have to bring him inside, We can't have him wandering off and alerting the militia. Well come on, get him inside!"

William picked himself up from amongst the split planks and shards of pottery that had arrested his fall. George helped him up and said under his breath simply, "Don't worry."

Isambard looked on helplessly from his perch on the wall above, inches from the sheer drop to the street below, watching as William was led into the house.

For a moment, silence returned to the rooftop.

"What's going on?" came McClavin's hoarse whisper through the darkness once the noise and movement had stopped.

"They've got William."

"God's bread!" came McClavin's helpless curse. "You need to come with me, boy. We can't help them now."

As Isambard clung to the freezing stone wall 25 yards above the ground, one thought rang in his head: his two best friends were now in grave danger and it was his fault.

"I'm going in after him," Isambard said. "Probably best if you go back."

"Suit yourself. No need to worry about me. See you on the other side," McClavin replied before starting the struggle back down the side of the building.

Isambard carefully dropped from his perch onto the surface below, where William had fallen. The roof was an odd kind of mezzanine construction which, in its heyday, may have been an Italian roof garden. It was about 20 feet across and its edge dropped away to a derelict courtyard garden, stacked with debris, two storeys below.

Isambard stopped at the door, levelled his breathing, put a hand on the door handle and began to twist.

Chapter 19

OPENING THE DOOR FROM the roof was painfully noisy - every movement brought with it an agonising graunch or squeak. Isambard squeezed cautiously through the door and found himself on a grubby, dimly-lit landing which led down a few steps to join a wider downward staircase. He closed the door behind him and stood motionless for a moment.

Opposite him a narrow doorway opened onto a bedroom containing a bare iron-framed bed and some dilapidated apparatus which Isambard guessed would have been part of Beddoes' medical experiments decades before. Isambard tiptoed as soundlessly as he could across the bare floorboards, clinging to walls with straining fingers as if he could somehow make his footfall even lighter. Cautiously he peered into the room, eyes wide, heart pounding, all senses on high alert.

"Isambard."

Isambard spun round, clinging to the wall to keep his balance.

"Oh my life!" Isambard said. "It's you."

"Course it's me," Millie whispered. "What's wrong? Looks like you're about to collapse."

Isambard placed his hand over his heart and took a few quick breaths.

"I just... Just you gave me a bit of a shock, coming out of the gloom like that."

"Soz," Millie said with a smirk. "How did you get here, anyway?"

"What do you mean how did I get here – what about you?"

"They grabbed me in the loft at Cato Street."

"Yes, I saw."

"But they dumped me as soon as they got out the back. They had carriages packed and waiting."

"Carriages waiting? As if they were expecting the soldiers to arrive?"

"Maybe. Anyway, I wasn't going to let them ride off into the darkness and disappear – I saw one of the carriages was full of baggage so I crawled in and went along for the journey."

"All the way to Bristol? That's the best part of a day and a night."

"I know – I didn't dare sleep in case they stopped to open the doors. When we got here I was able to slip out without being seen."

Just then there was a shout followed by some laughter from downstairs.

"William!" Isambard said. "He needs our help."

"They've taken him downstairs."

The two of them moved out of the room to stand in the shadows, straining to identify the sounds and voices that drifted up the stairs. Isambard realised that he was holding on to Millie's arm. He turned to Millie whose face was just a few inches from his own.

"My heart's going like a drum," she said.

Despite the shadows, Isambard could see that her eyes were fixed on his. He didn't admit that his heart was hammering too.

"We need to get William," Isambard said.

"I'll go. You need to take a look in that room. That's where they kept Beddoes"

"Kept?"

"He's dead, Sam. I think he killed himself. But he left clues, I'm sure he did. There's some sort of machine – maybe you can make sense of it..."

More noises from downstairs.

"Ok. You go down and get William. I'll try to find out what they wanted from Beddoes."

Millie nodded and they stepped out onto the landing, Millie crept down the main staircase and Isambard climbed up the steps on the other side of the landing.

Isambard pushed the door and it swept across the dusty floorboards soundlessly. Scanning the attic room, he could see it was cluttered with straw-filled tea-chests, books, papers and pamphlets arranged in piles against the walls. A desk stood against the wall opposite and, on the floor, lay the splayed body of Doctor Beddoes.

Isambard rushed forward and knelt next to the wretched looking man - even in the dim light, Isambard could see that his soft face had been corrupted by cuts and bruises.

"Sir. Are you there?" Isambard said, gently laying a hand on the man's wrist. The skin was cold. In the dark Isambard heard no breathing except his own. Withdrawing his hand Isambard felt something unusual and found a crumpled piece of paper in Beddoes grasp.

Isambard lit the lantern at the desk and prised the scrap of paper from the dead man's fingers. Opening it up he saw that it was a print from an engraving – it showed some kind of ornate tube labelled simply "The Scroll of Menhit."

More shouting from downstairs.

"They came here to get something from Beddoes – but he would rather die than give it away. What could be so important?" Isambard asked himself.

Isambard stuffed the drawing into his pocket and turned to the desk, where the lantern illuminated a series of beautifully made wooden cases adorned with wires, coils and switches. A hardback notebook lay open to one side - Isambard turned it over to read the inside cover by the light of the lantern.

"Experiences in Telegraphy," he read in a whisper. "Sending messages – but to who?"

Isambard put the lantern on the desk and began following wires with his hands, building a picture in his mind of how the parts of it fitted together.

"Battery. Switch – maybe a manual encoder. Some kind of energiser or amplifier? So this must be the signal," he muttered, following a cable towards the back of the desk where it attached to a pair of copper pegs, mounted on a board next to several others. Each labelled with a number – seven pegs in total. The connection was made at peg number three.

"Peg number three," Isambard muttered whilst leafing through the notebook. "Who is getting messages via peg number three...?"

Isambard found what he was looking for on the back page of the notebook - a table with the heading "Correspondents". He ran his finger down the list to number three and read the name: "Faraday, Iffley."

It was then that Isambard heard the cries of "Fire, Fire" from downstairs. What made it all the more alarming was that Isambard recognised the voice – it sounded for all the world like Millie.

A FEW MINUTES EARLIER Millie had watched Isambard disappear into the upper room and crept down the stairs, in much the same way she used to when, as a little girl, she couldn't sleep. The staircase had a full turn in it, and it was here that Millie sat and peered down through the railings. Below her lay a grimy hallway and the servant's entrance, with an internal doorway on the left wall. All was dimly lit by candles planted in jam-jars around the edge of the floor. Their flames danced in the draught, sending a kaleidoscope of shadows across the shabby wallpaper. She could hear voices but couldn't make out what was being said. She would have to get closer if she was to be any help to William.

A plan, or at least an impulse, a calculated gamble, formed in her mind. She glided down the stairs and stopped at the doorway off the hall.

She paused and peered into the room.

Inside, the drawing room was dark - at the opposite end of the room, another doorway opened onto a brightly lit dining room which seemed to be the source of the voices she could hear.

Out of sight and acting quickly, Millie collected the candles from the floor of the hallway and stuffed them into a single large jar. Doing what she could to shield the intense light that came from the jar now full of burning candles, she entered the empty room, walked around the perimeter and cautiously approached the well-lit doorway at the other end of the room. She put the jar down in the corner and peaked through the crack between the doors. There! She could see William, held with his hands pinned behind his back by one of Cato's gang. Every fibre of her body wanted to burst through the doors and wrench her brother away, but she knew that to do so would be to throw away the only chance they had for escape.

There was a clamour of voices – they were arguing about what to do with William - but Millie had heard enough. Taking the jar of blazing candles, she picked her spot and threw the wax fireball into a corner filled with peeling wallpaper and a wisp of cloth. The jar smashed and the candles scattered. Millie winced at the smashing sound but the conversation in the next room ran on unabated. The paper was beginning to smoulder, and smoke began to curl in ever-thickening fingers towards the ceiling. Millie stared, watching intently, willing the flames to catch. And they did, tiny yellow tongues at first, dancing from blackened smouldering edges of wallpaper. As she watched with the crazed look of a pyromaniac, she suddenly became aware that the conversation in the lobby had changed tone.

"...yes I can smell it now too."

"Did you set a fire, Ings?" One of them said looking towards the door into the dining room.

Millie would not have long. Now was the time. She ran from the drawing room, through the door on her left into the corridor.

"Fire, fire!" she shouted in as deep a voice she could muster, a cry echoed by someone in the dining room, who was also now calling out. Without time to consider who Millie was or what she was doing there, the fugitives succumbed to the instinct to defend themselves against the fire and flowed into the dining room to face the flames.

Whilst the commotion grew in the room next door, Millie crept down the corridor. She could see her brother and his captor standing next to a man Millie recognised from William's sketch. But they, like everyone else, were transfixed by the growing blaze in the adjoining room and had their backs to her.

Passing behind them, Millie reached for the heavy front door, worked the latch and pulled it open, before creeping steadily into the dining room behind Cato's line of sight. She squeezed her brother's arm. William's head flashed around and he stared in wide-eyed wonder at the miraculous apparition before him. With a look of urgency she nodded towards the open door. William tugged George's sleeve, making him turn sharply, concern on his face, barely able to suppress a gasp. He recovered his composure, and with an almost imperceptible nod of his head, gave them the signal to flee.

William began to run. But Millie didn't immediately follow him. An image had formed in her mind and she knew that she had to do something. Stepping forward she pressed the eyestone into Cato's pocket and, for a moment, she was intimately close to him - her senses were full of the side of his head, its wispy yellowy grey hair, the flecks of wax and skin in his ear, the chalky marks on the shoulder of his coat. Cato's animal sense of the presence of another made him look round, and as Millie back-pedalled towards the door, his ice-cold eyes locked with hers briefly before she turned and ran.

Although it had felt like time had stopped, she was just moments behind William. She leapt through the front door into the night, slamming it shut behind her as she went.

William was halfway down the overgrown pathway in front of her, both of them scanning frantically for an escape route, like foxes in the open field. And the hounds were upon them - just as they achieved the street the front door clattered open behind them, shouts and cries of their pursuers filling the air. The overgrown garden gave cover as the siblings ran headlong across the street to the garden in the centre of the Square. Hurling themselves over the fence into the dense greenery, they turned in time to see five or six fellows indecisively skittering around on the pavement. A voice gave orders and the men fanned out, two heading towards the garden. The men's progress across the street was interrupted by a flat-bed coal-lugger pulled along by a black mare. The men skipped impatiently round it, one joining the other in throwing off the coal-sacks that covered the lumpy black payload in the back.

"They're not here," one cried.

"What you lost, gentlemen?" the driver called out.

"Two thieving little rats, that's what," the other cried, jumping down from the back of the carriage.

"Well I'm just getting back to the coal-yard, so don't mind me," the driver muttered, to no one in particular, for his mate was fast asleep next to him.

Another man had run down from the house, bringing lanterns on sticks.

"We're for it now Will," Millie whispered. "We're pigs in a corner here."

"I'm just driving my buggy home back to the yard. Just checking the bridle," continued the driver as he dismounted and moved round to the front of the horse. Something about the ceaseless chatter made William freeze.

"Pulling up here so as to rest my bones," the driver was mumbling. "And thems of our nag Trudy..."

"McClavin!" William whispered with undisguised glee.

McClavin muttered on, now addressing the two fugitives in an unobtrusive murmur. "And you. Well yous two can just pop out and jump underneath like a couple of barnacles stuck on the bottom of my boat here. Nice and easy."

Lanterns flashed about in the garden, yet to work their way into the thick undergrowth where Millie and William huddled against the fence, but closing in. The coal buggy had stopped on the corner in front of them, the mare's bridle jangling with each toss of her majestic head.

McClavin moved back to the buggy, retrieving two sacks from the underside of the carriage and leaning against the spear-pole fence, within touching distance of Millie and William.

"I'll just stand here then whilst you jump into this sack," he said, holding one of the sacks open on the other side of the fence. "We'll have you out of here in no time," he muttered, unflustered.

Lanterns flashed all about them. It was now or never.

Millie shuffled into one of the sacks whilst the other two lifted her over the fence – once in McClavin's arms she was under the buggy in a matter of seconds. McClavin gave William the all-clear and he leapt under the carriage and secreted himself within the chassis as it pulled away. Millie was head first in the sack, stuffed into a shovel box on the side of the carriage whilst William clung with all his might to its freezing metal underbelly. Neither of them could see anything, but McClavin's continuous commentary was enough to make them feel like they had front row seats.

"And there they are, each one of them rummaging fruitlessly as we turn the final corner and, bravely led by Trudy the big black mare, we say goodbye to Dowry Square."

From a dark alley between the houses, Isambard had been watching as his friends clambered into McClavin's coal buggy. As it pulled into the street in front of him, Isambard realised that this could be his best chance of escape. Creeping as far as he could behind a low wall it was a few quick steps across the pavement before he could throw himself onto the back of the lugger. He came to a stop next to a pile of coal sacks and burrowed into them, hoping to God that he hadn't attracted the attention of Cato's gang.

A few turns and a good few hundred yards later, the carriage stopped – the street was blocked by a crowd of people with rows of stalls set up on each side.

"Can't go any further - looks like the night-fayre is in full swing," McClavin said, jumping down from the driver's seat. "I think it's safe - out you come."

William dropped to the floor from his perch under the buggy and stretched his fingers back into life. McClavin lifted Millie out of the tool-box and poured her out of the coal sack onto the ground.

"McClavin, you are amazing." Millie said, her cheeks blackened with coal dust.

But McClavin had produced a dagger from his pocket and his eyes were filling with aggression. Following his gaze Millie looked over her shoulder to the back of the lugger where a dark figure was emerging.

"McClavin, stop. He's a friend! Isambard!"

"Millie. William. You made it," Isambard said, jumping down from the buggy and embracing them.

"Come on - enough of that. We need to keep moving. That Cato Street lot could turn up any minute. Where you going next?"

"We should get back to London and let Ruthven know about Beddoes," Isambard said.

"Yes but how are we going to get back?" William asked.

But Millie wasn't listening - her eye had been caught by something familiar.

Chapter 20

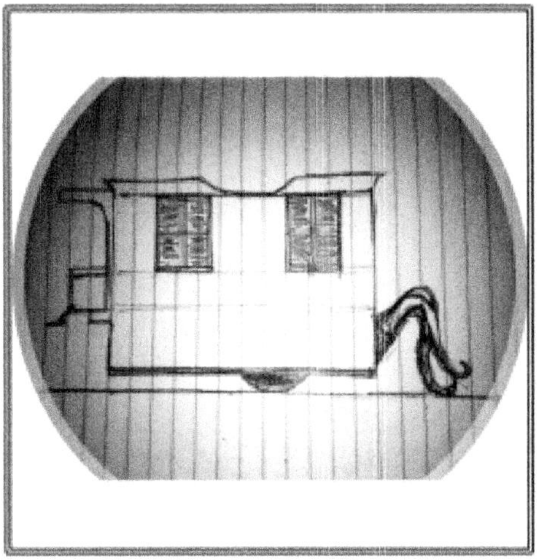

UP AHEAD, BETWEEN THEM and Dowry Square, lanterns hung on either side of the street and a large crowd had gathered, making a considerable noise. Stall-holders were calling out their wares: one stall selling lengths of brightly coloured material; opposite, a butcher's stall where pies and sausages covered the table and delicacies hung from a sturdy iron frame: a pig's head, a side of beef and its entrails.

But Millie wasn't looking at the goods on display - high on the awning of one of the stalls, an Egyptian cat sat gazing down at the messy human chaos of the night-fayre.

"That looks for all the world like the Candlewicks' cat," Millie muttered before pushing into the heaving crowds.

"She's seen a cat she recognises?" McClavin asked in disbelief.

Millie was in the thick of it now, surrounded by the scent of meat and perfume, hailed from every side by stall-holders' cries offering molasses and wheat-flour, rugs and wickerwork. The crowds heaved and pressed against them. Suddenly the smell of hot pies and gravy filled the air. Dirty-faced children weaved through the forest of legs.

"Keep your hands on your shekels. There are some light-fingers about," McClavin warned as they squeezed through the crowds in single file. The visitors from London didn't need a lesson on pick-pockets, but kept that to themselves.

"It's them," Millie muttered.

"Who Millie?"

"It's the Candlewick sisters – remember you asked me to return Trafalgar. Well I asked where he wanted me to go and he took me to their magic shop, somewhere out east. They're a very funny pair, but nice enough I think."

Millie made her way to the edge of the street where she could see the familiar faces of the Candlewick sisters - Esmerelda charming the crowds with her bright-eyed smile and exotic produce while Madagascar hovered ominously behind her, grudgingly laying out her fine bottles and specimen jars from the storage trunk onto the display tables.

"Hullo, who's this?" Esmerelda cried as she noticed the approaching party. Madagascar glanced up and a look of weary recognition soured her face even further. Esmerelda meanwhile had bustled around the edge of the table and was reaching for Millie's hand.

"Oh, we're so pleased you could make it," she beamed. "Aren't we Madagascar?"

Madagascar looked up and mustered a weak smile. "Delighted," she conceded.

"But what are you doing here?" Millie asked.

"Well," Esmerelda exclaimed, momentarily dumbfounded in a rare moment of speechlessness. "Well, we are shopkeepers and here we are selling our goods in an informal street-fayre setting. Is that right?"

"No, I mean, what are you doing in Bristol, this night of all nights? I thought you said you only go out of the shop for special occasions."

"That's right," Esmerelda replied flatly, staring seriously into Millie's eyes. "And who, pray-tell, are your gentleman friends?" Esmerelda asked, directing a coquettish smile at McClavin.

"This is my brother, William, my friend Isambard Brunel. And this is our... associate, Mr McClavin," Millie said.

"Delighted to meet you all. My name is Esmerelda Candlewick and this is my sister Madagascar." Madagascar bowed her head.

"Now, come come," Esmerelda continued, ushering them towards the stall. "Most of this is tittle-tattle, of course.

We keep the good stuff in the shop. But I'm sure you will find something of interest."

McClavin stood aloof, scanning the crowds for any sign of the gang.

Madagascar Candlewick was arranging the goods beautifully across a perfectly white cloth - ornate bottles, small snuff-boxes adorned with semi-precious stones, plain glass jars containing samples of exotic flora and fauna.

"Cawww, look at this Sam," William cried holding up a specimen jar. "Have you ever seen a scorpion like that before?"

Esmerelda shook her head ever so slightly.

"Put it down, Will," Isambard whispered forcefully. William did as he was told but quickly picked something else even gorier to marvel at, deciding this time to keep his excitement to himself.

"We need to get going. Shouldn't be hanging about here," McClavin said, looking anxiously down the street towards Dowry Square.

"How did you get on with the eyestone?" Esmerelda asked Millie.

"I dropped it into Cato's pocket."

"Oh what a good idea!"

"What's an eyestone?" Isambard asked

"It's a rather magical little rock that allows us to see whatever it sees," Esmerelda explained. "We can have a look when we get back to the caravan. We have got a motherstone in the caravan haven't we sister?" Esmerelda asked.

"Yes."

"Does it work?"

"Do they ever?"

Esmerelda gave a tight-lipped smile. "Let's go and have a look. Have you eaten? How are you getting back to London? Are you warm enough? You must be freezing. Come, come, we must get you out of the cold."

"Good idea," McClavin said. "No good standing around out here waiting to get caught again."

"Good yes. Come on Madagascar. We were just about to pack up anyway weren't we."

"I've only just finished laying out."

"Yes well, it's hardly a sell-out crowd is it."

"I've never seen it busier."

"Yes, yes, precisely. Far too many people. Best if we cut our losses and go home. Come along, plenty of room in the floating carriage isn't there Madagascar?"

"I'm not sure about plenty."

"That's a floating carriage?" McClavin asked of the hand-cart that stood overflowing at Madagascar's feet.

"No, that's a wheelbarrow," Madagascar replied mirthlessly.

"No dear, the carriage is around the corner. Here, bear a hand and follow us. But please do hurry!"

Madagascar and Esmerelda set off, each with a token package under their arm, leaving the rest for William, Isambard and Millie to carry.

"So what is a floating carriage?" McClavin enquired, newly puzzled.

"Well, based on what I know about the Candlewicks, it will be a carriage which floats," Millie said.

"Will it now?" McClavin wondered, one eyebrow raised. "Well, best leave yous to it then. God's bread, I shall be writing to Ruthven to ask him how long he's been recruiting from the lunatic asylums, looking at you lot," McClavin said with a crooked smile.

William leant over and shook McClavin vigorously by the hand. "Thank you Mr McClavin. I'm not sure how we will ever be able to repay you," William said with a broad smile.

"Yes, thank you. You got us, well, these two, out of a real fix there," Isambard said, grinning at Millie.

"Well, I look after my friends, see. And any friend of Ruthven's is a friend of mine."

"How are you getting on with that barrow, William?" came Esmerelda's commanding voice from the corner.

"We shall remember you to him with our fondest recommendations when we see him next," Millie said.

"That would be very kind. Now get on your way before Cato comes prancing by, looking for another Toffee Apple."

"Yes captain," she said before they turned, collected the last of the things and hurried after the others.

"What did you do that for?" Isambard hissed at Millie once McClavin had disappeared into the crowds.

"Do what?"

"Put that magic rock into Cato's pocket."

"Dunno, just had a feeling. Seemed like the right thing to do."

"We shouldn't be getting mixed up in this magical stuff, you know. I don't trust it."

"Not sure we've got much choice, you and me - we're in it whether we like it or not."

"What do you mean?"

But there was no time to answer – as they clattered around the corner together. Weighed down by the wheelbarrow and trestle tables, they found William standing still in a quiet side-street away from the crowds of the night-fayre.

"What is it?" Millie asked.

"I'm not sure – I suppose it's the Candlewicks' floating carriage."

Under a gas-powered streetlamp stood a tatty looking gypsy caravan.

Isambard noticed Madagascar taking up position on the driver's bench up top, and Esmerelda heaving her rather heavy frame into the carriage below. But instead of sagging in the way that carriages usually do when mounted by persons of Esmerelda Candlewick's considerable build, Isambard noticed how this carriage seemed to simply slide sideways, and would have slid further if it wasn't that the front and back were tethered to a rail like a moored boat.

"A floating carriage. Just like they said," Millie said.

"But how does it... how does it do that?" Isambard muttered.

Esmerelda looked up to see them approaching and called out a cheery "ahoy, there," accompanied by a tinkly wave as she hung in the doorway momentarily before disappearing into the carriage. As an afterthought she reappeared.

"It doesn't look like much from the outside - we deliberately keep it down-at-heel to avoid getting too much attention. People do tend to get curious when they see things...

defying the laws of gravity," she said, ducking back into the carriage. Within seconds, she re-emerged and pointed at the rear of the carriage. "Just pop the baggage into the back-trunk will you? Look out though - the handle is a bit stiff - just give it a spin, and pull," she said, directing them to the box attached to the back of the carriage.

As they approached, William put the wheelbarrow down and lifted the hatch to the trunk in the manner described. Hardly thinking to check the inside of the trunk, he set about lifting the wheelbarrow but was somewhat taken aback by the fiery glow that blasted from within, and altogether alarmed by the snake-like tentacles which emerged and explored blindly until they found the wheelbarrow and gathered it into the trunk. William stepped back and stood out of the way as the tentacles emerged again, slithered across the floor, and gathered in the trestle table in the same way. One tentacle with nothing to do prodded and probed William's feet for a moment before withdrawing into the trunk, delicately closing the top hatch behind it.

William, Millie and Isambard stared at the trunk for several moments.

"Obviously didn't fancy you," Millie said to her brother.

"Oh and beware of the octopus in the sump below the carriage," Esmerelda called from the doorway. "Sorry, p'raps should have mentioned that before. Tremendously useful for handling luggage. Come on, jump on board."

The inside of the carriage was much less ordinary looking than the outside. The wood panels were painted in bright, solid colours, and featured ornamental carvings of strange beasts. Plates and mugs sat in specially made cabinets at one end of the carriage and a large flat area covered in cushions took up most of the space at the other end. A life-size statue of a Greek soldier, his bow and flaming arrow poised for attack, stood guard just inside the door, causing Millie to yelp with surprise as they climbed on-board.

"Oh, don't mind Sagittarius, he's very friendly once you get to know him," Esmerelda joked.

A hatch opened above their heads. Madagascar peered in wearing leather-strapped goggles and a woolly cap.

"All aboard and ready to steam?" she called.

"Full steam ahead, Captain," Esmerelda replied, grinning at the siblings.

"Here, take a seat. It can be a bit jerky at the beginning," Esmerelda explained as she closed the hatch. They sat on the cushioned area and tightly gripped whatever parts of the cabin that came to hand, memories of the day-long bone-shaker that had brought them here from London still fresh in their minds. But there was just a slight surge as they pulled away from the kerb, and even then, it was hardly more than a swaying sensation, nothing like the constant swinging and jolting of the carriages which had brought them to Bristol. Millie and William loosened their grip on the fixtures as their wide eyes relaxed and they got used to the subtle movement.

"It's..... It's actually very smooth," Millie managed to say, suppressing her delight. "Compared to an ordinary carriage, I mean."

"How does it work?" Isambard asked in wonderment.

"Who knows?" Esmerelda replied. "Before you ask, I don't think it's anything to do with the octopus. The carriage floats, seemingly on a layer of disagreement with the earth's surface. It seems that the two of them had an argument some years ago and now cannot bear to touch. Their mutual animosity keeps us afloat. We bought this carriage from an old Magi in Morocco many years ago and put this gypsy frame on top. It often takes us for rides in the countryside. The dear old nag up front just has to give a little tug and we start to glide forward. The biggest challenge is holding the carriage back. Madagascar is up there with one hand on the brake lever. Ha!" Esmerelda concluded, with one of her 'fancy that' laughs.

"Now then," she continued, "Let's have a look at this eyestone. As I explained, the eyestone is constantly looking at its surroundings and telling us what it sees through the motherstone. Here, let me fetch it," Esmerelda said, trying to get up, but found she was rather too round to get out of the low, spongy day-bed. William jumped up to save her the bother.

"Oh thank you dear. It should be in that drawer there, on the left."

William opened a drawer only to find Bastet the Egyptian cat inside it, which distressed both cat and boy greatly. After hissing melodramatically, Bastet grudgingly leapt out of the way.

"Yes, next drawer down I would say. Is there a stone in there?"

William opened the second drawer which overflowed like a pirate's treasure chest, full to the brim with stones of incalculable variety. William blinked rapidly five times.

"There are lots of stones. Which one is it?" he asked, bemused.

"Ooh, that one there. The one on top," Esmerelda said, waving a hand vaguely and straining to peer into the drawer.

William shrugged and picked a stone at random from the top, fully expecting this to be the first of many failed attempts. "This one?" he asked, holding it up for Esmerelda to see.

"Yes. Yes! That's the one," she replied, almost clapping with excitement. Stunned at his immediate success, William returned to the day-bed and put the stone down. He was beyond surprise when he saw that it had grown to four, five then six times bigger than it had been when he picked it up. The stone had also begun to glow.

"Right, here we are. The motherstone will show us what the eyestone is seeing. We can see exactly where our quarry is, by seeing what the stone sees," Esmerelda said gleefully, tenderly adjusting it on the bed in front of them. The four of them stared expectantly. It began to pulse with a dull light, a light which got brighter, until it was possible to see a smudgy, largely brown, image.

"What are we seeing?" Millie asked.

Esmerelda stared uncomfortably at the stone. "Well. I..... I'm not sure," she eventually replied. "Where did you put it again?"

"In his pocket," Millie answered.

"It looks like movement," William said, applying his artist's eye.

"Perhaps they're travelling," Millie wondered.

"Look at the rhythm in the swirls. Looks to me as if they are cantering on horseback," William observed. The others peered closely.

"Well, if that's the case, we must speed ourselves up. We can't see where they are, but we know that they have left Bristol, and we know they are going at a fair lick! We will have to take a gamble that they are heading for London and redouble our speed to catch them up. Madagascar!"

Chapter 21

DESPITE THE HEAT AND the distance she had walked, Caterina could not remember a time when she had felt so alive. She strode up the hill from the river with energy and vigour, passing other pedestrians half her age along the way. As she crested the hill where the market stalls began, she found she had, for the first time in many years, a keening hunger. The food stalls were firing up for the lunchtime trade and the air was filled with swathes of aromatic smoke bearing the scent of hot olive oil, frying meat and rosemary that made her nostrils flare and her mouth water. She left her normal path down the middle of the dusty high street and browsed the food stalls, ignoring the cheerful greetings of their busy proprietors. With a grunt she selected a lamb kebab in focaccia bread, paying with a battered coin that she produced as freely as she might if it were one of hundreds at home. In fact, that lonely coin had been jealously guarded for years, possibly even by her father before her. But Caterina felt there was no need to be thrifty anymore. Since finding the amulet she felt as if she could have whatever she wanted and that, the more she wanted, the more she would get.

Caterina sat wordlessly savouring her lunch surrounded by the noisy crowds which gathered and drifted through the sunlit market square. As usual, she winced when children shouted and she kicked at any cats or birds that came into range. But instead of her usual fearful distrust, she now observed this swirl of people with serene contempt. Where she would normally look upon the blacksmith and his tools with fear, she felt a sense of calm superiority. Grandmothers who would normally stir jealousy in her breast now left her feeling only pity. Finishing her meal, she burped purposefully and took pleasure in returning the glances of those that objected. She wiped her mouth vigorously and stood, ready once again to push through the ebb and flow of the crowds towards Luca's shop inside the covered market.

The bazaar was nearly deserted as the majority of its shops closed for lunch. The cool air trapped by the vaulted stone ceilings made a pleasing contrast to the relentless heat outside. The smell of herbs and spices, displayed everywhere in colourful heaps, added their mosaic of rich scents. Despite the labyrinthine passageways, Caterina strode efficiently down aisle and corridor, until at last she reached her journey's end. She squeezed the amulet, which nestled inside her pocket, and went in.

"Luca's Cornucopia" was somewhere between a glorified junk-shop and a pawnbroker. That is to say, Luca, the owner, would buy anything from anyone as long as they were willing to accept his price. He liked to think that he had a prodigious ability to read the price that people would be willing to accept as if it were written on their faces. In reality, his reputation for low prices meant he simply ended up with a lot of low value bric-a-brac which he could sell for very little profit. This, however, did not concern him. He had, through a cousin with a particularly unsavoury history in the Saint Petersburg crime scene, become a significant supplier of antiquities (some genuine, mostly fake) to Tsar Alexander's court in general and to the Hermitage Museum in particular. This line of business, whilst risky, was also extremely lucrative, and the shop business had become little more than a smokescreen for his less legitimate activities.

"We're closed, Nona. Lunchtime," Luca called from the back room where he was transforming a recently purchased market vase into a plausible copy of a Roman artefact using a nail file and a small hammer.

"Luca. It's Caterina."

"I know. We're closed."

"Luca, I have something which you are going to like."

"Caterina, I've told you, I am never going to buy your mother's necklace."

"This is not my mother's necklace. You have never seen anything like this."

Luca lowered his tools and closed his eyes wearily.

"Last time you said this you showed me some broken crockery from Spain. Worthless." There was a long pause whilst Luca expected to hear Caterina make her excuses and leave.

"Luca."

It was just a name. Caterina had said it already a couple of times since her arrival. But something about the way she said it this time, not the volume but the power in her voice, made Luca snap open his eyes and shoot an uneasy glance over his shoulder. A short-lived smile flicked across his face and he placed his tools deliberately down on the workbench.

Luca emerged from the workshop cleaning the porcelain dust from his cracked fingers with a damp rag. He hardly recognised Caterina but was unable to pinpoint anything specific that had changed about her. It was just that, somehow, instead of the world-weary pig-like creature that Caterina usually resembled, she now had an air of authority, a kind of regal charisma. Luca did his best to conceal his reaction, but he couldn't stop a quizzical look crossing his face.

"So, what do you have for me?"

Caterina hesitated before laying the amulet on the table between them.

"I think it might be Roman. It looks Roman. Do you think it's Roman?" she asked, losing confidence with every second that she spent out of touch with the amulet.

"No," Luca replied, eyes fixed on the piece that now sat on his table.

The two of them stared at the amulet. Caterina's sense of weakness grew and she suddenly snapped into action.

"Maybe I ...." she began, but too late.

"Now this," Luca said, snatching the amulet, raising it to shoulder height and turning away from Caterina.

".... This really is something special. I shouldn't tell you that of course. My father would be turning in his grave. But Caterina, here you have something special. Very special indeed."

The two of them stared up at the amulet held aloft by the shopkeeper which now twirled slowly on the end of a cheap chain. It barely glinted, it was dull metal with no gem or leaf upon it. But in their eyes, it glowed and glowed. Overcome with longing, Caterina clambered onto the table and lunged at the amulet with one hand outstretched. Luca deftly held her off, turned and stepped backwards. Exhausted, Caterina fell to her knees feeling like a mother hen protecting her eggs from the circling snake. Her heart sank with the realisation that this snake always gets the egg.

Luca tutted and wagged a finger of one hand, hiding the amulet behind his back with the other.

"Now, now, Caterina. No snatching. I'm sure we can do a deal here. After all, this relic is of no use to you and yet to me... I'll give you thirty-two, if you promise to not tell a soul about it," Luca hissed.

Thirty-two. Caterina had never even seen so much money. She had arrived hoping to fetch five for the amulet. But despite her excitement, her desire to have it back gave her a strength she never knew she had.

"Forty."

Just saying the word gave her a feeling of vertigo. Caterina stared into Luca's eyes and for a couple of seconds neither of them spoke.

"I like you Caterina," Luca said with a crooked smile. He looked down at the hand which held the amulet whilst the other delved into a coat pocket and emerged with a bundle of notes. The money didn't matter to him as he knew he would make 10 or 20 times as much selling it to the Tsar's man in Saint Petersburg. He would leave for Russia that night.

He dropped four tens on the counter and made his way back into his workshop.

"Close the door on your way out."

Chapter 22

It was late morning by the time Isambard left the Candlewicks' carriage, slid through the window in the roof of his room and landed in a heap on his bedroom floor. He leant back against the bedpost and for a moment closed his eyes and listened to himself breathing. He would have fallen asleep were it not for the familiar sound of footsteps at the bottom of the ladder – he sat up and straightened his hair.

"Mother," he said as the hatch opened.

"Oh Isambard, I thought I heard you," she said, emerging from the trapdoor in the floor. She settled next to him and reached out to touch his cheek. "Oh I'm so glad you've come back. Your father and I have been worried sick about you. He didn't mean to throw you out you know – he's just trying to keep you safe. Whatever have you been up to?"

"I'm ok, mother. Don't worry," Isambard said, giving her hand a squeeze and pushing it away.

"Oh my Sam. Where have you been?"

Isambard thought about saying he'd been to Bristol and back but he knew she wouldn't believe him. Instead he asked "How's things been here?"

"You haven't heard? Your father's had a summons from the court."

"Courts? What for?"

"Debts. The money's run out. They say he'll be bankrupt."

"Debtor's prison?"

"Not for certain - your father is at the bank with the lawyer's, trying to fix it before the court hearing."

Isambard looked at his mother. "What's up?"

Isambard's mother looked at him and her face hardened. "This came for you. A messenger boy came by the workshop earlier," she said, tracing a finger over the wax seal on the back of the envelope. "Looks important."

Isambard suddenly felt like he did ten years ago when his mother had caught him stealing bites of the Christmas pudding.

"We need you to leave this Cato business and come back, Sam. Your father needs you back."

"I know that Mother. But I can't – I have an... obligation to the Government. I can't say any more."

"Obligation? What do you mean? Oh Isambard, you haven't done something wrong have you? Are you in trouble?"

"What do you think Mum?"

Isambard's mother returned her son's gaze with the same burning intensity, but she didn't answer. Isambard took the letter and cautiously cracked open the wax seal. But before taking the letter out, he looked back at his mother with a brittle, uncertain smile.

"What is it?" she asked.

"You know it'll be them. Calling me up again."

"Well go on. You going to open it?"

Isambard flipped the letter open and scanned the single line of carefully formed handwriting.

"Mr Brunel. Some news - meet me at 1pm at the Courthouse. Alone. R"

Isambard looked up. "Mother, what time is it?"

"Now? Well it's... it must be coming up half past twelve."

"I've got to go," Isambard said, stuffing some things into a bag and dipping to give his mother a kiss before diving down the stairs towards the workshop.

Isambard ran to his corner of the workshop, picked up the device that he had put together a few weeks previously, and made for the street outside. It was little more than a tray with some foot-straps, but with one foot stuck in a strap, Isambard grabbed a passing carriage and jumped onto the tray. The cab pulled him along whilst he directed the tray attached to his feet. It was hard work holding on, and the uneven road surface made balancing tricky, but Isambard was able to lean back and stay upright long enough to achieve a pretty respectable speed and make up valuable time. He had to change cabs once or twice along the way, as they stopped or went the wrong direction, but the last of these rides took him past the door of the Magistrate's Court where he let go and tumbled across the gutter in an exhausted heap, the battered tray on the floor next to him, just as the clock struck one.

"I've half a mind to caution you with my rod for joy-riding carriages," growled an angry voice.

Isambard gathered himself and looked up apprehensively.

"How do you plead?" Ruthven asked, bending over him, those yellow teeth breaking into a snarl behind the grizzled beard.

"Guilty as charged, your honour," Isambard replied through heaving breaths.

"Well boy," Ruthven said, offering a hand and yanking Isambard to his feet, "considering your honest plea, your otherwise good character and your excellent punctuality, I'll excuse you this time. How d'you get on in Bristol?"

"You heard that we found poor Beddoes dead?"

"Yes, well, not a bad thing if it means one less ally for Napoleon and Cato."

"He wasn't their ally – he died to keep a secret. He didn't give them what they needed."

"What do you mean?"

"I found him dead – poisoned himself to make sure Cato didn't get the full picture. But he sent a message before he died, through some kind of telegraph device."

"Message? Who to?"

"I don't know. But I've got the address," Isambard said, producing a scrap of paper. Ruthven squinted at it.

"Faraday. Iffley. I'll see what I can do," Ruthven said, pocketing the piece of paper. "Come on. There's someone that I'd like you to meet," Ruthven said, looking down at Isambard with a crooked smile. "I think I might have found a use for you."

Chapter 23

DIRK VAN POPPEL WAS reading. He spent a lot of time reading. He would sit in the back corner of the shop, when there were no customers, and read. His current book was entitled 'A History of the Literature of Ancient Greece'. Customers, actual customers, were few and far between. There were plenty of browsers, but each day there were only a few who actually bought anything. So there was plenty of time for reading.

The bell over the door clanged as one such browser came into the shop. Van Poppel didn't look up - he generally let people wander around by themselves. They would ask if they needed help.

But then something unusual happened; Van Poppel's neck began to tingle, or more accurately, the chain around his neck began to send a buzz into his entire body. It was a very strange, but pleasant, sensation like the feeling you get when, at the end of a long time underwater, you reach the surface and breathe again. Van Poppel inhaled deeply, drawing himself up and filling his lungs.

Van Poppel had become increasingly drawn to his amulet since finding it whilst salvaging an old sea-captain's cottage at the waterfront a few months previously. And then, a few days ago, the urge to place it around his neck had become irresistible.

He looked at the visitor for the first time and saw a wiry looking old-timer in a heavy cape, French buckle-shoes and a tricorn hat. The customer gazed around the shop in a perfunctory way as he walked towards the counter. Van Poppel watched as the customer approached. There was something inscrutable about his expression. As the customer drew closer, Van Poppel could see that his face was unusual - the chin looked for all the world as if it were made of pine.

"Good day," Cato said in French-accented Dutch.

"Good day." The tingling around his neck was now something of a warm buzz, accompanied by a growing sense of power and strength which surged pleasingly through his body.

"I wonder if you can help me," Cato said with a smile. "I am looking for something very particular and I have a very strong feeling you may be able to assist."

"...a very strong feeling indeed," Van Poppel said gazing into the customer's eyes with a look of defiance. "I will certainly try my best."

A weak smile spread unevenly across Cato's face, flickering like a single candle in a large room.

"I am looking for any trinket or... amulet that you may have from the Ptolemaic Dynasty. It's for my son you see. He hopes to go up to the university at Delft to study antiquities and I thought I might make a small present of it."

Amulets from the Egyptian era. The words darted around in Van Poppel's head, like swallows in a clear sky. The chain around his neck sent a buzz of power around his entire body.

"Well I'm sorry sir, we do not trade in trinkets or amulets in this shop; I suggest you go to the market if that is what you are looking for," Van Poppel said, signing off with a disapproving twitch of the eyebrows.

"Are you sure?" Cato asked. "I rather think this may be just the thing." He reached out and closed his hand around the amulet which dangled in front of Van Poppel's chest.

Cato instantly felt a flood of power flowing into him from the amulet. But Van Poppel felt a surge of his own and grabbed Cato's wrist with unusual force.

Van Poppel was, however, totally unprepared when Cato effortlessly hauled him over the counter and slammed him into a particularly fine Louis XIV dresser that he had been hoping to sell for a good price.

Van Poppel had taken many jobs in his life, coming as he did from a remote farmstead in the State of Saxony. He had been a shepherd of course, an auction house steward, a butcher's apprentice, an art dealer, a flower dealer and a jewellery trader. But it was during his time as a soldier that Van Poppel learnt about hand to hand combat and it was this that came to mind as he crashed onto the ground, surrounded by splintered wood and smashing porcelain. The adrenaline which pumped through his system, memories of past battles he had been in, and the surging power of the amulet all combined to give him an explosive urge to fight back. Even before the two men had regained their balance, Van Poppel was starting the attacking manoeuvre which had formed in his subconscious. He launched himself over Cato and, using his rotational momentum, threw him towards the wall with incredible force.

Unfortunately for Van Poppel, Cato's hand was still on the amulet, and the thin chain holding it onto Van Poppel's neck had already snapped like a thread.

Reeling from the collision, Van Poppel stood up unsteadily, and gazed down at the visitor who lay in a crumpled heap. He peered down past the rim of the tricorn hat to see the visitor's eyes glistening. A laugh began to form, somewhere within the black cape. The laugh grew louder and more menacing. The tricorn hat lifted to reveal the visitor's face, but it was not as it had been moments before – the entire lower jaw had disappeared, revealing a scar across Cato's exposed throat. Van Poppel recoiled in horror and realised that the amulet was no longer around his neck. As Cato stood, Van Poppel sank to his knees with an overwhelming sense of loss and powerlessness.

Cato stood over Van Poppel, and slowly extended a hand as if to help him up. Van Poppel hesitated, wondering what to make of the gesture, before lifting an arm and placing his hand into Cato's. There was a brief moment of kinship, before a pulse of energy flowed from one to the other and Van Poppel's lifeless body fell to the floor for the last time.

Chapter 24

ISAMBARD FOLLOWED RUTHVEN through the rain-soaked streets of Saffron Hill, the Officer occasionally acknowledging acquaintances who looked to Isambard more like murderers than Officers of the Peace. But Ruthven was in no mood to stop – he kept walking, until they reached Hatton Garden, the jewellery district.

Ruthven stopped outside a dusty looking shop with timepieces carefully arranged in the window. Isambard leaned back and peered at the sign which read "Horlogerie Fourier."

"A watchmaker's? Who are we meeting here?"

"Come in and see," Ruthven replied.

Isambard pressed up against the windows and squinted at the intricate timepieces on display on the other side. But Ruthven was impatient.

"Come on - no time for that," Ruthven said, disappearing into the shop.

"No pun intended," Isambard muttered.

Isambard followed Ruthven through the dark doorway into the shop, which was dimly lit by the weak morning sun. Isambard picked his way between the display cases full of carriage clocks and fob watches, following Ruthven into a back office. But once there Isambard found that they were no longer alone - a slender stranger sat slumped in a seat, booted feet resting on the desk and fingers steepled in front of his face. Flawlessly groomed and neatly dressed in a fashionable double-breasted jacket, his refined appearance was at odds with the angry scar on his right cheek. Beside him on the desk sat a beautifully constructed carry-case of the type usually used for the transport of scientific instruments.

"Ah Ruthven. You took your time."

"You can talk – not sure I've ever seen you awake before mid-day," the officer replied. "Anyway, I've been busy – got a revolution to stop, ain't you heard?"

"Of course – your raid on the Cato Street gang - I hear a few of them got away."

"Good news travels fast."

"Which ones?"

"Which ones what?"

"Which ones got away?"

"A few. We got Thistlewood at least."

"Unlike you to let your quarry slip the trap – do you think they had a tip-off?"

"You have a very suspicious mind," Ruthven said, twitching the curtains which stood between them and the outside world.

"Goes with the territory, old fruit."

"Talking of fruit, allow me to present Master Brunel," Ruthven said, turning his attention to Isambard. "Isambard, this is the suspicious Mr... well, perhaps you can let us know who you are today." Ruthven said with a crooked smile.

"A pleasure to meet you Master Brunel," the stranger said, standing up and giving Isambard an appraising look. "Nice and compact isn't he - all the better for crawling around. And he speaks French you say? That could be an advantage given the venue."

"And he knows mechanics," Ruthven added.

"Why are you talking about me as if I am a horse for sale in the market?" Isambard demanded.

"You should be more respectful," Ruthven growled. "If Catskill here don't have you, you'll be going up in front of the judge with Thistlewood and his gang."

"Oh, I don't think there's any danger of that happening – I think you will do perfectly Master Brunel," Catskill said with a twitch of a smile. "It is a pleasure to meet you at last. My name is Agent Catskill and I am a spy for His Majesty's Government."

"A spy?"

"I am told that you are a bit of an expert on the one they call Cato."

"I've seen a picture of him and heard his voice if that's what you mean."

"That's more than anyone else has been able to say for nearly ten years," the visitor said, smiling wistfully. "Isambard, I need you to help me in the fight against Cato."

"Sorry, I can't," Isambard said. "I'm not... authorised – I have express instructions from the Home Secretary to keep away from Cato."

"Not that that's stopped you before," Ruthven said.

"Master Brunel, I'm not talking about chasing Cato down – I leave that in the capable hands of Officer Ruthven and his men. As you may have gathered by now, Cato is part of something bigger and more powerful than a group of grubby revolutionaries in a barn loft. I have been brought in to combat the very source of Cato's power."

"Brought in by who?" Isambard asked.

"The Duke of Wellington. The Prime Minister. King George himself," Agent Catskill said without a trace of irony in his voice. "Is this the kind of authorisation that you need?"

But Catskill could see that Isambard was far from convinced.

"Isambard," Catskill continued, "Cato is not your Common or Garden revolutionary. He has much grander plans – plans to..."

"Collect and deploy the three Amulets of Ra and bring Napoleon to power as Emperor of Europe," Isambard preempted.

The visitor raised an eyebrow and blinked.

"Ruthven told me that you were well informed but I was not expecting you to be able to tell me that. How the deuces did you know?"

"A man."

"A man? Did he have a name this man?"

"I think he said... Hardleygrieve."

The visitor flashed a look at Ruthven. "Then you understand the world in which we are operating..."

"More than can be said for me," Ruthven muttered.

"...if Cato gets hold of these amulets, there will be no point swashbuckling up to him on a stallion expecting him to give himself up peacefully – our conventional defences will be useless. We need to prepare for the worst."

"What do you mean?"

"We believe that the amulets have an Achilles' heel – a weak spot. We need your help to find it."

Isambard looked at Ruthven, who responded, for once, with sincerity.

"We need you son – wouldn't be asking if we didn't."

"Okay, I'll help," Isambard said.

Catskill went to the bookshelf and pulled out a book-shaped lever, twisted it a quarter-turn and used it to pull the entire bookcase open, like a door.

"Bring that box, would you old chap? This way."

Chapter 25

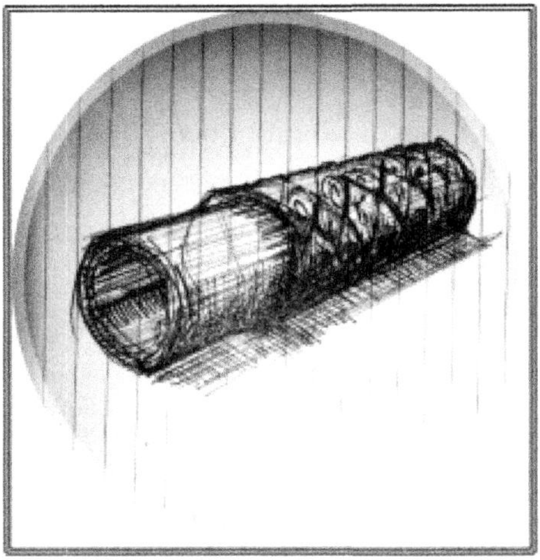

"YOU NOT COMING?" ISAMBARD asked Ruthven as Catskill disappeared through the doorway.

"I've got to get back to work – thieves to catch. I'll join you later. Don't worry, you'll be alright," Ruthven said with a solid nod, before disappearing back into the shop, the way they had come.

Isambard grabbed the large and surprisingly heavy box that Catskill had pointed to and followed him into the hidden back-room. But instead of dusty dark corners and antique looking timepieces, this room was full of intricate steel assemblies which glimmered in the lamp-light. Isambard gazed around the edges of the room where there were areas for fine metalwork, fabrication, braising and assembly. Small, cloudy windows admitted a watery light from outside but Isambard noticed how concave mirrors were being used to concentrate the candle-light and create well-lit areas just where it was needed.

The large workbench in the middle of the room was divided into four workspaces, two of which were occupied by workers tilted forward on stools, hunched over their work, surrounded by neatly laid out components and tools.

"Isambard, allow me to introduce Mr Fourier, watchmaker extraordinaire."

Fourier gave a tiny bow and clicked his heels together. He wore small wire-framed spectacles, his beard was neatly trimmed and his hair oiled.

"He, together with Mr and Mrs Bodes here are our finest watchmakers turned encryption artisans. They build and maintain encryption machines and other devices for the Secret Intelligence Directorate," Catskill explained.

"It is a pleasure to make your acquaintance," Isambard said, exchanging cautious smiles with each of them in turn.

Fourier stepped forward and spoke to the two watchmakers. "Mr Brunel is here as a special envoy from King George. He will be assisting Agent Catskill for... a while." Then, with a sharp intake of breath, Fourier drew himself up and returned to business, indicating to the carry-case. "In the meantime, it seems that Agent Catskill has managed to break his encryptograph."

"Again?" Mrs Bode said in disbelief, giving Agent Catskill a reproachful look.

"Would you mind helping him to remember what it is he's managed to do to it and get it fixed?" Mr Fourier asked rhetorically.

Mrs Bode paused only to give Catskill an icy stare before clearing a space on her desk, moving cylinders, drawings, dials, gauges and miniature screwdrivers to make way for the cumbersome case, before taking it from Isambard and lowering it into the newly-created space.

Not knowing quite where to look, Isambard caught the eye of the other watchmaker who dismissed the squabbling with a playful shrug.

"I think it may have happened when I jumped from that blasted carriage in Vienna," the agent explained.

"Could you not dismount the carriage with more care?" Mrs Bode replied, somewhat grudgingly.

"Well there's only so much care you can take when a fellow pulls a knife and you're spinning along at seven knots, but yes I take your point. Allow me to explain..."

But before Brunel could hear the full story, Fourier had taken him by the elbow and edged him to one side.

"It is none of my business," the watchmaker began, "I am simply a humble servant, but I would never have recommended you participate in this operation. It is too dangerous," Fourier hissed, fixing Isambard with a sharp stare.

"I'm sure Agent Catskill will look after me."

"I'm not talking about your safety – I am talking about this room. What you see here is extremely sensitive and highly confidential. You do not say a word of this to anyone outside this room. To do so would be an act of treason, do you understand?" Fourier demanded.

"Yes sir," Isambard replied warily.

"But, to your credit," Fourier said with a boyish smile, "I understand that you are the son of the great French engineer – this is good. Now that you are here you may as well learn what you can do to... look after yourself. Perhaps you should take this," he said, hesitantly. "I hope you will never have cause to use it."

From his jacket pocket he produced a smooth black object and handed it to Isambard.

"A fountain pen?"

"Look at the nib."

Isambard did as he was told and removed the lid.

"Watch. I attach this wire to the back of the nib. Loosen off the coil. Now, point the pen at that door and twist the end. Attention!"

There was a loud bang and the smell of cordite hit Isambard's nostrils. The tip of the pen was now embedded in the door but it remained attached to the body of the pen by the fine wire.

"Deadly, yes, but also useful when you are in need of a lift," Fourier smiled, giving the wire a firm tug. "High tensile steel wire. Here are some fresh charges – to create the pop-bang. And you will need to learn how to rewind it," Fourier said, handing Isambard the pen, ten slender metal cartridges and the bundle of wire.

"Master Brunel, if you please..." Catskill called from across the room.

Isambard pocketed the charges and wound the miniature pen-harpoon as he squeezed through the warren of tables and chairs. Agent Catskill was leaning against a workbench with his arms crossed, watching Mrs Bode working on the encryptograph.

"They are amazing you know, these chaps," Catskill said in wonder. Mrs Bode glared up at Catskill who added with a nod "...and chapesses. Anyway, let's get down to business. Come over here and take a look at this."

Catskill turned to the bench behind him and gestured for Isambard to join him. There on the desk lay an ornately engraved cylinder.

"What do you see?"

"It looks just like..." Isambard said, jamming a hand into his pocket and pulling out a crumpled bit of paper, flattening it out onto the desk. "The scroll of Menhit."

"Where did you get this image from?" Catskill asked.

"I found it in Beddoes hand – it was the last thing he looked at when he died."

"Hmm, poor Beddoes. If only we'd listened to him."

"What do you mean?"

"For years he's been writing rather hysterical letters to Lord Wellington's office, warning of the dangers of relying on the amulets, and sharing his research on how to destroy them. I'm afraid we'd rather dismissed him as something of a crackpot – but now it seems like he was right all along."

"So what do we do with it, now we have it?"

"Have it? We don't have it that's the thing. This is just a copy. A facsimile that the chaps... and chapesses here have come up with."

"So how do we get the real thing?"

"The scroll is on display at the French Ambassador's official residence. And *we* are going to switch it for this copy - steal it from under their noses."

"If it's at the Ambassador's house it's on French soil – there will be guards. You can't just walk in there and take it."

"Precisely. And this is where you come in."

Catskill turned, released a latch and lowered a hinged board from vertical against the wall to the horizontal, like a fold-out table. On the table and on the wall above it were pinned several blueprints which Isambard began devouring with his eyes.

"Tonight, the Ambassador is hosting a ball for a visiting dignitary – some minor French Royal or other. Usually the scroll is kept in a safe, but for the ball it will be the star attraction in a display case right here," Catskill said, dotting the plan with a delicate finger.

"And this is the display cabinet?" Isambard asked, pointing to one of the other drawings. "Iron cladding– it's impenetrable."

"There is one way in," Catskill said.

"From the top!" Isambard said with delight. "An overhead hatch – accessible... from the room above."

Catskill raised an approving eyebrow.

"Quite so. We just need someone small and mechanically astute enough to dangle into the cabinet and replace the scroll with the replica."

"I'm not small," Isambard objected. "I'm... compact."

Catskill smiled but something on the workbench caught his eye.

"Ah here it is, you'll like this," Catskill whispered to Isambard, before turning to Fourier. "I say Fourier, is this the universal lock-pick that you've been working on?" Catskill picked up the device and turned it over in his hands – to Isambard it was a baffling collection of metal blocks, rods and knobs.

"Nnnyes, but it is not finished," Fourier said without looking up from the drawing that he was studying. "Do not take it."

"Of course I won't," Catskill said, making a face and indicating to Isambard to hide it under his coat. Isambard responded with an anguished look, but stowed the lock-pick all the same.

"Right, well Fourier old man, we shall leave you in peace. Isambard, all the equipment we need for this evening's spectacle is in a warehouse in Greenwich. Come on, we'll need as much practice as we can get before we go on stage tonight."

Chapter 26

“WOAH BOY,” ISAMBARD said, bringing the horse-drawn barouche to a halt.

“What's up?” Ruthven demanded.

“There it is. I just thought we should take the opportunity to have a look before riding on in there.”

Isambard peered through a gap in the trees and over the fence at the magnificent house and manicured lawns, all washed by the watercolour light of a three-quarter moon. The polite laughter of a hundred guests drifted towards Isambard over the lively sounds of a string quartet.

"Quite right Brunel," Catskill said. "An agent should never approach an encounter without a clear plan and a good knowledge of resources available. Having said that, plans usually go out of the window at the first turn, so let's not spend too much time on the detail."

"We get in. We get this tube thingy. We get out," Ruthven said, scowling at the big house which sprawled behind the 10-foot-high gates.

"Precisely, Officer Ruthven. I couldn't have said it better myself."

Isambard took a long look at the French Ambassador's estate and looked over his shoulder at his two passengers.

He then started to laugh uncontrollably.

"What's so funny?" Ruthven growled.

Isambard couldn't decide which was funnier, Ruthven (in his frock-coat, cravat and ivory handled cane) or Agent Catskill (in a fulsome silk ball-gown, complete with beauty spot and powdered wig). The two of them looked at each other quizzically.

"I do declare M'Lord Duke of Chessington that you are cutting quite a dash tonight, even if I did have to dress you myself," Agent Catskill said.

"You don't look so bad yourself," Ruthven said, with a sincerity which took them all by surprise.

And whilst it was true that the Agent had done a good job of scrubbing Ruthven into a decent impression of a Landed Gentleman, the agent's own transformation into a Lady of Means and Beauty was disconcertingly convincing.

“Anyway, I don't know what you're laughing at,” Ruthven said to Isambard, who was wearing a sky-blue silk Footman’s outfit.

“Yes, yes, we all look rather lovely, but let’s not sit around much longer. I’m getting cold shoulders,” Agent Catskill said. Isambard cajoled the horse into motion.

“Remember, Master Brunel, when you drop us off they'll direct you round into the paddock over there on the left. Any sign of a panic, you get out here on the drive and start circling. If they smell a rat, the only way we are going to get out alive is if you have a rolling start. Leave it to us to figure out how we get on board.”

They passed through the lantern-lit gateway and joined a procession of elegant carriages which followed the gravel drive in a loop around a lawned fountain, until it was their turn to stop at the stone stairway leading up to the great door. Paper lanterns and decorative awnings brought extra colour to the already breath-taking facade. Isambard couldn’t help noticing that there were also dozens of soldiers stationed about the place.

“Not a bad little bolt-hole,” Ruthven mused.

“News of the French Revolution obviously never made it this far,” Catskill quipped as they came to a halt.

Agent Catskill coughed delicately and extended a gloved hand.

“Oh, my. What an unforgivable lout I have been,” Ruthven said, trying his best to put a polish on his cockney accent whilst taking the gloved hand and helping Agent Catskill to the buggy door.

"I think it best if you go first and assist me down," Agent Catskill said firmly, whilst smiling effusively at anyone who cast a doubtful glance in their direction.

"Of course, my lady," Ruthven replied, dropping heavily to the ground. Agent Catskill looked somewhat dismayed, but took a tentative step onto the footplate. But he could barely suppress a yelp of surprise when Ruthven bodily lifted him down onto the floor, in a quite unconventional manner. Catskill soon regained his composure and smiled again at the tittering crowd that was now watching their somewhat unusual arrival. The Master of Ceremonies, however, was not amused, and had taken an immediate dislike to this couple who he did not recognise and who therefore clearly had no business being there. With a flick of his eyebrow he signalled his suspicion to the Guardsman at Arms, who straightened up accordingly.

"The Duke and Duchess of Chessington," Isambard announced from his seat on the buggy.

"Leave this to me," Agent Catskill said quietly as they approached the Master of Ceremonies.

"Duke and Duchess of... Cheesington?" The Master of Ceremonies enquired through a sickly smile. "I'm afraid I was not made aware of your invitation."

"Francois. So nice to see you," Agent Catskill said with a mischievous smile.

The Master of Ceremonies was visibly shocked to hear his own name, and his whole body seemed to go rigid. He cocked his head to one side, waiting to hear what Agent Catskill would say next.

"We've been missing you in the *Cloture des Anciens Jacobins*," Catskill said, fixing the Master of Ceremonies with a playful look.

The Master of Ceremonies held the gaze for a moment before blinking sharply and allowing a smile to twitch across his lips. Taking a moment to collect his thoughts, he drew a piece of paper from a pocket and seemed to change his mind about the Duke and Duchess.

"Chessington, Chessington, of course... I will beg your ladyship's forgiveness, my English is quite lamentable and... my poor eyes are also.... Please forgive me," he said with a bow and a hand gesture which ushered them to proceed.

Agent Catskill took Ruthven's arm and together they climbed the wide granite steps, pushing past the motionless guard.

"What did you say to him?" Ruthven whispered urgently once they had safely passed the guardsman.

"I just let him know that I am aware he's acting as an insider for an illegal gang of anti-aristocratic revolutionaries. I hope my techniques don't offend you."

"I'd be lying if I said I'd never used a dose of blackmail once or twice myself," Ruthven said with a theatrical laugh, the two of them looking every inch the happy couple to anyone in the crowded reception area who might care to look.

Isambard drove the barouche around the back into the paddock and set about stabling the horses. Most of the other footmen and drivers were clustered in small groups or joshing around at the back door hoping to charm some of the wine or fine food from the maids who came in and out. But Isambard was not here to make friends or procure victuals.

Grabbing his bag, he made his way to the back of the house and found the coal shed just where Catskill had shown him on the floorplan in rehearsals. Because of the light and noise that streamed out of the vast ballroom windows, the coal shed was almost invisible until Isambard was within its shadows. His breaths were shallow and frequent, a kind of electricity flowing through his veins as he pressed himself into the shadows and tried to steady himself.

"Just need to climb the roof," he whispered with his eyes closed, "get the scroll and get out."

From his bag he pulled on dark overalls, threw the bulky rucksack onto his back and peered up at the profile of the grand house, silhouetted against the midnight blue sky. A good night for fireworks he thought to himself.

Isambard clenched his jaw and turned to face the wall. He found a toe-hold and began climbing. Hidden by the mellifluous sounds of the string quintet, peals of laughter from the ballroom and boisterous conversations of the footmen, Isambard climbed undetected across the coal shed roof, up some well-established ivy and to a dark window that seemed to open into the eaves of the building. To his relief Isambard found that he was able to ease the window open and, with a final rush of adrenaline, wriggle through it into a heap on the floor.

Isambard froze and held his breath. Something was moving. There, in the corner of his eye: a rustling; a scuttling. The unmistakable fidgeting of a nest of rats. Isambard allowed himself a sigh of relief and closed his eyes.

The moon cast a beam of blue light into the dusty room – a large rug lay rolled up at one end and the wooden floor was littered with the ghostly shapes of furniture draped in dust-sheets.

Isambard thought back to the architectural plans that Catskill had shown him and made his way as quietly as he could across the floor towards the southern service stairs.

"LOOK AT THE STATE OF this place," Ruthven said as he entered the foyer, overawed by the glittering crystal chandeliers and jewel-draped guests. But Agent Catskill had seen the like before and was busily scanning the scene for routes in and out of Fouché's study.

"The study was up that staircase when I came here last. Down the east wing corridor," Catskill said, whilst smiling politely at an elderly Comtesse across the way.

Catskill gazed into Ruthven's eyes and whispered as romantically as he could manage. "There is a guard blocking the stairway."

"I'm sure he could be persuaded to leave his post, especially if asked by a beautiful Duchess," Ruthven suggested mischievously.

"A fellow believer in the old 'Cadogan Remove' I see," Agent Catskill said with a gracious smile.

"We call it the Shoreditch Switch, but I'm sure the effect is the same. That passageway over there would do the trick," Ruthven said, nodding almost imperceptibly towards the dark recesses under the East staircase.

"Spot on. Now I don't know how you normally do it," Catskill said in a low voice, pushing a small vial into Ruthven's hand, "but I find this essence to be a silent and eminently effective sleeping-draught. Just make him inhale it from a cloth."

Just then the Comtesse (a large woman resembling a sugar plum fairy) and her wiry partner approached them noisily from the cloakrooms. The lady delivered a rapid fire introduction in French which Ruthven suspected he would not have understood even if it had been in English, whilst her partner acknowledged Ruthven with a weary smile. Agent Catskill made a brave effort to fend off these advances, citing language as a barrier, but undeterred, the woman explained that her husband would translate. He spoke hesitantly, with an accent that made him sound like he had a small apple in his mouth.

"A very good evening. My wife and I ... would like to extend our most.... warm welcome to you, our friends from across the channel."

The large woman laughed energetically, fixing Officer Ruthven with a wide-eyed grin, willing him to agree that her husband really was a fantastically talented man. Agent Catskill smiled graciously before excusing himself to pursue a passing tray of champagne leaving Ruthven to fend for himself. Of all the many exciting and memorable experiences Agent Catskill would enjoy in his years of adventures in the field, the look of sheer panic which passed across Ruthven's face as he was left wearing someone else's clothes and speaking in two languages he didn't understand was a memory that the Agent would cherish above most others.

Ruthven was finally able to extract himself from the conversation with the sugar plum fairy and her long-suffering husband by explaining that he needed to "avail himself of the utilities." He made for the water closet under the east staircase, exchanging a solicitous nod with Catskill who was busy giggling coquettishly for the benefit of the guard at the foot of the stairs. Ruthven was once again struck by the credibility of the agent's disguise, noting that the poor young soldier was well on his way to falling prey to the agent's 'feminine' wiles with nothing more than a bump on the head and a charge of 'dereliction of duty' to look forward to in return.

Before long the agent had landed his fish, luring the hapless guard into the dark corridor where Ruthven administered the sleeping drug. Moments later Ruthven emerged dressed in the soldier's uniform.

"Oh good Lord," Catskill said on seeing Ruthven in the borrowed outfit. "You look like a scarecrow."

"I'm bigger than him," Ruthven retorted.

"In every direction," Catskill smirked, before adding, "it will have to do. Come on."

Ruthven took up his position guarding the stairs and, in a moment when the foyer was clear, Agent Catskill emerged from the shadows, brushed past Ruthven and glided up the stairs at great speed and in total silence, despite the skirts that Catskill held above his knees.

At the top of the stairs the air was still thick with music, smoke and noise from the crowded ballroom below. Catskill strolled down the east wing corridors as if he had every right to be there. The only light came in through the corridor's end-window from the lantern-lit terraces below. The Agent peered through the gloom and looked into each room in turn with the easy haste of a guest looking for somewhere to powder her nose, before chancing on the room that he was looking for.

Finding the door locked, Catskill reached into the capacious bustle of his ball-gown and from it produced a pouch containing the lock-picking device from Fourier's secret workshop.

Suddenly there were voices. A pair of men were approaching from down the corridor. With not a moment to lose, Catskill unwrapped the device from its oily wrapper, and began putting it to work, adjusting the lock picking tools with steady hands before snapping the unit onto the lock with magnets. Crouching down and breathing hard onto the device, Catskill worked the rods and levers until, with a satisfying click, the bolt on the other side of the door shot open and the door gave way. With the conversation in the corridor getting dangerously close, Catskill slipped through the door and closed it silently behind him.

Like all good studies, this one smelled of polish, woodsmoke and valuable books. Bookcases hung heavily from every inch of wall. By the light of the moon pouring in through two large windows at the front of the house, Catskill could see that the study was spacious and orderly. A large globe stood between a magnificent desk and a grand fireplace where a small fire glowed. Catskill lit a taper and transferred the flame to a nearby lantern. Holding it up, he peered up and down the bookshelves to get a feel for the layout of the books. He then sat in the carved chair, carefully placing the lantern down and leaning on the desk, deep in thought.

Suddenly, three sharp knocks at the door. Catskill retreated into the shadows. The door creaked open and a short dark figure crept in.

"Brunel. Over here. Well done. Unseen I hope."

"Yes sir."

"Right, you see if you can locate the hatch. I'm just having a nose around - there's something else I'd like to pick up whilst I'm here."

Whilst Catskill sifted expertly through the desk and shelves, Isambard produced a bundle of string from his pocket. Unwinding it, he walked to one corner of the room and attached it to the bookshelf. He then tied the other end of the string to a point in the other corner of the room. With both ends tied, the string was slack, but towards the middle he found the knot that was the marker – holding it he walked towards the fireplace, repositioning himself until both ends went taut. There, under his feet, lay a small rug, and, after moving a few pieces of furniture, he was able to roll it away and reveal the bare floorboards.

"Catskill. The triangulation worked. It's here," Isambard said, pointing to the trapdoor under the rug.

"Of course it worked. Here, you may need Fourier's lock-pick."

Catskill joined Isambard at the edge of the trapdoor and pressed his skirts behind him, out of the way. Kneeling down, they worked with the lock-pick until finally, the lock popped open.

"Right, let's see what we've got."

Catskill held on to the lock-pick and opened the trapdoor a crack – a mixture of tobacco smoke, perfume and music poured in through the tiny gap and Catskill quickly pressed the trapdoor shut.

"Well. That works." Catskill squinted up, between the door and the bookcase, at the great clock laboriously marking the seconds.

"Four minutes until fireworks are announced – Ruthven will get them all cleared out. Come on, let's get the rig ready."

Isambard put down his rucksack and pulled out six limbs of wood and a lump of metal, just as he had in rehearsals that afternoon. The limbs looked like table-legs, thick and sturdy cylinders, but Isambard and Catskill soon had them screwed together into three long legs which were then attached to a wooden block forming a tripod, six -feet tall, with a geared pulley at its apex. Isambard shuffled into the harness whilst Catskill unravelled the rope.

The minutes passed slowly until finally, the Master of Ceremonies rang a bell in the ballroom, the clamour of the crowd reduced to a hum and an announcement was made. An audible wave of excitement rippled through the building followed by the sound of people moving towards the back of the house.

"The herd is on the move. Good. Now we just have to wait for the all clear from Ruthven."

Several moments later they heard Ruthven's authoritative voice ushering the last of the party-goers out of the room below, before banging three times on the ceiling with a pole.

"Time to lower away," Catskill said, playfully flicking an eyebrow at Isambard.

Catskill turned the lock-pick and removed the trapdoor whilst Isambard took the rope and attached it to the loop on the harness at the small of his back.

"Got the replica?"

Isambard replied with a sardonic smile and began to crawl through the trapdoor. He felt Catskill taking up the slack in the rope, holding him comfortably through the harness around his middle.

"Well done son, easy does it," Ruthven said as Isambard appeared through the hole in the ceiling. "There's no key in the door so I'll have to stand guard - make sure no-one comes to watch."

Outside the string quintet were working themselves up to full power – suddenly the air was punctured by what sounded like a platoon of gunners loosing off their muskets. The fireworks, Isambard thought to himself – he had three minutes at most.

As he was lowered serenely past the cut glass chandeliers, Isambard could feel the blood throbbing in his head, not just because of the terror that boiled in his belly, but because he was now upside-down, as if diving under the surface of the water. He looked down at the white tiled floor and into the middle of the display case directly below him where the scroll was kept. Isambard could see now what Catskill had meant about the case being effectively impenetrable from the sides - it was made from an ornamental floor-to-ceiling lattice of wrought iron and encased in a large glass tube. But being directly above it, Isambard was able to reach into it from the top.

"Down another foot or two Catskill," Isambard whispered. "I can't reach the scroll yet."

Isambard was now dangling face-down, holding the fake scroll in one hand, being lowered haltingly into a glass tube which was only just wide enough to accept his shoulders.

Isambard took a deep breath and blinked – the sweat rolling into his eyes was beginning to sting and he didn't have space to raise his hand and wipe it away.

Isambard could hear Ruthven dismissing some of the partygoers who were keen to re-enter the room.

"Hurry up," Ruthven complained. "Fireworks are nearly over. Crowds are on their way back this way."

"Another couple of inches and I'll have it," Isambard said.

With a jerk, he dropped another few notches, until he was able to grab the scroll with his free hand and replace it with the replica.

"Come on. They're coming"

But the fake scroll had toppled over.

"Stop. Down. Down two inches."

"Open this door at once," came an officious voice through the door that Ruthven was guarding. Ruthven recognised the voice of Francois, the man who tried to stop them coming in the front door.

"There seems to be a problem with the latch, sir," Ruthven replied, pushing against the door handle with all his might whilst glaring up at Isambard. Isambard stretched his fingers and, compensating for the swaying motion, reset the new scroll on its stand.

"Got it! Haul away. Go go go."

Above him, Catskill pulled rapidly on the rope – Isambard gripped with his ankles and disappeared into the black cavern of the room above just as the door handle finally snapped off in Ruthven's hand. The officer stepped to one side and Francois collapsed onto the floor in front of him.

"See," Ruthven said, waving the door handle at the dazed Master of Ceremonies, "I told you it was broken."

Above Ruthven's head, Catskill had secured the rope suspending Isambard and was replacing the hatch when suddenly there was a thunderous bang on the door.

Catskill grabbed Isambard as he hung helplessly in the harness, a yard above the floor.

"Sink me, sounds like soldiers," Catskill whispered. "Rest assured that I will rescue you if needed, but unless they are actually about to kill you, you will find me hiding behind this chair."

Catskill dived behind a large armchair just as the door burst open and half-a-dozen soldiers flowed in, followed by two men dressed in civilian clothes.

"Here, this is the... who the devil are you?" the first gentleman asked in French. Isambard was used to speaking French to his father and answered without hesitation.

"Sir, I was asked to recover the..."

"Ah excellent, you have it already – very efficient, Fouché," the other man said, reaching out with a pudgy hand. Isambard stared at the man, his brain awash with the recalled images of thousands of portraits. The man in front of Isambard was unmistakable –Napoleon Bonaparte.

"Well hand it over boy," Fouché said from over Bonaparte's shoulder. Hardly able to breathe, Isambard slowly edged a trembling hand forward, offering the scroll. Napoleon took it with a half-smile, slid out the rolled parchment and unrolled the paper, giving it a cursory glance. Isambard caught a glimpse of the hieroglyphics as Napoleon folded the scroll and placed it in his breast pocket.

"Here," Napoleon said, glancing at the fireplace. "Pop this on the fire for me would you? Very good Fouché," Napoleon said, making for the door. "Let's get everyone out of here."

"You heard him," Fouché hissed before following the Emperor out of the door. Within a few moments the whole party was gone, and Isambard was left holding the tube, suspended above the trapdoor in the middle of the room.

"Bad luck old boy," Catskill said, emerging cautiously from behind the chair. "Could have been worse - you're still in one piece at least. Be thankful for small mercies. Now, no point us all getting caught. You'd better cut along and bring the transport round the front. I'll get rid of this lot," Catskill added as he released Isambard and started unscrewing the parts of the tripod.

"Aren't we going to try to get it back?"

"From Napoleon's jacket pocket – not a chance my old fruit. Half the battle is knowing when you're beat my boy – we wouldn't get close to him. Now, off you go, retrace your steps and meet us out front."

"What about this?" Isambard asked, finding he was still holding the tube of an ancient Egyptian scroll.

"Keep it as a souvenir. Now get out there and get the barouche."

Isambard didn't stop to argue – he opened the door silently but straight-away pushed it shut.

"Somebody coming," he whispered urgently.

"Can you make it?"

"I think so."

"Then you go. I'll deal with this and meet you as planned."

"There's a plan?" Isambard asked as he slipped out of the door.

"Cheeky blighter," Catskill cursed, unable to completely suppress an admiring smile.

Catskill had just enough time to blow out the lantern and drop behind the desk before the door swung open. He watched the newcomer's feet through the low archway formed by the desk – in the half-light they looked like soldier's boots and breeches and they were getting dangerously close.

Once he had established that there was only one pair of feet, Catskill opted to go on the offensive and grabbed the only substantial object within reach - a particularly weighty volume of Greek History. He stood up and smashed the soldier over the head in one smooth motion. The soldier collapsed to the floor, clattering into the globe as he went - but Catskill could instantly see that he had made a terrible mistake.

"Ruthven, my dear fellow!" Catskill cried, dropping the book and falling to the Officer's side. "Are you quite alright?"

Ruthven groaned and cradled his neck.

"I would have hit you first, but I thought you was a lady," Ruthven growled.

"Ever the gentlemen," Catskill replied with a wink.

"Our guard woke up downstairs - your sleeping draft must have ran out. He's groggy and floundering around in his underclothes but it won't be long before they're onto us."

Just then, an alarm bell began to ring and the unmistakable sound of soldiers mustering added to the cacophony of the ballroom downstairs.

"Quicker than we thought! Come, we will have to defenestrate."

"Defenny-what?" Ruthven asked, hauling himself to his feet and repositioning his somewhat collapsed cap.

"Defenestrate - leave by the window. Here, shove this down the back of my dress will you?" Catskill said, handing Ruthven a journal that he had scavenged and turning his back on him.

"What's this?" Ruthven asked whilst doing as he had been directed.

"Fouché's diaries from the Revolution – could be useful."

Ruthven followed Catskill to the window just in time to see Isambard pulling out onto the circular driveway in the empty barouche.

"Good lad, right on cue," Agent Catskill murmured, whilst performing some mental calculations based on Isambard's speed and trajectory.

"What do you think you are doing?" Catskill demanded of Ruthven, who was fiddling with the latches on the windows.

"Opening the window," Ruthven responded, mystified.

"Oh dear, so old fashioned," Catskill grinned, holding Ruthven's hands and drawing him back into the middle of the room. "Do exactly as I do and you will be fine."

"I don't understand," Ruthven said warily. Just then a pair of soldiers burst in through the study door.

"Go!" Catskill yelled before running headlong at the window. Throwing caution to the wind, Ruthven followed suit. The scarecrow-soldier exploded through the windows seconds after the Duchess of Chessington and began falling towards the ground below. Catskill's fall was arrested by one of the ornamental awnings which covered the terrace. The angled canvas catapulted the agent into the air, only to land him in the back of Isambard's barouche as it completed its circuit of the drive.

Ruthven was not so lucky, and found himself crash-landing on top of half a dozen unsuspecting house-guards, sending them to the floor like as many skittles. As the guards recovered themselves, they began regarding Ruthven with increasing suspicion. Thinking fast, Ruthven decided that he would do his usual in this situation – divert the attention.

"Stop them," he cried, breaking into the best run his aching body could manage, chasing after the carriage which Isambard now had galloping at full tilt towards the gates. From the steps behind them, the Master of Ceremonies began to cry out that the Duchess was an imposter, which encouraged any of the unconvinced soldiers to follow Ruthven and join the pursuit.

The carriage was now racing down the home straight of the gravel drive and, although there was much yelling and jangling of ornamental buckles, it seemed to be out of harm's way.

Until the shots rang out.

Ruthven saw Catskill recoil and collapse, just as the carriage disappeared through the gates.

Ruthven shambled to a halt, breathless and distraught at what he had seen. The acrid smoke of spent gunpowder burnt his nostrils. The rest of the soldiers straggled on but there was little point chasing a horse-drawn vehicle on foot. A guard on horseback galloped up the drive and wheeled around the men, shouting orders. Ruthven copied what the others did until the horseman chased after the carriage.

Dazed and battered, Ruthven followed the search party until he was able to slip away into the woods and start the long walk back to Catskill's quarters. But all the while he was haunted by the memory of the gunshot, and Catskill's slumping body.

Chapter 27

CATO OPENED HIS EYES and found that he was lying on his back, staring up at the grey-black sky above. He could see lights moving about in his peripheral vision. Turning his head, the sound of gravel filled his ears. He lay still for a moment, listening to the familiar sounds of a busy market town on a pleasant Spring night. The scent of grilled meat and fresh bread stirred a deep hunger in him.

His clothes were wet through - water lapped around his legs, up as far as his waist. It wasn't cold but Cato found it unpleasant, like being licked by a dog. He lifted his head, pressing his wooden jaw against his chest as he strained to learn more about his surroundings. He looked across the glassy surface of the water where a tethered row-boat split the stream of flowing water.

"My good man, are you in order? What makes you in the water?" came a friendly voice from behind him. Cato had enough German to understand that the enquiry was one of friendly concern, but he did not have the rather specific vocabulary required to make an adequate response. He scrambled to his feet and, pragmatically deciding that it would be easier to convince them that he was mad than sane, started barking, looking directly into the German's eyes. This seemed to have the desired effect, and the friendly interloper and his partner hurried away.

Knowing that Bavarian night-watchmen were infamous for their mistreatment of vagrants, Cato moved off in the opposite direction, and climbed a grassy bank onto a pontoon. In the shadows of a deserted docksider's cabin he crouched and tried to remember how he had got there. He recalled that, since collecting the first amulet two days ago in Antwerp, he had felt an irrepressible urge to wander southwards. He remembered stumbling on a hillside. Crossing a bridge. Being unable to continue. He remembered feeling at once euphoric and nauseous, standing on the bridge overlooking the fast moving water. The grey-green of the water had become blue, ever deeper and more beautiful. He remembered smiling as his gaze followed the flowing water eastward. The water turned green, yellow, orange and gold and seemed to reshape itself into a spiral, then curves and stripes, filling the valley and the skies above in one incredible kaleidoscope. Cato remembered breathing it all in through smiling lips before closing his eyes and collapsing over the wall, into the cold embrace of the river.

Just then, several raised voices echoed around the river valley. Cato looked up to see two men in capes, carrying lanterns on sticks, hurrying towards the spot on the bank where he had landed. These were the watchmen he had heard about. Behind them, the couple who had offered to help him now gave away his position by shouting directions. Although the watchmen were overweight and slow moving, the determination and authority with which they approached, would, for most people be intimidating. Cato, however, found himself filled, not with dread, but with a certain relish as they approached.

Focusing on the furthermost watchmen, he imagined the word "stop." The watchman fell, as if he had run into a glass door or an invisible wall. Cato's eyes closed themselves and he found that he could visualise the remaining watchman being flicked across the riverbank. Cato opened his eyes to see both watchmen clutching their damaged bodies and groaning.

Cato closed his eyes again and allowed his mind's eye to take him on a path from the docksider's cabin, through the small market town to a smoke-filled beer hall. Opening his eyes, he found that he was now standing in that beer hall, next to a showgirl and her heavy-set suitor, neither of whom seemed pleased to see him. He excused himself and gazed around. It was poorly lit and noisy, full of sweaty men and screeching women. To Cato's cultured sensibilities it appeared to be an unholy combination of playground and cowshed. The smell and tobacco smoke made him sneer. Serving girls pushed through the crowds with overflowing beer-jugs.

Cato closed his eyes and enquired inwardly for direction from the amulet. With unseeing eyes he began to push through the crowds round the side of the bar where the human crush was even more oppressive. Cato decided that he would not have contact with anyone. So he didn't. Instead he repelled bodies without contact, walking steadily through the crowds, untouched.

A moment later Cato's eyes opened to lock briefly with a man whose tanned face and leathery skin set him apart from the pale-faced locals. Cato's repulsive aura extended steadily forward, pushing the revellers aside and creating an empty channel between him and his quarry. Luca, sensing the arrival of a predator, stood with as much conviction as he could, and for a moment a rising sensation of invincibility flooded his being. But as the crowds looking on fell silent one by one, Luca began to sweat and found himself swallowing hard. Cato lowered his head and was beginning to raise an arm when Luca bolted, scrambling through the crowds as best he could.

But by a force which even he didn't understand, Cato simply plucked Luca out of the crowd, pulling on the amulet around his neck.

Luca thrashed ineffectively, like a trapped rabbit, legs flailing and arms clinging onto the amulet to stop it throttling him. Cato savoured the moment, pulling the second amulet close, dragging Luca into the space that had formed between them.

Fighting for breath, Luca threw off the amulet and held his throat. The amulet lay on the floor. The silent horror of the crowd was spreading in a wave throughout the hall. Cato stepped towards Luca, who cowered, backing away from the amulet on the floor.

Cato bathed in the gaze of a hundred terrified spectators, picked up the second amulet and disappeared.

Chapter 28

Guided by the stars, Ruthven journeyed all night through woods and villages and then along the dusty roads towards London. He found streams to drink from, but as the night drew on, hunger, fatigue and bruises began to take their toll. He had given his valuables to Catskill to look after, so was unable to buy himself even a piece of bread when later the bakers' ovens filled the morning air with their tantalising aromas.

The sun was rising by the time Ruthven climbed the stairs to Catskill's lodgings on the seventh floor, where he found Isambard asleep on the floor outside the room.

"Isambard! What are you doing on the doorstep?"

"Ruthven!"

"Where's Catskill? Is he dead?"

Ruthven was breathless from the stair-climb, mad with hunger and mentally exhausted. He made for the door before Isambard had a chance to stop him.

"Don't go in!" Isambard called. But in his daze the officer stumbled over Isambard and through the door into the room where a bed stood pressed against the wall opposite. In it lay a short-haired lady who abruptly sat up, drawing bedclothes over her naked shoulders.

"Pardon me ma'am." Ruthven said, respectfully averting his eyes and drawing the door closed.

"Who the devil is that?" Ruthven demanded of no one in particular.

"Ruthven, come back in here," the woman said from inside the room.

Ruthven recognised the voice and began to feel nauseous, sea-sick, disorientated. He groaned and tried to focus on Isambard before confusion and exhaustion got the better of him.

"Catskill?" he wondered out loud before slumping to the floor, unconscious.

Ruthven woke with a start and anxiously scanned the room. He found himself lying under a blanket in a corner between the door and the foot of a single bed. Sunlight filled the room and the sloping ceilings suggested he was in the eaves of a tall building - he remembered coming up to Catskill's lodgings on the seventh floor. Ruthven sank back onto the floor, groaning with the aches from the previous night's exercise. Above him the woman from his dream appeared and sat on the edge of the bed. Something about her was strangely familiar. Then he remembered.

"Good morning Officer Ruthven," she said.

"Catskill. I thought you were shot dead."

"Shot. But not dead. Isambard patched me up - this book took the brunt of it," Catskill smiled, showing the 1794 journal that she had hidden in the dress, now peppered with gun-shot.

"I'm sorry we had to make your bed on the floor. Isambard and I couldn't move you so we had to just cover you up where you fell. Will you take the bed now?"

"No," Ruthven growled bashfully, heaving himself to his feet with a grimace. "Quite comfortable standing thank you... my Lady."

"Oh, yes sorry about that.... deception. I've found it's almost impossible to do a job as an Agent of His Majesty's Special Intelligence Directorate as a woman. So I have to go around pretending to be a man. Most.... inconvenient. But it does sometimes work to my advantage," she smiled, looking at the ball-gown heaped on the floor. "My real name is Madeleine. Madeleine Grant," The agent continued, proffering a hand. Ruthven shook it, tentatively, still not sure whether she was real or a figment of his fevered imagination.

"So, at the ball when I thought you were a man dressed up as a woman, you were actually a woman dressed up as a man dressed up as a woman?"

Catskill raised her eyebrows and looked into the corner of the room. "I suppose you could put it like that," she said. But then she turned and fixed Ruthven with a hard stare. "Of course, I'd appreciate it if you could... keep it under your hat. Not sure how the Admiralty would react if my secret were to come out."

Just then footsteps came hammering up the stairs. Ruthven instinctively took up a defensive position behind the door as it swung open, but Catskill raised a relaxed hand just as Isambard appeared carrying several paper bags.

"Breakfast anyone?"

WHILST RUTHVEN AND Isambard restored themselves with coffee from the stove, scones and cheese, Catskill leafed through Fouché's journal, occasionally laughing and reading sections aloud.

"It looks like Fouché was the one who introduced Cato to Napoleon back in the nineties... Cato gave Napoleon a bit of a leg-up early in his career. So maybe Napoleon would have helped Cato escape the guillotine - Cato would be forever in Napoleon's debt,"

"So Cato was mates with Napoleon, eh?" Ruthven pondered.

"Right up until the Emperor's precious Egyptian amulet mysteriously went missing. Napoleon held Cato personally responsible and vowed to kill one member of Cato's family every month until it was found."

"Sounds like an old wives' tale," Ruthven said.

"It happens to be true."

"How do you know?"

"Because I was the one stealing the amulet," Catskill said.

Isambard and Ruthven stared at Catskill, dumbstruck, but she had already returned her attention to Fouché's journal.

"Ha! Here we are!" Catskill cried. "Here's a loose end if ever I saw one." The agent stood up holding the journal and began to read.

"*Cato guillotined today. He was in a sorry state - his face disfigured from a gunshot wound, according to Doctor Souberbielle.*' There! How about that for an open door?"

Ruthven and Isambard exchanged blank looks.

"Guillotined sounds pretty final to me," Ruthven said.

"*Face disfigured.* His face. How else can we know a man but by his face?" Catskill asked from the sunlit corner of the room.

"Even faces can hide secrets," Ruthven said, raising an eyebrow at Catskill.

"So, what are you saying?" Isambard asked.

"Don't you see? Cato was injured during his arrest – half his jaw was shot off – he would have been disfigured and covered in bandages – the perfect cover for a stand-in."

"That would explain his strange wooden jaw," Isambard pondered. "But who would want to go to the guillotine in his place?"

"They were desperate times. People would do anything to protect their families – some desperate prisoner would have done a deal and taken Cato's place at the guillotine."

"All sounds highly unlikely," Ruthven grumbled.

"And you think it more likely that Cato has come back from the dead, do you?" Catskill demanded. "We need to find this Doctor Souberbielle – I'll have to go back to France," she added, searching about as if she'd lost something. "If you'll excuse me gentlemen, I need to get dressed. Now, what's a girl to wear?"

RUTHVEN AND ISAMBARD were slumped outside Catskill's door when the sound of footsteps came drifting up from the stairwell.

"Ruthven," Isambard whispered, realising that the Officer was dozing.

"Hmm, what?"

A boy appeared at the top of the stairs, breathing heavily from the rapid ascent up seven flights.

"Officer Ruthven," the boy said. "Message for you."

Ruthven grunted, put tuppence in the boy's hand and watched him disappear down the stairs. Ruthven coughed, hauled his slumping frame upright and tore into the wax-sealed envelope.

"Hmm. Good news for you."

"What's that?"

"That address you asked me to trace, the one you got from the dead man's house in Bristol. It's a house in Iffley, near Oxford."

"Where's that?"

"Halfway between here and the middle of nowhere." Ruthven said, thrusting the note into Isambard's hand.

"I could take a coach."

"It would take you half a lifetime to get out to that bit of country. Unless you can fly – you're not going to tell me you've invented a contraption that can make a man fly now are you?"

Isambard's heart sank and he cursed inwardly. Then a thought occurred to him.

"Not me – but old Lunardi might be able to help."

"Who's Lunardi?"

"According to my father he's the greatest balloonist that ever lived – and he's also my Godfather."

Chapter 29

"ISAMBARDO! MY FAVOURITE Godson. What happen? How do you do?" Vincenzo grabbed Isambard by the hand, shook it vigorously and used it to pull the somewhat abashed Brunel close for an impassioned hug.

"Oh. Vincenzo. I'm. Fine. Thank. You," Brunel replied, between thumping back-slaps and as the breath in his lungs returned.

"Look at you," Vincenzo cried, stepping back for a wider view. "What a fantastic boy you are? You have a girlfriend, yes?"

"Well, no not exactly..."

"Not one girlfriend but many girlfriends. Of course. When I was your age I also had many girlfriends," Vincenzo beamed proudly. A long string of Italian syllables came streaming down the corridor from the kitchen, which seemed to wipe the smile off Vincenzo's face.

"*Mama, che, non sono affari tuoi*," Vincenzo called over his shoulder whilst pulling the door closed behind him.

"So. How is your father? He still making the holes in the ground?"

"Yes, we're building the stage two prototype for testing at the end of..."

"And Sophia. How is your beautiful mama?"

"She's... very well. She..."

"Does she still talk about me? You know I had to stop coming to your house because I think that if not she is gonna get herself into the trouble with me and your father! Eh? A beautiful lady, Isambardo. A beautiful lady. Your father a very lucky man, eh?" Vincenzo, who had been holding Isambard by the shoulders during the whole conversation, now steered Isambard into the house.

"So what we can do for you? You don't come round here just to show off all your girlfriends and tell me how much your mama miss me, eh?"

"No. That's right. I actually need a bit of a favour."

"Of course you do. Anything. Anything Vincenzo Lunardi can do for a Brunel, I do for Brunel. What is it you need? A nice suit?" Vincenzo asked, standing in front of a vast brocade framed portrait of himself with a cat and a dog. In the picture, Vincenzo held a pamphlet which read "Into the skies" and sported the same winning smile that Isambard saw today. The painting stood absurdly large in the small shabby room which overflowed with bric-a-brac from a lifetime whose glory was all in the past.

"You wanna drink? Grappa, coffee? *Mama! E Isambard. Per favore, prendere qualcosa da bere.*"

"Isambardo!" she cried in delight before emerging at the doorway, rubbing floury hands on her apron and beaming. The little round woman extended her arms and gathered Isambard up, all the while babbling the international language of aunties everywhere. Vincenzo translated as she went.

"She say she very happy to see you. She say how you have grown. She say you very handsome. She say you very thin. She say you want some gnocchi?"

"Gnocchi?" Isambard asked, peering out from the bundle of hugs.

"It's the little dumplings. Potato with the bit of cheese. She say the cheese is not the right cheese but she use the Cottage Cheese and it's alright. I say it's the best gnocchi in the world but, you know, that's my mama."

Mama stepped back, wiped a tear from her eye and held up an out-stretched hand still chattering away.

"She say three minutes."

Mama retreated to the kitchen and the brief whirlwind was over.

"So," Vincenzo said, leaning back on the sideboard. "What can I do for you?"

"Vincenzo. I need your hydrogen balloon."

Vincenzo's face dropped and he suddenly looked every one of his 61 years.

“But Isambardo, this balloon no fly for 15 years.”

“I need to get somewhere urgently. It's the fastest way.”

Mama called from the kitchen. Vincenzo looked hard at Isambard.

“We eat. We're gonna need something in the tummy.”

The two of them talked about the balloon trip almost incessantly whilst devouring the delicious dinner; Isambard had hardly eaten all day so was happy to do most of the listening. Mama simply hunched over her plate and, with a spoon in her fist, devoured her small portion in twenty seconds before attacking the washing up with renewed gusto. Vincenzo helped himself to generous glasses of wine, but was good enough, or at least pragmatic enough, to notice that Isambard was not enjoying the vinegary brew and did not need his glass topping up.

By the end of the meal, they had talked through all the major obstacles to relaunching the balloon, and, increasingly emboldened by the wine, Vincenzo was beginning to sound more optimistic about their chances.

“Ok Isambard. We do it. Tomorrow going to be a perfect day for ballooning. We load the carriage and get some sleep and get up early and we be in Oxford for lunch with The Earl of Berkely.”

Isambard felt frustrated, but he knew that Vincenzo was right.

“He will be very pleased to see me. You know, he once paid me a thousand shillings to take off from his back garden during his daughter wedding. And you know, Lunardi always find a bridesmaid who want to come with me, yes?"

Chapter 30

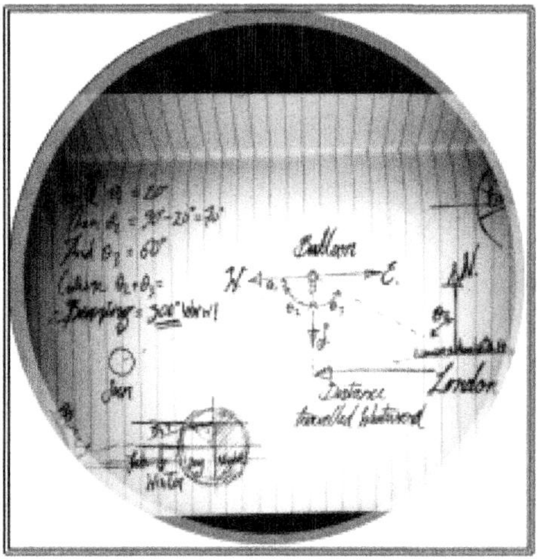

WHEN THEY FINALLY BECAME airborne, surrounded by a small crowd at around lunchtime the following day, Isambard and Lunardi found themselves being whisked along at an exhilarating speed - 18 miles an hour by Isambard's reckoning. Isambard had convinced Lunardi to let him bring his "reverse windmill" on-board, which Isambard said was the only way to guarantee that they progress in the right direction.

“Is working, this contraption of yours?” Lunardi asked when he could no longer hear the delighted cries of the onlookers below.

“I think so,” Isambard replied, between rhythmic puffs of breath. Isambard was seated in a reclining chair, pedalling a crank at a near-constant speed, which in turn drove a sixteen-bladed windmill. “I can definitely influence the direction of the balloon using these levers,” he added, demonstrating. “It’s a shame you don’t have a map. I took a bearing at take-off, and as long as we can keep reaching our way-points we should be there in a few hours.”

“At least you keep yourself nice and warm,” Lunardi said with an amused smile.

They made steady progress in what seemed to be the right direction - the lack of a map was only slightly less frustrating than Lunardi's geographical observations, which were almost always misleading. However, when the breeze was blowing in the right direction Isambard took a break from pedalling the windmill and sketched a triangulation arithmetic using the position of London (which could still be seen as a hazy dome on the horizon behind them) and the estimated point of sunset.

“According to this, we’re making good progress in a North-Westerly direction,” Isambard said, showing the calculation to Lunardi.

Lunardi snatched the paper from Isambard’s hand and squinted at it. “Of course we are – what you expect? Lunardi always on target,” Lunardi said. “Look, there - Reading.”

“I think that must be High Wycombe actually.”

“Reading. High Wycombe. All the same.”

Lunardi had at least had the good sense to keep a supply of mink collars, rabbit-skin hats and silk gloves in the aeronauts' basket, which were doing a good job of keeping him warm. Most of these items had belonged to lady passengers, and the sight of each one gave Lunardi an excuse to recount another romantic story until eventually the combination of their warmth and the early start got the better of him and he fell asleep on the basket floor. But the sun was getting lower and weaker. Isambard squinted out across the featureless fields, woods and pastures. They would have to land before nightfall.

Suddenly a crack ripped through the air and echoed down the valley. Lunardi's eyes flicked open. Another crack and Lunardi was on his feet.

"*Dov'è? Dov'è?*" Lunardi cried as he scrambled about the basket looking wildly over the sides.

"We not the French!" he yelled repeatedly.

"What's going on?"

An unfamiliar whistling sound followed by another crack. Lunardi spoke rapidly. "Bonaparte and the French used military balloons many years ago. Now everyone see a balloon they think it a French invasion. There they are! We Not Are French!" Lunardi screamed over the side, waving a white handkerchief on a stick which had obviously been used for this purpose on many previous occasions. Isambard peered over the basket and could make out a group of two or three figures wielding firearms. Two of the guns flashed, followed by the whistle of shot passing the balloon and then the delayed report of the discharge. Another flash.

"Look out!" Isambard called, ducking back into the basket.

"Is alright, we out of range now." But his expression turned to panic when the shot whistled through the rigging chords attaching the balloon to the basket. Isambard could see that two of the cords had been snapped.

Lunardi screamed, visibly shocked, and yelled down at the snipers, who were busily reloading but fast receding out of range.

Isambard clambered onto the sill of the basket and yanked the two ends of a broken cord and attempted to bring them together. Of course, the tension that they had been under was considerable and Isambard could not retie the chord.

"Do you have any rope?"

"Yes!" Lunardi replied, rummaging through a box at his feet and triumphantly producing some short lengths of rope. Isambard used these to join the ends, then twisted the new rope using a fork from the picnic basket to make it progressively shorter until it was a similar length to the original. Isambard repeated this process for the other snapped cord and before long they were able to relax and look around them. Which was fortunate, because if they hadn't they would perhaps not have noticed that they had lost about 500 feet in altitude and were continuing to fall fast.

"The ground, Lunardi. We're going to hit the ground!"

"Full overboard!" Lunardi yelled, taking first the picnic hamper, which was still generously furnished with contributions from the crowd at take-off and hurling it overboard.

Next went the ballast (10 bags of sand carried for precisely this reason), followed by the toolkit, Elderflower Champagne, spare mink scarves and the landing ladder.

The descent slowed but the balloon was still gliding downwards, towards the forbidding darkness of a dense forest.

"Those shots must have put a hole in the balloon," Isambard remarked, squinting into the distance. Through the early dusk, he was able to see, for the first time, a very distinctive skyline of rooftops, spires and domes.

"Is that...?"

"Is Cambridge," Lunardi said with brio.

"Oxford?"

"Yes, Oxford. I say Oxford."

For a moment the balloon's descent was halted and it scudded along about 500 feet above the ground. But the breeze was still pushing them along at a rate which was suddenly terrifying, especially at this height; the trees and fields below rolled past in a dizzying stream.

"How do we land at this speed?" Isambard asked.

"We need a nice open field. We bounce a few times."

"A field?" Isambard repeated in dismay. "Aren't we going a bit fast to land in a field?"

"Yes we going a bit fast! What you want to do, find a giant pillow to land on?"

"We need to slow down."

"Ok, ok, but we don't have a brake. How you wanna slow down?"

Isambard thought for a moment.

"We'll have to clip the trees to slow down. Have you ever done that?"

"Yes I done that. It's a disaster. It make a great big mess of the basket."

"Have you got a better idea?"

Lunardi was silent for a moment.

"No."

"Right, well it doesn't really matter because right now we are going to plough straight into those houses whatever we do."

Isambard was right. They were beginning to lose height again and seemed to be heading for a populated area on the outskirts of Oxford.

"Listen, Isambardo. This last flight, it make me very happy you know. You give me happiness like I haven't seen since 1804. No 1799, when the Spain people make me a saint. But now, you know, I an old man. I am just ballast you know?"

"Lunardi, what are you talking about?" Isambard demanded with a slightly wild look in his eye.

Lunardi gripped the basket and put one foot on the sill.

"What are you doing?"

"You got to save you self, Isambardo. I'm just ballast you know. I lived my life."

"Lunardi, you have got to be joking. You are not going overboard. We still have a load of things we can throw out." Isambard ventured, desperately looking about for anything they could throw overboard. He picked up his case.

"Here this weighs a bit. This could go."

"Goodbye Isambardo. You are the son that I never had. I very proud of you."

"Why does this case weigh so much?" Isambard asked himself. He put his hand in to have a rummage and found a large cold jar.

And then he remembered.

"Goodbye Isambardo," Lunardi said, one leg swinging over the edge of the basket.

"No! Lunardi get off there and wait a minute," Isambard said, pulling out the jar and plucking the cork out of it with a satisfying pop. "I can get us out of this mess. Trafalgar?"

"Hello," Trafalgar said, turning a light green colour behind Isambard's left shoulder. Lunardi gave an involuntary shriek.

"Trafalgar, what are you doing out of your jar?"

"Helping you get to Iffley – you don't think your pedal powered windmill has been doing all the work do you?"

"You mean you've been helping... I thought you were asleep."

"Asleep? Whilst you've been making such a song and dance about it. I could hardly sleep through it could I." Trafalgar's slow, almost melancholy voice was somehow hugely reassuring to Isambard.

"Listen I'm sorry I haven't got you back to the Candlewick's shop before now. It's been a bit busy and..."

"No, no that's alright. It's been quite fun travelling about a bit. I don't tend to get out so much these days so it makes a nice change."

Lunardi was staring at the jar and the green, misty shape that hovered above it.

"Oh sorry Lunardi. How rude of me not to introduce you. This is Trafalgar, the talking gas. Trafalgar, I suppose you've picked up who this is."

"It's an absolute pleasure, Mr Lunardi. I can't tell how grateful we gasses are to you for raising our profile in the public imagination and for generally spurring interests in the study and application of all things gaseous."

"The.... The pleasure is all mine, I assure you Mr Trafalgar," Lunardi replied, with one of his trademark smiles.

Isambard glanced over the side of the basket and calculated that they had about 20 seconds before smashing into a small village. He spoke with renewed urgency.

"Gentlemen. I hate to be impolite, but there is the matter of our dangerously rapid descent which does not seem to have slowed. Trafalgar, is there anything you can do to help?"

"Certainly. Sorry. I tend to be a bit chatty after being bottled up for a while..." Trafalgar replied whilst snaking his way around the outside of the balloon. The wind whipped at his edges but he seemed to be able to hold his wispy form together as he oozed over the entire surface of the balloon.

Suddenly, the basket gave a sharp jolt and there was a snapping sound as it hit a tree at the edge of the village common-land. The balloon was dropping fast and two hundred yards across the common stood a church which Isambard thought looked dangerously solid.

"I've found just one hole," Trafalgar boomed over the roar of the wind. "I'll go in there and block it from the inside, then reduce my density a couple of times."

The green gas disappeared into the hole in the side of the balloon, like water down a plug hole just as the basket smashed into the grassy ground, hurling Isambard into Lunardi's arms. The balloon bounced crudely as the enormous thrust of Trafalgar's buoyancy gripped the balloon and hauled it into the air, causing it to ride up the face of the church, across the tiled roof and to graze one side across the spire, opening another gaping hole in the balloon which Trafalgar rapidly filled.

"Erm. Everything was going well until that second hole appeared. I'm not sure how long I can hold it. It's the fabric you see. It's sort of tearing and I'm not really built for holding things together," Trafalgar said, his voice now echoing in the chamber formed by the taut balloon.

Isambard scanned the path ahead; they had at least gained some height and would clear the village buildings. However, ahead of them stood the densely populated collection of buildings that was Oxford, and there would be no obvious landing targets there, especially at this speed. They continued to rise, but the ascent was slowing.

"You ok Trafalgar?"

"Hnngh. I'm not convinced that I'm keeping all this gas in," Trafalgar replied mournfully.

"There! We shall slow down against those trees and land there!" Lunardi cried, pointing forward at a large grassy area that could just be made out through the evening gloom.

"Ok. Well, looks like we'll need to lose altitude pretty quickly to avoid overshooting." Isambard said.

"Don't a worry. I got a release valve." Lunardi said, grabbing the valve cable and tugging hard.

"Wait!" Isambard called. But it was too late. The cable opened a valve at the top of the balloon allowing the buoyant hydrogen to escape. The effect was immediate as the balloon's ascent rapidly turned into descent.

"Trafalgar," Isambard yelled, "have you got any lift left?"

"I could expand a little bit more I suppose."

"Great. Just before we hit those trees we need to level out. Ok Trafalgar, now. Give it all you've got."

Trafalgar expanded, the balloon stretched wider and began to slow its descent. Isambard and Lunardi braced themselves against the side of the basket. The balloon was levelling out as the bottom of the basket crashed into the tree canopy. It rocked forward violently, tipping the basket over before disengaging from the trees at about half the original speed. The basket swung wildly like a pendulum drifting across the treetops.

"Dump! Dump both of you," Isambard called, realising that this was their opportunity to drop into the relatively springy arms of several ancient oak trees from ten feet.

Lunardi grappled for the release valve cable and Trafalgar pulled himself away from the inside wall of the balloon by shrinking to his original volume. The balloon was now holed like a perforated handkerchief in the wind. It collapsed around the escaping hydrogen and streamed behind the basket as it dropped into the trees. The basket and its contents dropped like a wayward trapeze artist into the tree-canopy, bursting through the upper branches but collecting more and more resistance as it went. Above them, the tangled mass of deflated balloon became increasingly ensnared in the branches and began to heave on the basket ropes. The noise of branches snapping and silk ripping filled the air but at least the basket was gradually slowing. There was a lurch as the basket slipped through the last of the major tree limbs and went momentarily into free-fall, but in the canopy above, the balloon had become so entangled in a broad array of branches that the fall was arrested by the connecting ropes. The basket finally came to a halt, swaying in the air suspended 20 feet from the ground, surrounded by a quiet rain of falling winter leaves and dislodged branches large and small.

"Is everybody alright?" Trafalgar asked dolefully, snaking back into the jar, which still lay on the floor of the basket. Isambard checked his hands, front and back and looked up to see Lunardi's ecstatic expression beaming back at him, made all the more alive by a stream of blood running down the side of his leaf-covered face.

"Lunardi, you're hurt!" Isambard cried.

Lunardi smeared the blood with his hand and gave it a cursory glance.

"If I bleeding I must still be alive, which already is a good thing," Lunardi said, throwing open his arms and crossing the basket to envelop Isambard in a heartfelt hug.

As each slapped the other on the back and started to make sense of what they had just been through, they became aware of the sound of horses approaching.

"Ahoy there, are you alright!" two riders yelled from amongst the trees.

"Well at least they don't think we're French," Isambard said, only half joking. "Yes, we're ok. We're just a bit... stuck"

"We no stuck. We just not fully landed yet," Lunardi corrected.

Two horsemen pulled up in the clearing below, each carrying a lantern.

"We saw you swinging around a bit up in the skies and thought that you might be in trouble, but if you really are alright, we can leave you to it..." one of the fellows said politely, doffing his riding cap.

"Mr Sadler, is that you?" the other said, holding up his lantern and peering up through the gloom.

"*Sadler sia dannato*. No this no Sadler. This the great Lunardi, truly England's first aeronaut!"

"Oh, terribly sorry I thought it was that Sadler chap out of retirement, messing about in his balloon again," the second man said to the first, turning his attention away from the basket suspended above them. "D'you remember him? Oxford chap. Townie, mind you."

"Oh of course, 'the Flying Baker.' He has that pastry shop."

"The Lemon Hall Refreshment House...."

"...on High Street. Jolly good flan cases in there."

"Really? So his baking is better than his flying is it? What?"

"I should hope so!" And with that, the two of them began roaring with laughter, their horses bridling beneath them.

A loud popping noise brought them to their senses.

"There it is again. It's a gun I tell you!" one of them said. Isambard heard it too. And now there was a rhythmic wheezing and squeaking sound from beyond the trees which seemed to be getting louder. The horse riders stopped their chatter and looked behind them.

They all turned to see a wicker bath-chair mounted on large wheels approaching. In the chair sat an old lady with a blanket over her legs and a smart fur hat on. Her gloved hands each rested on a brake lever, one each side of the chair. Behind her was fixed a vertically mounted cylinder which seemed to be the source of the motive power of the wheeled-chair. The lady applied the levers and the chair came to a halt. The four men stared at her intently.

"I'm glad to see our aeronauts are not broken. And it's a good thing you young chaps have turned up. Undergraduates?"

"Yes, ma'am." The two horsemen chorused, suddenly obedient.

"Well, consider this an initiative test of the most practical kind. You are in a wood with two horses, each of 16 hands, accompanied by a second man of average intelligence. Two fellows, clearly with less than average intelligence, have contrived to suspend themselves from the trees at a height of 21 feet from the ground. How do you rescue them? Points for efficiency, effectiveness and ingenuity. Your time starts now."

"Ma'am I am a student of the classics and as such have very little notion of the physical nuances...."

"Did not the classicists give us geometry? Fluid dynamics? Simple mechanics?" she asked sternly.

"Ma'am, they did. I was merely...."

"Please ask yourself: in what way is this current intervention assisting you?"

The classicist fell silent.

"If you please ma'am," Isambard called gingerly from the basket.

"It speaks! But what does it say?"

"Ma'am you forgot to mention the presence of a distinguished lady in a carriage propelled by what looks like an internal combustion engine. These may turn out to be useful."

"Indeed I did," the lady conceded with a tight-lipped smile. "One point for obsequiousness."

"Well, we could stand on the horses and reach up," one of the lads suggested, heaving his boot onto the saddle, taking the strain and attempting to stand. "I'm sure I've seen Quarrington doing this down on the farm...." he muttered.

"Please bear in mind that points can be lost for poor performance."

The acrobat's friend with the riding cap reached across and put a disapproving hand on his friend's shoulder, encouraging him to retake his saddle.

"Surely you have some rope up there don't you?" the riding cap called.

"No. We throw it all out as part of the.... controlled descent," Lunardi replied.

"What about those ropes supporting the basket? If you cut some of those wouldn't you tip towards the ground a few feet? And then those ropes would dangle towards the floor. That would put you just 15 feet from the deck," the acrobat suggested.

The riding cap looked at the old lady.

"A point for ingenuity," she eventually conceded.

"Then you could drop onto my shoulders if I can get this horse to stand below you," the riding cap added with a marvellous grin.

They all looked at the old lady but she looked on unmoved.

"It better than sitting up here all night. I needing the lavatorio." Lunardi confessed.

Although it was pretty dark up in the basket, Isambard was able to find his knife (which he had chosen not to jettison even in their most desperate moments) and clamber up to start work cutting the cords.

"Cut them as high up as you can," the acrobat called.

One by one the cords were cut, and with each cut, the basket's rebalancing reaction was more violent. The observers below looked on intently as Lunardi clung on for dear life and the basket floor tipped closer and closer towards the vertical.

"P'raps you should tie yourself onto one of the trailing cords in case you fall," the riding cap suggested. Isambard took the advice and tied one of the lower lines to his belt. He carefully shuffled around the top edge of the basket and put the blade to one of only 5 remaining chords. But the tension was so great that in a few short strokes the cord exploded into two parts, sending the basket into a frenzy and dropping Isambard into free fall.

A split second later Isambard was jolted to a halt by the rope he had tied to his belt and he became part of the enormous, compound pendulum which swung ominously from the trees which were now adding creaks and whines to the shower of papery brown leaves.

Recovering themselves, the horsemen moved into position underneath Isambard, who now dangled like a rag doll, suspended in mid-air.

"Can you reach?" the riding cap called. Isambard gingerly extended an arm and their hands made contact, but he was at full stretch.

"I'm not going to be able to undo this knot. It's tied on behind me. My only option is to cut it but then I'll fall..."

The two lads looked at each other, each having the same thought.

"How did Quarrington do it, d'you think?"

"Ma'am, would you mind pulling up over here to hold onto these horses? It'd be dashed unsporting of them if they were to wander off whilst we were mid-rescue," the acrobat joked to his chum. The lady did so, taking both sets of reins and giving each horse one of her no-nonsense stares. From their sitting position in their saddles, the lads linked an arm each, right hand to right hand and used their remaining six limbs to clamber onto their respective saddles. Standing on horseback, they then created a cradle with their arms, directly below Isambard's suspended body.

"Right, boy. Why don't you cut yourself free? We're here to catch you. Don't you worry about that."

With one last terrific effort, Isambard was able to twist around himself, grab the restraining rope at his back, and hack at it with the knife in his free hand. After some frenzied sawing, the rope snapped, and Isambard flopped into the human cradle below. The horses adjusted their footing somewhat, but otherwise stood firm.

"Oh bravo, boys. With a bit of practice you could give the Palladium Circus Troupe a run for their money," the lady in the chair called, clapping sincerely with a twinkle in her eye. She looked up at the Italian still clinging to the basket, and added, "And now you, Mr Lunardi. Let's see if you really can fly."

Chapter 31

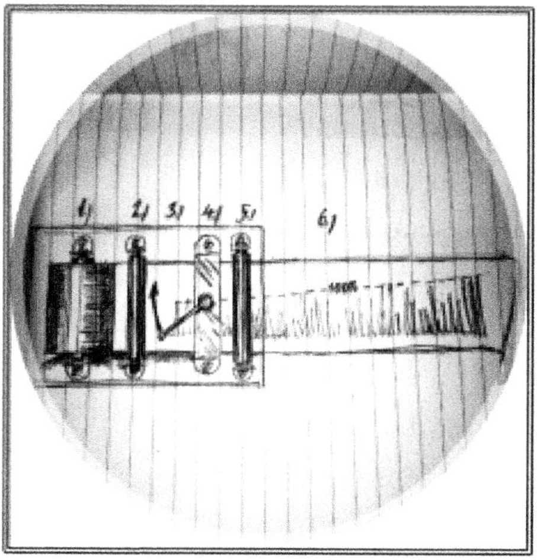

LUNARDI COMPLETED HIS descent from the precariously suspended basket with all the grace and elegance of a sack of Borlotti beans, ending up in an untidy but undamaged heap, on the floor in the dust at the back end of the acrobat's horse. Picking himself up, he managed to swallow his pride and smile with relief as the students dismounted, lifted him onto their shoulders, and lavished him with praise for his magnificent and brave descent.

"Thank you for your help Mrs..." Isambard said, extending a hand to the old lady in the wheeled chair.

"Mrs Faraday," the lady responded with a smile. "It was my pleasure."

For a moment Isambard didn't know what to say.

"Faraday? Mrs Faraday of Iffley. What luck - exactly the person that I had come here looking for. Or at least your husband is."

"If it's my husband that you're looking for, then I'm afraid you've come a long way for nothing."

"What do you mean? I mean, where is he?"

"He's dead, young man. Very dead," she said with a defiant smile. "Perhaps I can help."

"I'm... I'm sure you can. My name is Isambard Brunel, I am an apprentice engineer in London and I have been sent here on a matter of the utmost importance."

"Indeed?"

"Mrs Faraday, I have just come from the house of Doctor Thomas Beddoes who I believe you know."

"Yes he is a great friend of ours."

"I'm afraid I have some bad news. A gang of anarchists broke into his house a few nights ago."

"Anarchists... well is he quite alright?"

"I'm afraid not ma'am - they killed him."

"Killed him? But... but why?"

"It seems they were trying to force him to help them in a terrorist plan. A plan to... kill members of the government. But I believe that before he died, he sent you an electrical message, some kind of distress signal down a wire – is that possible?"

"The telegraph machine. Yes, yes of course," Mrs Faraday said vaguely, lost in thoughts of her dear old friend, murdered. "You must... you must come back to the house," she stammered.

"That's very kind of you."

The moment was shattered by a loud round of laughter from Lunardi and the students.

"I wonder what your friend will wish to do," Mrs Faraday said, indicating Lunardi with a raised eyebrow.

Isambard looked over at Lunardi, who appeared positively diminutive next to the burly graduates who had rescued him.

"Isambardo!" Lunardi cried as if he hadn't seen the boy for years. "My brave co-pilot! Come here. Have some..." Lunardi hesitated, peering at the plain brown bottle that the graduates had handed him.

"Morrell's Varsity. The finest ale known to humanity," the riding cap boomed.

"No. Really, thank you but no," Isambard said. "I feel it is my duty to chaperone Mrs Faraday back to her home to make sure she gets there safely."

"Of course!" Lunardi cried.

"Although it strikes me she could look after herself pretty well in most situations, what?" the acrobat said in a stage whisper, to gales of laughter from the other two.

"Will you be ok getting back on your own?" Isambard asked Lunardi. "What about the balloon?"

"Don' worry about me. I have lots of friends in Oxford," Lunardi called back brightly, gesturing at the pair of students.

"Just wait 'til we get you back to the Turf Tavern," the acrobat said. "They will not believe their ears."

By now, Mrs Faraday had long ago moved off - Isambard had to follow or risk losing her.

"Well please look after him. And thank you again for plucking us both out of the tree," Isambard called as he broke into a run towards the distant glow of the lantern on Mrs Faraday's chemical carriage. The cries and booming laughter of Lunardi's group drifted off towards the bright lights of Oxford town, whilst the hissing and popping of Mrs Faraday's hydrogen engine acted as Isambard's distant guide.

"I must say I'm very impressed with your self-propelling chair," Isambard said once he had come up next to Mrs Faraday. "Is it some kind of internal combustion engine?"

"What's that? Yes, yes. Excuse me, I was miles away. Yes, it burns hydrogen in a piston and converts the energy into gravitational potential in the weight at the back. I have a nervous condition you see, which means I can no longer walk. To be honest I've no idea what's wrong with me - even the finest minds at the University admit to being centuries away from really understanding how the large sponge we call the brain actually governs such complex tasks as walking. Suffice it to say, whatever coordination that I had in that department is long gone, has been for years, hence this contraption which I designed with my husband and manufactured in the lonely years after his death. He was called Monty which is why this machine bears the sobriquet 'Monty's Carriage'. Silly really. Here, give me a shove."

They had arrived at the house and Mrs Faraday was pulling on the doorbell tassel. Once the carriage had mounted the small step in front of the main door, it opened, seemingly of its own accord. Isambard felt a draught of warm air rush out.

"Hullo! What magic is this?" Isambard grinned as the door swung open.

"No magic, my boy. Just a counterweight under the threshold flagstone. Come on inside, you're letting the heat out."

By skillful use of the brake levers, Mrs Faraday directed the wheeled chair through the door which closed behind her with a click. Isambard stepped onto the threshold flagstone expecting it to swing open but it stubbornly refused, however much he jumped up and down.

"Step off and pull the doorbell to open the latch first," Mrs Faraday called from the other side of the door.

"Would you like a cup of tea?" she asked once Isambard was safely inside. "Or something a bit stronger?"

"Tea would be lovely, thanks." Isambard replied. He rarely drank tea and didn't really know what all the fuss was about, but it was hot and wet and that was just what he needed at that moment. He gazed around the brightly lit cottage, walls of bare Cotswold stone, cosily appointed with rugs and fine furniture. He wandered through a book-lined sitting room and found Mrs Faraday in a U-shaped kitchen, where all the tabletops and objects were at the right height for her sitting position in the wheeled chair.

"So you can't get out of the chair at all?" Isambard asked.

"Well, I can. But I'm a bit stuck if I do. Here, hand me that milk."

Mrs Faraday lifted a pan of steaming water, revealing a sheet of glass which was glowing red hot. Isambard could feel heat radiating from it even though he was several feet away.

"Wow, what is that?" he asked in wonder.

"This? This heating plaque?" Mrs Faraday said, pushing a lever causing the red to fade instantly. "This is just a couple of sheets of tempered glass around a coil of copper that glows hot when electricity passes through it. I've got more electricity than I know what to do with in this place, so I use it for heat and light. You see all these lamps about the place," she said, waving a hand around the room. "Those are all coils of different types of metal. I'm trying to find the element with the right mix of radiation frequency, energy efficiency and durability."

At that moment there was a fizz and one of the electric lamps went out with a spark. Mrs Faraday stopped what she was doing and squinted at the offending lamp.

"They tend not to last very long," she said privately, as if not wanting to offend them.

Gazing around the room for the first time, Isambard now discerned seven wire lamps hanging on the walls, linked by a braided cable. Each glowed shades of white, orange and red, even some blue. He had noticed the heat in the room and felt how it emanated from each of them.

"Are they dangerous?"

"Very. See that corner over there?" she said pointing over Isambard's shoulder. "We had a nasty little conflagration there due to a spark from a failed wire."

Isambard peered at the blackened walls. "Perhaps you could encase the wires in glass. Like a bulb, a glass daffodil bulb."

"It's a good idea, but one for your generation I fear," she said, looking up from the tea cups with a weary smile. Suddenly her face was twisted with pain and she reached a bony hand out to grasp the table-top and coughed violently. Isambard leaned towards her as she recovered herself, turned to face him and smiled through the pain.

"Are you ok?" Isambard asked, genuinely alarmed. But she just shook the question off.

"Here, come and have your tea," she said quietly, collecting herself, grimacing bravely. "And you'll be wanting a bacon sandwich. Just wait 'til you see how we make toast around here. And in return, you can tell me how you came to be stuck in a basket halfway up a tree with that histrionic Italian Prima Donna."

Mrs Faraday applied herself to the task of refuelling Isambard with sandwiches and cake, whilst he told the story of the balloon trip. But her keen mind was not satisfied starting the story with Lunardi, and whilst Isambard chewed through a restorative range of refreshments, she concentrated on eliciting details about Robespierre, Napoleon and the Amulets. When Isambard got onto the subject of Bristol and Beddoes, she dabbed a tear from her eyes.

"Ah, poor dear Thomas. You know, he gained his Readership here at Oxford back in the late Eighties. He was a real eccentric. And a bit of a Republican. Oh, he got himself into such trouble with the Establishment over his sympathies with the French Revolution. But he was never the sort to conspire to incite a revolution. Goodness, I doubt if he would even attend a public assembly," she chuckled.

"He died trying to protect the only thing that might save us from these cursed amulets."

"Hmmm. I'm afraid this is all looking rather serious," Mrs Faraday mused, with no hint of irony in her understatement. "I could get you back to London, of course. But, it's late, it's dark and that would be a long journey. We will leave at first light. You will sleep in the clock-room. But before that, I must show you how we are going to travel," Mrs Faraday said, finishing with a smile that gave Isambard a fleeting image of Mrs Faraday as a little girl. "You are going to like this."

She set her chair in motion and led the way through the mill-house towards the river. The sound of the waterwheel, which up that point had been a distant, rhythmic gushing sound, became suddenly deafeningly loud as Mrs Faraday opened the door to the old mill. As elsewhere, the room was lit and heated by several electric wire lamps and Isambard entered the room with eyes wide in wonderment. Through a window on the wall opposite he could see the waterwheel turning tirelessly. The drive shaft broke into the mill-room through a rough hole in the ancient stone wall, turning a large bobbin wound in copper wire.

"This is the electrical generator where our energy is created. Sorry, converted. It's simple really. The generator is just a coil rotating in a magnetic field creating a current which flows to a distribution board over here. It really does create an incredible amount of electrical energy. You should talk to my son Michael about it."

"Michael Faraday – I'll be sure to look out for him. And what happens if you don't use all the energy?" Isambard asked.

"I switch off the drive-gear. Or switch on more lights. It can get rather hot! We used to run it off as heat in the river, but that created some very strange conditions in the water which didn't do the fish any good so we stopped doing that," she replied, with a cheeky smile.

"Anyway," she continued, propelling herself to the far side of the room. "This will be our mode of transport for the morning," she said, pulling at a canvas tarpaulin to reveal the polished wooden hull of a small river cruiser, freighted with a large engine.

"This is *La Myrtille*, the big sister of the chair I am sitting in. A river boat powered by a hydrogen combustion engine. This engine is another rather clever French design from the same year as the de Rivaz engine – a pair of brothers this time, used hydrogen to power a water pump to propel a boat. Those Frenchies would be quite useful engineers if they could just stop squabbling about Governments and Royalty..."

"My father would completely agree with you. And he's French," Isambard replied dreamily, his mind completely captivated by the beauty and intricacy of the device that had been revealed to him. "He would love to see this."

Isambard approached the boat reverently, walking slowly towards it and peering at it from different angles.

"She's beautiful," he said, gingerly touching the edge of the gunwales and peering at the engine. "But doesn't it have a paddle wheel to push it along?" he asked.

"Ah, well, you see, that is where the real genius is," Mrs Faraday said, that cheeky smile again playing on her lips. Her eyes gave Isambard a clue, pointing him to the rear of the boat.

"A water screw!" he cried, on seeing the propeller. "I've read about these. Is it really as efficient as Mr Watt says?"

"I've no idea," Mrs Faraday snapped, doing her best to suppress a cough as she passed the canvas back up onto the boat with one hand, gripping her chest with the other hand. Isambard leaned over and helped slide the cover into place. Mrs Faraday gave an apologetic smile and caught her breath.

"We had planned to do a series of rigorous tests to prove the screw against the paddle wheel but in the end we just followed our instincts. Another one for you young ones to sort out, what? Come on. Time to go to bed. Early start."

She was about to trundle off down the corridor, when she came to an abrupt stop.

"Wait a minute. All this talk of contraptions – we've forgotten the most important thing."

"The telegraph," Isambard said.

"Come with me."

Mrs Faraday's chair seemed to turn on the spot before darting down another corridor, illuminated by the lantern on her carriage. She navigated the doorways and ramps with expert speed whilst Isambard struggled to keep up. Mrs Faraday spoke as she went.

"The professor and my husband remained great friends even after Thomas' effective expulsion from Oxford in the early Nineties. A combination of frustration with the postal service and a love of new-fangled contraptions led the two of them to devise an early form of telegraph communication. It wasn't very good but it kept them amused. I haven't looked at it for years but if he was under duress, there is a chance that Beddoes may have tried to send a message. Here, turn that lever would you?"

Isambard did as he was asked and one of the light heaters began to buzz, filling the room with a reddish glow and an instant warmth. She wheeled into the room and came to a stop surrounded by dusty piles of folios, papers and folders.

"There, on that desk. You'll know it when you see it," she said with a flick of her bony finger. She coughed and gripped her abdomen tightly with the other hand. But the adrenaline got the better of Isambard's manners, and he plunged into the grotto formed by the inclined roof beams, walls and towers of paperwork.

In the middle of it all, towards the back of a small square of clear desk space stood a flat object about the size of a large reference book. A strip of paper covered the object from left to right, ending in a roll on the left-hand side which formed a spool. This band of paper fed across the machine under a kind of bridge before running between two rollers clamping the paper like a mangle.

"Is there a kind of line drawing on the loose end of the paper roll?"

"Yes!" Isambard cried, noticing a faint pencil trace running along the length of the paper.

"Pull the paper through so you can see the entire message. Don't leave any of it behind in the machine. Press down on the guillotine to be able to tear the paper off. Give it a sharp tug as if you're breaking a pheasant's neck."

Isambard had never broken a pheasant's neck, but he got the idea. He carefully pulled the paper through, pressed down on the bar which trapped the paper, and gave a sharp tug, tearing the paper clean off. He passed the ribbon of paper to Mrs Faraday and stood behind her, looking over her shoulder as she stretched the paper out like a scroll.

"Oh dear. It's very short. Probably because he has very little electrical potential. Look at the opening test signals. He is losing power rapidly."

"I'm sorry," Isambard confessed, "I really have no idea what I'm looking at."

"Of course, of course," Mrs Faraday murmured, distracted. "Oh dear me. Poor dear Thomas." She paused and pressed the cryptic message to her heart for just a moment. She cleared her throat and shuffled in her seat.

"The height of each spike can be decoded into a letter of the alphabet. The first three spikes indicate that the message is beginning: this allows both parties to see the strength of the signal and to calibrate accordingly. You see here the first one is reasonably high, but the next two are progressively lower; this is typical where the power source is deteriorating rapidly. And look here at the closing test signals: these should all be at full height but look how low they are. I would say he is losing three or four percent of his power with each letter signal. We shall test this. It's going to be difficult to accurately decode the message, especially towards the end as the power gets low. The sender receives an echo of each signal so Beddoes will have been aware of the limited power at his disposal. He will have made this message as compact as possible. Now, I haven't checked this machine for years so we have no way of knowing when this message was sent, but let us work on the assumption that this is a cry for help and decode it with the utmost urgency and accuracy. We will need a measuring rule, pencils and a sheaf of paper. Have a look in the desk drawers. And pick up that deciphering book there."

They moved back to the kitchen, cleared the table and laid out their work. They started by drawing on the "100% line", a smooth curve which linked the tops of the opening and closing test spikes.

"He will be using the Limited Character Set due to this lack of power. It's on page 12 of the deciphering book, if memory serves. This allows the encoding of only 24 characters, each one corresponding to 1/25th of the 100% height. It gives us a better chance of getting an accurate reading when the signal is weak."

"But there are 26 letters in the alphabet." Isambard said impulsively.

"Yes, so there are some casualties. I think "x" or "z" are missing. But there is a work around: if you want to send "x" you send two "v"s, that sort of thing. So, as an example, if the signal height is between 0% and 4% of the 100% height, you look that up, and it means...."

"A," Isambard answered. "But it's not simply a, b, c as the percentage increases," he observed, reading down the deciphering table.

"No. In their wisdom the men split up letters that could be commonly interchanged. For example "dome" and "done"; m and n are not next to each other in the deciphering table to make any doubts a bit easier to clarify. You'll see when we start deciphering."

They set about decoding every "letter" by measuring the height of each spike against the 100% line and looking up the spike percent in the deciphering table. The message did not make any immediate sense and, towards the end, the signal was so weak that it was difficult to see which letter was being indicated.

"Well, this last one is about 10%, but it could be "d", "e" or "f." It's difficult to tell."

"Patience, patience. We write it down and then see what we've got. The message is usually pretty obvious once we have the letters roughed out."

But the message was far from obvious. As Isambard decoded and called out each letter, Mrs Faraday wrote the letters across her page from left to right; where the signal was ambiguous, she wrote the options above and below the line.

"This method makes it possible for your eye to take different pathways through the letters to find the message," she said, holding the page at arm's length. "Have a look will you? My old eyes can hardly make out the page, let alone the letters," she chuckled.

"Okay, well, the first bit is pretty clear – S E C R E T A R I U M – does that mean anything to you?"

"Secretarium? No. I'm pretty sure it's Latin – bit rusty on that score I'm afraid," Mrs Faraday beamed, whilst manoeuvring herself and the chair to a bookshelf heaving with dusty volumes.

"Get on with the next bit whilst I..." Mrs Faraday said, placing the selected book on her lap and driving back to the kitchen table where they were working.

"Well. Then it seems to be a collection of numbers – ONE FIVE ZERO SIX ONE THREE."

"150613 – one hundred and fifty thousand six hundred and thirteen? What's the good of that?"

"No idea – maybe it's a pointer. You know, points to a location or place."

"A point in time," Mrs Faraday wondered.

"A date. 15th day of the 6th month of..."

"The year 13 – 1813. Maybe. But what of it?"

"Something in the newspaper?"

"Could be anything."

"Something only you, or your husband, would know about."

"Well, I haven't seen Beddoes for... fifteen years. What could possibly have happened on the... wait a moment," she said with a dawning realisation. "Here, take this – look up 'Secretarium' while I..." she said, disappearing down the corridor before her sentence was complete.

Isambard took the book and placed it on the table.

"Dictionary. Right. OP... Q... S... Secretarium, secretarium..."

"Well – have you found it?" Mrs Faraday said, reappearing from the corridor with what looked like a bundle of letters in her lap.

"Yes... Secretarium - a remote, solitary or secret place."

"Remote, solitary. Is that all? Very well, perhaps it will make more sense if we crack the number code. Here, these are the letters that Beddoes sent to my husband. Let's see if there's one dated the... what was it?"

"15th June 1813."

"Quite, yes. Here, you take these."

The two of them tore through the letters as carefully as their excitement would allow.

"These are too early," Isambard said.

"It must be in here – take this half."

"1812"

"Oh good, I'm still in 1816."

"Here. 15th of June, 1813," Isambard said, holding the letter up in triumph.

"What does it say?"

"My Dear Faraday..."

"Here, what's this?" A scrap of plain paper had emerged from between the pages.

"That looks like a picture of Menhit's scroll – the one I was telling you about. The one that has the power to stop the amulets. What does it say?"

"It says – steganography – the answer may be more patent than we think."

Isambard flicked through the pages of the dictionary.

"Steganography: the practice of concealing messages or information within other non-secret text or images."

"It's the tube," Isambard muttered. "The message is hidden in the tube."

Chapter 32

Before dawn the next morning, Isambard padded into Mrs Faraday's kitchen, bleary-eyed and yawning.

"Presumably if you ran some of these heating wires under the flagstones you would be able to heat the floor," he said, noticing a stark difference in temperature between the air and the floor.

"That would be the height of poor taste," Mrs Faraday replied testily.

"The Romans had underfloor heating..." Isambard protested.

"And look what good it did them. Now, gobble one of these down and I'll start loading the launch for the journey," she said, thrusting some bread filled with still sizzling sausage-meat into his hand. She heaved a large bag off the table onto her lap and headed off in the direction of the mill-room. A moment later she reappeared on her way to the study. "Well come on then. We'll never catch the tide at Richmond at this rate."

Isambard dressed hastily, chewing through the sandwich as he went. In what he considered to be pretty short order, he appeared in the mill-room to find Mrs Faraday checking the straps which now fixed her wheeled-chair to the midpoint of the launch. The boat had been lowered into the water and the engine was running. Everything appeared to be ready.

"Where do you want me?" Isambard asked tentatively, stepping onto the pontoon which ran alongside the boat.

"Jump on the back. You'll be driving us out. I can sit here and pilot, but I'm afraid you will need to do exactly as I say until you get the hang of the control mechanism. Here - put one of these oilskins on. It's looking pretty moist out there."

Isambard donned the waterproof and then, under detailed instruction, disengaged the water-wheel drive, cutting the power and casting the grotto into darkness apart from the orange-blue glow of the bow-lamp on the boat. He then loosened the lines, engaged the propeller and cast off. The boat began to glide through the archway in the side of the building, cutting through the mirror-smooth surface of the water, sending thick, dark ripples away from the bow as it went.

The time was just after seven o'clock and the eastern skies were beginning to lighten with the dawn. Without a word, Mrs Faraday extended a hand to one side, which Isambard followed as a direction, pushing the tiller, swinging the launch to the left until it aligned with the reeds and grasses which flowed along with the clear running water. The launch had joined the river downstream of the roaring water-wheel, and the modest power of the propeller added its speed to the steady current.

Before long, the noise of the mill had given way to the deep silence of the cold clammy air under the rhythmic popping and clanking of the engine.

"A challenge for you, young man. Using what you know of our speed and the flow of the river, what time do you think we will arrive?" Mrs Faraday asked, craning her neck to look at him as best she could. Isambard thought briefly before replying.

"Between four and five o'clock this afternoon," Isambard said with some borrowed confidence.

"I'm impressed. I presume you calculated the average flow rate of the river based on precipitation, land area and river depth assuming a U-shaped river bed and a meander ratio of three to one?"

"No. I just noticed that you have packed provisions for both lunch and tea, which suggests we will be in the boat until at least four pm and assumed we would wish to be there before dark, which will be five pm."

Mrs Faraday chuckled. "Well, I suppose that is an equally valid, and very practical solution. Your prize is a jar of hot tea which you will find in the knapsack on the floor between us. You will find one in there for me as well. You should be able to reach them without taking your hand off the tiller."

They made steady progress through Oxfordshire and into Berkshire, flanked on each shore by bare, black-limbed trees and foggy meadows. Isambard watched various bargemen starting their day: the early risers, hanging off their boats to wash in the icy water, others stoking their stoves and feeding the horses, and later, cruising along under the pull of their horses on the towpath. *La Myrtille* cut between them all, having its own drive and no oars, propelled only by the occasional pop from the combustion chamber, attracting a great deal of silent study from the bargees as it passed. Squeezed together when passing through the occasional locks at Abingdon and Goring, the barge-men found their voice - sometimes they were enamoured of the new technology, sometimes disdainful, sometimes aggressive. Mrs Faraday dealt with them all with the same gentle benevolence.

The rising sun had turned cold mist into cold drizzle and they ate lunch without stopping. Mrs Faraday sang chamber music to herself and pressed Isambard to share ever more bawdy carols from the East London slums, relishing the wicked pleasure of their forbidden rhymes and the gruesome tales they told.

Later that day, the weir at Marlow played its trick on Isambard as it does on all novices, standing between the open water and the safety of the lock around the corner. Without realising it, Isambard steered *La Myrtille* towards the hazard, until bystanders on the bank began offering advice and barge poles. A combination of manually assisting the engine, some frantic work at the tiller and some judicious tugging on bystanders' poles pulled them out of danger. It was not pretty, nor elegant, but it gave a crowd of bystanders some afternoon entertainment.

On any other occasion, Isambard may well have enjoyed the final leg of their epic journey, from Windsor Castle to Westminster. But night was falling and he was chilled to the bone. He fell to thinking about the grim task ahead.

"So, upon arrival, we simply throw a rope to the Lord Chancellor, ask if anyone has seen a long-dead French Revolutionary and conduct a citizen's arrest, is that the plan?" Isambard asked sardonically.

"That would be nice. But I'm not sure it's going to be quite as simple as that. However, my nephew sits in the House of Lords so I think we'll start with him. He may also be able to provide a bowl of hot broth."

At last, they approached the Parliament Strand, hidden behind a maze of ships which lay at anchor in the channel. Isambard retched at the river stench, which had been growing steadily worse since Teddington – it was more powerful here where the foreshore was coated with the effluent from the factories and sewers up-stream.

There was a gravelly graunch as the boat grounded on the muddy riverbank outside the House of Commons. For a moment neither of them moved. Filthy waves stroked the muddy bank, and the current pushed at the back of the boat, easing it around. Isambard locked off the engine and clambered past Mrs Faraday, whose head hung down towards her folded arms in exhausted sleep. Isambard hauled the boat up the bank and secured it to the anchor ropes before re-boarding and crouching in front of Mrs Faraday. She was nearly doubled over in her sleep and suddenly looked very old. Her waterproof oilskin stretched down from her neck like some kind of funeral gown.

Isambard shuddered and said her name several times, shaking her forearm gently.

It was a long while before she woke, and when she did it was with deep rasping coughs which she smothered with a handkerchief covered in spots of blood.

"Mrs Faraday. Are you alright?" Isambard asked. She replied with a weak smile.

"We're going to need to use the ramp. Would you mind?"

Isambard re-moored the boat against the wooden pathway that led up the perilously slippery mud bank to the shore. Ingeniously, the bow of the launch was hinged and could be unfolded to form a ramp onto the landing path for Mrs Faraday's wheeled chair. Once unloaded, Isambard anchored the launch out of the way and joined Mrs Faraday as she progressed up the slipway.

A couple of guards had been watching the landing and now clattered down the Parliament Stairs to attend.

"Gentlemen," Mrs Faraday said to the guards in a return to her more robust manner. "I am here to see my nephew, Lord Petersham, Lord of the King's Bedchamber, and would very much appreciate some assistance."

"Yes ma'am," the guards replied in unison, doing their best to haul the wheeled chair up the stairs whilst keeping their scabbards and helmets and ornamental appendages from snagging in its muddy machinery.

Once safely on the paved path, one of the guards gave his name as Corporal Chadwick and offered to escort the pair through the building.

"That would be most kind," Mrs Faraday said graciously. "I am sure we will only have to go as far as the Parliament Library to find him hard at work," she added with a knowing smile.

Under the auspices of Corporal Chadwick, Mrs Faraday drove with such purposeful authority that none of the fresh-faced guards or aged counsellors had the wit or the courage to stop her along the way. With a smart salute, Chadwick left them in the care of the Library Butler, who stood between Mrs Faraday and the library.

"I am afraid ma'am, that this library is for gentlemen only. You would perhaps wait here whilst I pass on a message?" the butler asked politely.

Mrs Faraday winced slightly but yielded.

"Of course," she replied through a sardonic smile. "Would you please find Lord Petersham and tell him that the Duchess of Iffley is here to see him at his earliest convenience?"

The butler straightened at this, nodded stiffly, muttered "...Your Grace," and strode into the library. As they watched from the doorway, the warmth of the library began to seep into Isambard's clothes, raising his spirits.

"I didn't know you were a duchess," he said, bending over to whisper into Mrs Faraday's ear.

"I'm not," she replied with a vague smile. "That's just what the family call me. I say, counsellor!" she called to an elderly bewigged man sitting behind a desk nearby. "Would you be so kind as to arrange a message to Officer Ruthven of the Bow Street Runners asking him to... to....?" Mrs Faraday faltered, looking to Isambard for inspiration.

"Er, well, he should come here with... with reinforcements."

"Right, yes, ask Ruthven to bring a squad to the Houses of Parliament immediately. To ask for Lord Petersham. Tell him Cato is here. Here. In capital letters. Take these two shillings to make sure it gets through."

On sight of the money, the counsellor appeared to take the instruction doubly seriously, and began transcribing the note onto headed paper.

Isambard thought about contacting Millie and William, wishing they were here to help – but he quickly dismissed the thought when he remembered how close he had come to losing Millie last time.

"Your Grace!" a voice boomed from inside the library, ruffling the newspapers of some and disturbing the sleep of others. The voice belonged to a compact little man sporting a yellow tail-coat and a puff of grey hair, waving a delicate cane as he approached. "Is it really you, Aunty? Fancy you coming here to visit me," he continued. "How simply marvellous! You must come to my chambers for tea. How the deuces are you?" Lord Petersham said, bending down to kiss Mrs Faraday on both cheeks. "And who is this young chap at your side? Your new husband I'll own?"

"No Freddie, this is not my new husband. This is Isambard and he brought me here down the Thames in *La Myrtille*. Tea sounds like an excellent idea. We're going to need your help."

"Of course. Tea this way. *La Myrtille*. Good Lord, is that old thing still going?"

Lord Petersham led the way down the dimly lit corridors giving an intermittent tour of the place as he went, commenting on the paintings by the Dutch Masters and the much needed renovations recently completed by James Wyat. At one point, as Lord Petersham led them through the Undercroft Chapel, Isambard whispered in Mrs Faraday's ear. "Is now really the time for taking tea with his Lordship?"

"Patience, Isambard. He can be extremely effective but he's always much better when he's had a slice of cake."

At last they arrived at Lord Petersham's chambers and tea was ordered. Frequently interrupted by her own rasping coughs, Mrs Faraday told the story of Robespierre and the Cato Street conspiracy with a degree of accuracy that impressed Isambard. Lord Petersham devoured the drama, relishing every detail as if it were a Penny Gaff.

When Mrs Faraday had finished, Lord Petersham sat with a mixture of glee and dread on his face. He blinked and took a large bite of cake.

"The weekly Cabinet Dinner is usually on Tuesdays and I am sure that the Prime Minister will be in attendance tonight. Perhaps that is the target" he said thoughtfully, spitting cake crumbs as he spoke. He drained his teacup noisily and stood up.

"Now, where is that Westminster Gazette?" he asked rhetorically, glancing around the room vigorously as if he were trying to catch a fly. "I'm sure I had it this morning. Aha. Here it is, carefully archived," he cried presently, pointing and lurching forward into the waste paper basket. "Now let's see. Yes, tonight in the Chapter House of St Stephen's, starting half-past five." Lord Petersham consulted his fob watch. "They will have already started," he said with a pensive stare. "What about this Officer Ruthven?" he continued, fixing Isambard with his piggy eyes.

"We have already sent word to request his assistance," Isambard responded.

"Good. Assuming this rabble make a second attempt at their original plan, they will attack the assembled party as they dine. I'm afraid we will have to defer your hot bath and buttered kippers until later. We must find the Prime Minister and save the Cabinet."

Chapter 33

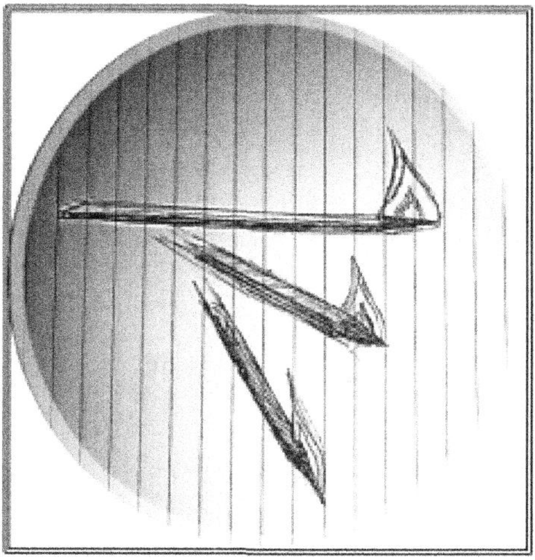

LORD PETERSHAM APPROACHED the guard at the Chapter House of St Stephen's with his customary bravado.

"Good evening officer. I am Lord Petersham of the House of Lords and it is imperative that I see the Prime Minister on a matter of grave importance."

"With respect, my Lord, my orders are to prevent anyone from entering the premises whilst the Cabinet meeting is in session," the officer replied, staring unflinchingly into the middle distance.

"My man, this is a matter of National Importance. It is imperative..." Lord Petersham said, winding up for a full-blown oratory on the reasons why he should be allowed to pass through, but he was interrupted by the sound of a loud bell peeling, and raised voices.

"Sounds like the fire bell." The guard said with a look of panic in his eye.

"Look! The Jewel Tower is on fire!" Lord Petersham cried.

"This may be part of the attack. A deliberate distraction." Isambard said.

"Quite so. Officer, stay at your post. We will inform the Prime Minister," Lord Petersham said, leading the way into the chapel. They pushed through the heavy oak doors into a large chapel full of high spirited voices and the sound of a string quartet playing a German waltz. The chapel was in darkness at the entrance end, but brightly lit by candles and fire-grates at the other, where the assembled party were seated around a long dining table. Lord Petersham strode purposefully down the aisle, calling as he went.

"Prime Minister. My Lords. The House is under attack and you are in grave danger." Lord Liverpool stood up. The string quartet came to an ungraceful halt and nineteen of the most powerful pairs of eyes in the country turned to look at Lord Petersham and the intruders. In the newfound silence, the alarm bell and the shouts of the militia guardsmen from outside could be heard. The Prime Minister's anger turned to concern.

"What's this about?"

But there was no time to answer - a metal canister smashed through one of the stained-glass windows and skittered across the floor. Then another. And a third. Almost immediately the canisters burst into life, one after the other, spraying a pungent liquid randomly about the chapel, spinning wildly with the force of their jets. Isambard's nostrils filled with an acrid smell and he instantly began to feel light-headed. Thinking quickly, he reached into his case and opened a large jar - Trafalgar poured himself out and made a stretching noise.

"Hello," he said in his customary monotone.

"Trafalgar, can you do anything about this?"

"Well. It's what we call a volatile liquid. Liquids are a bit tricky. I don't think it's poisonous. I think it's some kind of hydrocarbon."

"What does that mean?" Isambard asked.

"It means it burns easily and is filling the room with flammable vapours."

"Vapours are gases aren't they?"

"Yes."

"So you can catch those?"

"I suppose I could create a blanket on top if you like. If you get off the ground I might be able to keep you safe."

The crowd was becoming agitated, so Isambard attempted to take control.

"My Lords. We believe that this is some kind of gas attack. Please make your way calmly onto the altar behind you."

Following the Prime Minister's lead, the gentlemen of the Cabinet rose from their seats, coughing and covering their faces with handkerchiefs as they did so.

"Prime Minister," Isambard said, putting himself next to Lord Liverpool. "We believe they are here for the Amulet."

"The Amulet?" the Prime Minister hissed. "They'll never get it. It's in the Secretarium, guarded day and night by a company of The King's Own Guard."

"The Secretarium?" Isambard said remembering Beddoes' message. "That's exactly where they want it to be."

Suddenly, the heavy oak doors creaked open and a dark figure appeared in the doorway; a short, stocky man in a dark cape. He walked slowly towards the altar, gazing up at the walls and ceilings appreciating them as any visitor might.

"That's not Cato," Isambard said in a whisper to Mrs Faraday.

"No," she replied. "It's Bonaparte..."

Bonaparte began to address the captives in a soft, accented voice.

"My Lords, Ladies, gentlemen. Thank you for coming to this historic event, the dawn of the creation of the British Republic. And thank you for providing such a beautiful venue. Do not fear, the citizens of the British Republic will honour and respect your civilised finery. But they will not tolerate undeserving privilege. Some things will have to be sacrificed on the journey to the Second Enlightenment." Bonaparte said, approaching the altar to inspect the captives.

"Our people would rather die than side with you," the Prime Minister said.

"In normal circumstances, perhaps. But once I have all three amulets, I will destroy you, your government and your monarchy. Your people will have no choice but to embrace me as the new Emperor of a united Europe. But, as even you must know, there is no power without mercy," Napoleon said, looking Lord Liverpool in the eye. Napoleon walked around the altar and pointed to one of the captives, Earl Bathurst. "You will come with me," Napoleon said.

Napoleon left the altar and flicked one of the canisters with his foot, considering it as it rolled across the floorboards, glistening with flammable liquid.

"In the Second Enlightenment the citizens will be the new Kings. Science will be the new religion."

At that moment, a line of Parliamentary Guards filed in behind the altar from the vestry door and began to approach.

"Now we've got him," Lord Petersham muttered, triumphantly. But both he and the Parliamentary Guards came to an abrupt stop when Napoleon produced a pistol and held it against Lord Bathurst's panic-stricken brow.

"Prepare yourselves, gentlemen of the government. A renewed Empire will arise from the ashes of this rotten hegemony. Welcome to the dawn of the British Republic – I hope you will live long enough to see it in all its glory." Bonaparte grabbed Earl Bathurst and backed him towards the door with the pistol against his head. But as they reached the door, he did something that Isambard was not expecting – he threw the pistol towards the middle of the chapel. Isambard watched as it flew through the air, pausing at its apex before accelerating towards the glistening flagstones.

A primed pistol, Isambard thought. A hard floor. Flammable liquids.

The pistol made contact and the flint-hammer was instantly released. The spark didn't need to find the gunpowder - a blue flame had already ripped like a wave across the entire floor of the chapel with a boom, creating a lake of blue-yellow flame.

TWO HUNDRED YARDS BELOW them, in a poorly-lit underground tunnel, the last of the King's guards lay dying in a pool of his own blood. His sword had swept unnoticed through their unearthly bodies. Untroubled by his blade, they simply sliced his life in half, just as they had his comrades whose bodies littered the tunnel in a wretched trail behind them.

When the killing was complete the attackers stood motionless, dispassionate, no hint of humanity in their eyes. Cato swept past them to the end of the tunnel and placed his hands on the solid oak door. As it began to moan and turn to dust, a smile grew across Cato's face.

IN THE CHAPEL ABOVE them, the trapped flames boiled unnaturally, as if under a sheet of glass and, for a moment, everyone watched in wonder. Trafalgar had spread himself across the gas-liquid mixture, creating a lid and forcing the flames into a layer on the floor. But thick smoke and the smell of burning alcohol was filling the air and Isambard was beginning to find it hard to breathe. It was impossible to see a path through the field of flames.

But, just then, the main door opened and a crowd of figures appeared - in the ghostly blue light of the flaming floor, Isambard recognised one of the faces.

"Ruthven!" Isambard called. "Bonaparte was here but he's got away. He has Earl Bathurst with him as hostage."

The flaming blue liquid drained out of the doors, creating a river of flames outside the chapel, and leaving a path through the smouldering wreckage.

Isambard and the others spilled out of the chapel doors to find Parliamentary Guards running in every direction - the clear night sky had been made day by the blaze from the Jewel Tower and the air was filled with smoke and raised voices. The guards had formed a human chain, passing buckets of river-water up to the flame-front.

"Spread out," Ruthven commanded. "He can't have got far. But be careful – he's got a hostage," Ruthven told them as they fanned out across the Strand lawn.

Within a few moments there was a cry from one of the Runners who stood at the wall above the river's edge.

"There they go!" The runner yelled, pointing out towards the river. "They're on that steam-launch."

The search party converged at the spot and they scanned the scene. The inferno behind them lent a stark orange glow to boats of every size and shape that cluttered the river in front of them. Isambard spotted Bonaparte and his hostage on board the launch as it steamed noisily out into the main channel. Within minutes the boat would disappear behind the larger vessels which lay at anchor.

A gunshot rang out as one of the Runners fired off a pistol. Ruthven quickly forced down the Runner's arm.

"Don't shoot! You've as much chance of hitting the hostage as Napoleon. Get down to the water and requisition whatever craft you can. Follow him down river scouring as you go. Dock-up at Wapping and report back to Bow Street. Go!" Ruthven roared.

But in his heart, he knew Napoleon was gone.

Isambard and Ruthven looked out over the oily black water which flickered with flashes of orange reflected from the burning building behind them.

"We'll get 'im. It ain't over 'til the fat lady sings."

"What does that mean?" Isambard asked, puzzled.

"It means... it ain't over."

Isambard nodded, none the wiser.

One of Ruthven's men arrived out of breath. "Sir. The Secretarium – it's been plundered. You'd better come, sir."

Ruthven straightened up and stared out over the river.

"Alright. I'll join you in a bit."

When the Runner had disappeared, Ruthven turned to Isambard.

"Not to add insult to injury," Ruthven said, wincing slightly. "Bit of bad news about your old man I'm afraid. He was up in court for them debts. Bankrupt. Debtor's prison until he can repay."

On top of everything else, the news crushed Isambard like a wave.

"Cheer up son - debtor's prison i'nt so bad. As my old uncle used to say, if you ain't been in debtors' prison once or twice, you i'nt trying hard enough," Ruthven said with a robust pat on Isambard's shoulder. But he could see that his attempt to lighten the mood was falling flat. "You best... you best go see him first thing in the morning," Ruthven said as sympathetically as he could. Isambard looked up, blinked and focused on Ruthven.

"Which prison's he in?" he managed to ask.

"Marshalsea," Ruthven replied, heading off towards the Secretarium. "And take pies – food's terrible in that place."

Chapter 34

Lord Sidmouth stepped through the door into the Hinterland and found Hardleygrieve waiting on a wooden platform next to a lake.

"My Lord, what a pleasant surprise to have you on my side for a change. Something important?" Hardleygrieve asked breezily.

"What the blazes is going on?"

"My Lord?"

"You saw what they did at the Houses of Parliament. We were lucky there weren't more dead."

"Lord Bathurst will be fine – hardly a scratch on him."

"And they made short work of the Secretarium – it was designed to be impenetrable. This situation is out of control." Sidmouth stopped himself, took a breath and looked out over the placid water. Hardleygrieve watched expectantly from the other side of the wooden platform.

"This is your mess Hardleygrieve – not mine. You need to clean it up. And soon."

"I understand your sense of urgency, my Lord. But I think to act now would be to miss an opportunity. For you in particular."

"What are you talking about?"

"Once again our Nationhood is being threatened by the most hated man in the country."

"Napoleon."

"And now that Napoleon has all three amulets, even our hero Wellington will not be able to save us - Wellington's armies will be crushed like toy soldiers. But the amulets are not unstoppable. With my help, Napoleon can be vanquished even as Wellington fails."

Lord Sidmouth gave Hardleygrieve a long, cold stare. "What are you suggesting?"

"I recently took the liberty of initiating an operation through the Special Intelligence Directorate to recover the Scroll of Menhit. Untraceable, of course."

"The scroll - so it really does have the power to destroy the amulets," Sidmouth said, before narrowing his eyes at Hardleygrieve. "Listen to me Hardleygrieve. His Majesty's Government has not sanctioned the use of dynamic magic for over 400 years and I'll be damned if I'm the Home Secretary remembered for plunging us into the next Dark Age."

"Forgive me sir, but this is not Dynamic Magic – the scroll and the amulets are already imbued with these powers. It is in their nature. They are magical whether the government sanctions it or not."

"And your proposed course of action... I suppose you're going to tell me that it doesn't break the Covenant?"

Hardleygrieve shook his head patiently. "There is no need for you to actively align yourself to the magical exchange – it is enough that you allow it to prevail and position yourself to benefit from the outcome. I'm sure a man of your political skill will be able to use this episode to your own benefit. Wellington, if he survives, will come out of it looking inconsequential and irrelevant. This could turn out to be Wellington's downfall, and for you, a stepping stone towards the Prime Minister's seat."

A bird flew serenely across the surface of the water. Sidmouth clenched his teeth and drew a long slow breath in through his nose. "I will leave it to you for now. But I will not be able to hold the Council back for long," Sidmouth said, heading for the portal. "Do not fail me."

"If I fail," Hardleygrieve said once Sidmouth had disappeared through the portal, "you will not be alive to see it."

Chapter 35

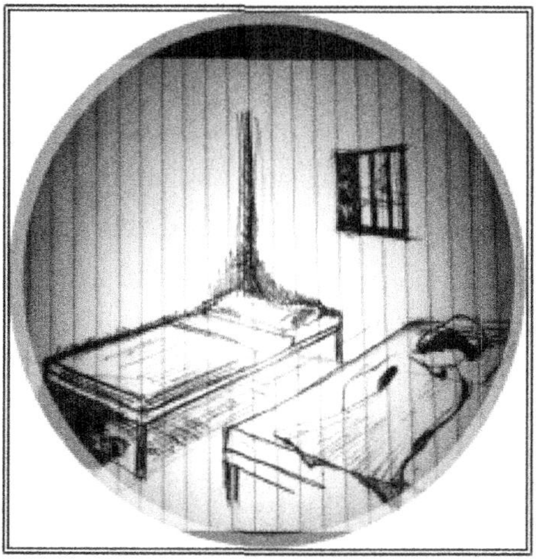

"OH! ISAMBARD!" SOPHIA cried. "What are you doing here?"

"*Mon fils! Mais qu'est-ce que tu fait ici?*"

Isambard approached his parents with a broad smile lighting up his boyish face.

"Oh my little Sam. It's been such a long time - why didn't you write ahead?" Sophia said, embracing her son as if trying to make up for all the missed hugs.

"You shouldn't have come to see us in this... place," Marc said looking around the cramped quarters with an anxious look on his face.

"Well, you know what they say," Isambard said. "If you haven't been in debtors' prison once or twice, you i'nt trying hard enough."

"Ha," laughed a man sitting at the back of the room who Isambard had not noticed.

"Ah, this is Mr Harrison, my... room-mate," Marc said, gesturing towards a flamboyantly dressed man sitting cross-legged at the other end of the bed. Mr Harrison saluted Isambard with his toothpick and flashed a brief smile.

"Them is certainly wise words, my boy. But I believe I should be taking a stroll to leave you in some privacy," he said, picking himself up and making for the door.

"Oh Mr Harrison, you needn't have. Thank you so much. This is Isambard, our son, Mr Harrison," Sophia added, almost as an afterthought.

"A pleasure to meet you I'm sure, master Brunel. Until the next time," Harrison said absently, as he left the room through the low doorway.

"Lovely man, isn't he Marc. Poor thing lost all his money when his shop burnt down," Sophia confided in Isambard. There was a slightly awkward pause, nobody quite knowing what to say next.

"Well this is... cosy," Isambard fibbed, gazing around the stone-walled room which was barely bigger than the two single beds squashed into the corners.

"Yes. We even have running water," Marc joked, pointing to a rivulet running down the wall.

"And a view of the ornamental gardens," Sophia added, gesturing through the barred window to the dusty courtyard outside.

"But enough about my good fortune...." Marc countered.

"Oh Sam, it's so good to see you."

Isambard felt a stab of remorse at seeing his parents in these wretched surroundings.

"We must get you out of here, father. As soon as possible. How much do you owe?"

"Oh now Sam, you can't ask your father..." Sophia objected, but Marc gently raised a hand, paused and then answered.

"Five thousand pounds."

Isambard's eyes fluttered at the sum.

"Five thousand eh? Well, I've got six pounds and fourpence I have been able to save, so we are nearly there," Isambard joked, holding the money out in a grubby hand.

"Oh Isambard," his mother smiled, "how we've missed you. How have you been?"

But Isambard would not be diverted. "You're owed money aren't you? Have you been paid for the structural inspection at Leicester Fields?" Isambard asked, pressing on with his questions.

"No," Sophia replied, suddenly energised. "We jolly well haven't. I went over there myself every single day for several weeks. In the end they said the investors had got cold feet and wouldn't be coming up with the cash."

"What about selling the boot factory?"

"Nobody wants an old boot factory," Sophia explained, with a nervous glance at Marc.

"I try to sell the machinery," he explained. "Give it a new purpose. I have taken the plans to several bootmakers. Remember our work on the lacing machine..?"

"Nobody is willing to pay, Sam. We're going to have to scrap it off and give up the building," Sophia added.

Isambard looked at his father.

"Is this true?" he asked.

Marc simply raised his eyebrows and gave a forlorn smile.

"What about the Ministry? They still owe us money from the wars, don't they?"

"Of course they do. But they'll never pay." A glum silence fell in the room. The shouts and raw laughter of the other prisoners echoed around the stone building.

"I have written to Tsar Alexander," Marc said, with a mischievous flick of the eyebrows. "He liked my bridges. He is keen for me to... visit him."

"Marc, we are not going to work for the Russian Royal Family! England would never let you go," Sophia objected, compressing her passion into a strained whisper. Marc withdrew into a sulk.

"Never let you go – of course," Isambard repeated dreamily, with the first genuine smile of the day.

Chapter 36

ISAMBARD ACCOMPANIED his mother from Marshalsea back to the workshop on Poultry Street and found a copy of his father's bills to Wellington for the boots. After a bowl of thin vegetable soup, he made his way over the rooftops to Millie and William's house. He was delighted to find them sitting in the late morning sunshine amongst the chimney pots on the roof of their house.

"Isambard!" Millie called as soon as she saw him.

"Ah, Monsieur Brunel!" William echoed, "this is a far from disappointing development. How the devil are you?"

"We've been worried, Sam."

"Speak for yourself, Mill – I knew he'd be alright. I presume that mess at the Houses of Parliament was your doing?"

"Well, I can't take credit for all of it... You got my letters?"

"Yes Sam – I can't believe you came face to face with Bonaparte."

"Neither can I. But listen, I need your help. Or to be precise, my father needs your help."

"Tsk, we don't see him for days and when he does turn up, it's only because he needs us to do him a favour!" William teased.

"What's up?" Millie asked with a note of concern in her voice.

"My father's been taken into debtors' prison - we need to get him out."

"You mean a smash and grab? Get in there in the dead of night, whisk him away and go on the run?" William asked gleefully, his imagination running away with him.

"No, I mean pay off his debts."

"Oh," William said, somewhat crestfallen.

"How much does he owe?" Millie asked.

"A lot. But we're owed a load of cash by the War Office. Father was never paid for the boots he made for Wellington's armies during the war."

"So, what do we do?" Millie asked.

"We go straight to the top. I need two minutes with Wellington."

"The Duke of Wellington, hero of Waterloo?"

"Yup."

There was a silence whilst the siblings thought this through, Millie and William exchanging uncertain glances.

"Even if we could get you in front of Wellington, what are you going to say when you get there?" Millie asked.

"Leave that bit to me," Isambard replied with a twinkle in his eye.

"So how do we get you in front of him? Need something pretty extraordinary," William pondered.

"Maybe the Candlewick sisters would have some ideas," Millie said, nodding across the rooftops.

"Do you know how to find them?" Isambard asked.

"No. But that's kind of the idea."

HAVING GOT THEMSELVES thoroughly lost, they found Madagascar in the courtyard, wearing a sailor's oil-skins, watching a large ball of wet linen which hung in mid-air, spinning gently.

"Hullo young people," she said, hardly taking her eyes off the rotating drum. "Well don't look so surprised, even the magically endowed have to do laundry you know," she continued sharply. With a flick of her wrist, the rotation began to accelerate and water began to spray outwards in every direction.

"This is the spin cycle," she cried, above the rushing noise. "I suggest you go inside if you're not wearing water-proofs."

They ran for cover and crammed through the back door of the Candlewick's shop. But they soon cannoned into each other when William, at the front of the line, came to a sudden stop and braced himself against the corridor walls to hold the others back.

"Don't make a sound," he whispered, keeping as still as he could.

Doing her best to follow her brother's advice, Millie screamed.

"Now, now, whatever is going on? What's all this noise? You must be careful not to frighten Abendigo," Esmerelda Candlewick said, emerging from the room behind the three of them.

"Who's Abendigo?" Isambard asked in a strained whisper.

"The lion, of course. Had you not noticed him? Well, it doesn't look like he's noticed you, so I suppose it's not that surprising. Come on Abendigo, come and say hello," Esmerelda said to the magnificent beast. The recumbent lion's head lifted wearily to assess the newcomers but quickly returned to the pillow made by his paws.

"Well I would think you should make a little bit more effort than that for your new clients, don't you?" Esmerelda scolded.

The lion responded by standing and nonchalantly leaping onto one of the glass display cases where he drew himself up to his full, magnificent height and gave a deafening roar of majestic proportions. Having discharged his duty, he slouched back into his snoozing position as deftly as a water-snake slipping back into a stream.

"I heard you needed something to bring Lord Wellington's coach to a standstill and I thought that's the sort of thing that Abendigo does very well."

"No no no," William stammered, realising the implication of the situation. "We can't be responsible for taking this beast out onto the streets of London."

"Oh he's really very obliging, there's no need to worry. He's just a little sleepy having eaten next door's dog," Esmerelda said, emerging from the corridor where the three of them were taking refuge. "Only joking," she smiled. "You couldn't hurt a fly could you Abendigo...."

Esmerelda reached down to stroke the lion but her hand went straight through the animal as if it were smoke.

Isambard gasped. "An apparition," he murmured.

"Not technically an apparition. He's actually a miasmara, a visible spirit. Part of the Urudayabo tradition of folk-magic..."

As Esmerelda continued to explain, the back door rattled behind them and Madagascar clattered into the corridor carrying a basket of clean laundry. Affrighted, the lion leapt to his feet and, covering the length of the shop floor in two giant strides, began an attacking leap which sent Isambard, Millie and William diving for cover.

But before the lion reached the apex of its trajectory, it dissolved into a cloud of sparkling dust which drifted into nothing above their heads. All three of them gawped at the space where the lion had been with various shades of terror on their faces.

Esmerelda began a laugh, which she attempted to stifle.

"I'm sorry," she spluttered, losing her battle with the laugh. "I'm sorry... It's just the look on your faces...."

"We are not amused, sister. A miasmara it may be, but a degree of caution should always be exercised in these matters. And, no doubt it will be me that ends up paying for it when the ParaChemical Society finds out."

"My sister is right, of course, this is no laughing matter," Esmerelda said, pulling herself together. "Indeed, this teaches us a valuable lesson. I will need to do some reading to find out how one controls the miasmara. So far I have only found the on-off switch," she said, waving a small carving of a lion's paw. "Which one of you is going to be in charge of him?"

"I can't do it. I'm... allergic to... cats," William said pitifully.

Isambard shook his head in dismay. "Well, I'll need to concentrate on my little chat with Wellington."

"I'll do it," Millie said, stepping forward.

"Here," Esmerelda said, as the lion reappeared in the middle of the room. "You see, he likes you."

Esmerelda gave Millie the ceremonial bone carving and explained how it should be used to make the lion appear and disappear. The lion itself padded around, circling and nuzzling against Millie. She put a hand out to touch and, although there was nothing solid to push against, she felt a very subtle warmth where the lion's fur should have been.

"Here, lie down. Lie down," Millie said gently. To everyone's surprise, the lion did as he was told.

"Well, this should make the whole thing a little more manageable," Esmerelda said, smiling across at her sister.

Just then a seagull came flapping in through the open back door.

"Ah Jasper. What news?" Esmerelda said, reaching out for the bird. A messy chase ensued, involving a lot of flapping, sliding around on the shiny surfaces and some smashed pottery. Even Abendigo joined in, with a few irritated swipes of his enormous paw. A moment later, Madagascar emerged into the shop with a smelly fish which calmed the gull (and therefore Esmerelda) considerably. The bird stood on a display case and carefully regurgitated a ball of paper onto the glass surface before taking the fish from Madagascar's hand with a snap.

"Aha!" Esmerelda said, unravelling the ball of paper whilst keeping one suspicious eye on the bird.

"According to this, Lord Wellington will be making his way to see the Lord Mayor at the Mansion House in.... 20 minutes. You can catch him en-route if you run. Here, as this is a special occasion," Esmerelda said, with a sharp glance at her sister, "take the front door. And Isambard, remember to ask Wellington about the hieroglyphic scroll. I have a feeling that he may be able to help."

The three of them bundled out of the door and found they were on Wallbrook Street. There was very little traffic and they heard the Ceremonial Carriage approaching as it turned the corner from Cannon Street.

"This must be him," Millie said, noticing the plumed horses and armed guards.

"Well go on then," William said impatiently.

"Wait 'til they get a bit closer," Millie replied in a low voice. With the carriage approaching, Millie wandered across the uneven road. Abendigo appeared where Millie had activated the carving, and simply stared intently at her.

"Stay there, Abendigo. Sit. Sit!" Millie said as she backed off the road and into the shadows. Alone in the middle of the street, the lion relaxed and swung its heavy gaze towards the approaching carriage. The horses were close enough to see him now, and began rearing and whinnying wildly. The driver wrestled with the reins and the postilion held on to the bridle for dear life as the horses trotted forwards and backwards on the spot.

"What's going on?" came an authoritative voice from inside the carriage.

"There appears to be a... a lion on the road, my Lord,"

"Right-o. Do hurry it up," came the matter of fact response.

This was Isambard's chance and he jumped at it, opening the carriage door and leaping in.

"Hullo! What's this, juvenile highway robbery?" Wellington chortled.

"No sir. All I would steal, sir, is a moment of your time."

"And I suppose that is your lion impeding my path."

"Yes sir, I'm afraid it...."

"Jolly good wheeze, boy. Jolly good wheeze. Hold on one moment. Guard!"

Isambard's blood turned cold as his arrest suddenly seemed the inevitable outcome of this half-baked idea.

"Be sure as not to damage the lion, will you. No blood if you don't mind," Lord Wellington said.

"Yes, my Lord," came the somewhat uncertain response from the soldier outside.

"So, who are you and what do you want?" Wellington asked, settling back into his seat and fixing Isambard with an appraising look.

"My name is Isambard Brunel, my Lord..."

"Impostor!" Wellington cried. "You cannot be a Brunel. When I last saw you at your father's factory you were but a child!"

Isambard's rising feeling of panic turned to hope as he realised Wellington remembered his father's factory.

"When was that? 1811. The dark days of Napoleon's March through Europe. I must say, your father's factories kept our ships on the water and our boots on the ground my boy. You should be proud. And what is he doing now, your father?"

"Well, my Lord, that is what I've come to talk to you about."

Just then the guard called into the carriage, "my Lord. The lion doesn't appear to be open to persuasion but Driver is prepared to execute an about-turn if it you please?"

But Wellington ignored the guard and pressed on.

"Come on boy. Your father. Cat got your tongue? Or has the lion? Ha!" Wellington asked, rewarding himself with a sharp laugh.

"Well, my father is in Marshalsea, my Lord, debtors' prison and..."

"My Lord, should we turn?" The guard asked again.

"A retreat? At my age? I think not! Brunel here will clear the way. Come on, you got us into this fix, you get us out. Up you jump," Wellington said, ushering Isambard out of the door.

Once again, Isambard's heart sank and he stepped down from the carriage onto the dusty street with a keen sense of failure.

"Off you go, Abendigo, off you go," Isambard called. There was no immediate impact, but the lion's ears twitched and Isambard could tell that Millie was giving instructions from the shadows. Abendigo shambled lazily towards Millie and out of the road. Isambard stood, listless, out of the way of the carriage, waiting for it to pull away, his hopes of his father's release going with it.

"Well come on Brunel. Jump back in boy. You were telling me some nonsense about your father," Wellington bellowed.

Isambard leapt back on board and, as they drove past, managed to exchange slightly panicked glances with Millie who hovered in the shadows with William and Abendigo.

"However did your father end up in the Clink?"

"Well sir, as you may be aware, although my father is a fine engineer..."

"The finest!"

"He has not much of a business head on him..."

"Ha! That much is surely true. When I made that visit to the boot factory he was clearly operating at a loss. I told him to put the prices up by a penny! He said, and I shall always remember this, he said, 'a penny per pair?' And I said, 'no, a penny per boot!'" Wellington said, with a generous laugh.

"Well, sir, my Lord, sir, he may or may not have done that, but in the end we were never paid for the last shipment of boots, which, given the production rate, meant we were quite considerably out of pocket."

"Well, yes, I dare say you were. Not paid, eh?"

"Of course, my father is doing his best to generate new projects. Tsar Alexander seems very keen to have my father do more work on the bridges over there and is prepared to pay my father out of prison."

"The Tsar? Of Russia? Employing your father. No, no, no, we can't have that," Wellington said, looking flustered for the first time. "And how much is it you say we owe you?" he continued.

"I have a copy of the bill here sir," Isambard said, hiding a smile as he delved into a pocket. Wellington snapped the piece of paper open, gave a cursory glance, and stuffed it into his jacket with a grunt.

"I can see I've been rather outmanoeuvred by you, my boy," Wellington said, fixing Isambard with a piercing stare. "Admirably done," he continued, the gaze turning into a smile. "Anything else I can help you with, now that you've got me thoroughly over a barrel," Wellington grinned.

"Ah, well sir, there is perhaps one thing," Isambard said, producing the wooden tube holding Menhit's scroll.

A look of alarm flashed across Wellington's face. "Well, you are full of surprises aren't you - and where did you get this from?"

"Sir, I was the one who retrieved it from Fouché's residence. Assisting agent Catskill."

Wellington looked puzzled for a moment before a smile began to form on his lips.

"Brunel, Brunel... of course - I knew I'd seen your name somewhere recently. This nasty Cato business. You're one of our key sources aren't you?"

"Well sir I'm, I'm not sure about that sir."

"Yes, yes, now this... tube. I thought we'd lost it to our old friend Bonaparte."

"We had sir, I mean, he took the scroll. But he didn't take the tube. I have reason to believe that the secret is hidden in this tube, somewhere in this intricate carving."

"Here, give that thing to me," Wellington said, taking the tube and looking at it closely. "No idea what this is supposed to be," he mumbled, unfolding a monocle and pressing it against one eye. "Some kind of code? Hieroglyphics you say?"

The carriage came to a stop and Wellington squinted out of the window.

"Ah, here we are. I must dash, I'm afraid. Not sure an excuse about a lion in the road will wash with The Lord Mayor of London," Wellington chortled, collecting himself and dismounting the carriage. Handing the tube back to Isambard, almost as an afterthought, he added, "take it to Thomas Young. He'll be either at Saint George's Hospital or the Observatory at Greenwich. He's something of a genius in this sort of thing, although whenever I hear him speak, I'm sure I haven't a clue what he's getting at. If memory serves, he's discovered a way of translating these pictograms so he may be able to help. Give him this," Wellington said, jabbing one of his calling cards into Isambard's hand. "And consider your father's debts paid!" Wellington called as he disappeared across the gravel towards the palace steps.

Chapter 37

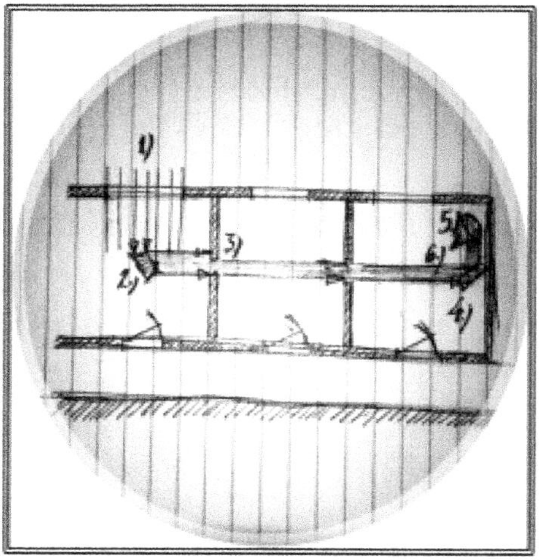

"MR YOUNG. MR YOUNG!" Millie called.

"Are you sure that's him?" Isambard whispered urgently, wincing at her raised voice and looking around the marbled entranceway for someone to apologise to.

"No, I'm not sure. But we're not coming all this way for nothing. Mr Young!"

On Wellington's instructions they had looked for Mr Young at St George's hospital and, when that failed, they had boated downriver to the Greenwich Observatory where Mr Young was Superintendent of the Nautical Almanack. Along the way they had studied the portraits of him that hung on the walls of these eminent institutions, so they had a fair idea of what he looked like. But the two of them were not prepared for the scruffy, wiry-haired little man that now waddled purposefully ahead of them.

"Mr Young," Millie called again, now from much closer range. The man stopped and looked over his shoulder, squinting through wire-framed spectacles.

"Ah! Aha! Well, hello," he cried, turning towards them, his face a mix of confusion and delight.

"Are you Mr Young? Mr Thomas Young?"

"Well yes, almost certainly. I mean yes, but what a very quaint question..." The man replied, gazing into the middle distance.

"Mr Young, my name is Millicent Woodington, and this is my associate Master Isambard Brunel. Lord Wellington said we should come and find you here."

"Brunel, Brunel... isn't that the chap who is tunnelling under the Thames round hereabouts? Aren't you?" Thomas pondered resting a finger on his podgy lips.

"He is sir, that is, my father is. I am helping him build the machinery," Isambard said.

"Indeed. Very good. A Thames tunnel really is a very good idea, you know. Bridges are all well and good but, well, they're very... limited. No no. In a city such as London, we will need to exploit the vast spaces underground. It won't be long, you see, before we have horseless carriages travelling on rails through a network of tunnels underneath every capital city in Europe, mark my words. And London will be the first!" Young said triumphantly.

Millie and Isambard exchanged baffled glances before Mr Young gathered his thoughts and papers once more.

"Sunny outside?" Mr Young demanded abruptly.

"Very," Millie replied.

"Jolly good," Mr Young beamed. "Well come along then. You've come all this way, you may as well help me with my experiment," he said before setting off down the corridor, littering papers along the way.

Isambard and Millie looked at each other quizzically before running after Mr Young, picking up his loose papers as they went.

"Now, one of you will need to go into that room there. Not there, the next one," Young said, flicking an agitated finger at Isambard who sheepishly edged along the corridor as instructed. Young ducked into the first room.

"Shall I come in too?" Millie asked, but Young did not seem to hear her.

"Are you in?" Young called through a rough hole in the wall which led through to the next room. The next room had a similar hole in its wall, which broke through to the room beyond. Millie could see all the way through to the third room.

"Yes sir," Isambard said, his smiling face appearing through the window-like aperture in the wall, two rooms away.

"Splendid. Now. You see the mirror at the window and the one mounted on the wall behind you. Simply direct those in such a way that a beam of light strikes this mirror here," Young said, adding what remained of his sheaf of papers to a pile of similarly disordered files before waving his arms, as if transmitting his instructions to Isambard by sign language.

"Aha!" he cried, as a beam of light leapt from Isambard's mirror like a spotlight, across the empty room to Mr Young's target mirror.

"Thank you. Splendid. You can come back through now."

Whilst Millie waited for Isambard to join them, her eyes wandered around the room, noting various lenses, glasses, retort stands and screens that made up Mr Young's optical laboratory. In one corner she saw a heap of rolled maps and a globe, huddled below a blackboard covered in geometric diagrams. Millie made her way toward the board and gazed at it.

"What is it that you are studying, Mr Young?" she asked.

"Well, all this nonsense represents the most important advance in optical theory for two hundred years. But you didn't come to speak to me about that I'm sure! You came to see me about the hieroglyphics didn't you?" Mr Young said as Isambard came into the room.

Isambard and Millie looked at each other.

"How did you know that, sir, if I may ask?" Millie enquired, a look of astonishment on her face.

"When I heard about Lord Liverpool's amulet going missing, I thought it was only a matter of time before their Lordships sent someone to see me. When you said you were from Wellington the only question in my mind was, 'what took you so long?'" Mr Young said with an indulgent smile.

"He did send us to ask you about the hieroglyphics, sir, you are quite right. But he didn't say how you might be able to help," Isambard said.

"Well, I was one of the first persons in England, and possibly the modern world, to decode the hieroglyphic alphabet. I say one of the first of course because there was that dratted Frenchman. I suspect Wellington thinks I can help translate whatever artefact you have relating to... relating to..." Young said, waving a hand loosely towards the two of them. Exasperated, he rested his knuckles on the tables and gave a sigh before continuing in a slightly different direction.

"Keep it under your hat, but we've understood how to read hieroglyphics for nearly a decade without telling the wider world. Not really in the spirit of scientific collaboration I know but, well the Prince Regent and the Prime Minister seemed to think that the fate of Europe was more important, so we had to keep it all a secret from Napoleon's France. However," Young said, pressing his spectacles back into position on his nose, "it turns out, the French were at it as well - it is now clear that Napoleon's academics were translating hieroglyphics as far back as 1804 without declaring, which is a bit naughty. When Napoleon systematically plundered antiquities in his Egyptian campaign of 1799, he didn't do it to advance our understanding of human civilisation, or even simply to expand his military influence. He did it to acquire the key to hieroglyphics and the fabled power of the Amulets of Ra. We believe he tracked down one of the amulets a short time thereafter which helped him become the most powerful leader in Europe and, well, the world.

That is, until one of our spies captured the amulet instantly sending Napoleon's 1812 attack on Moscow into calamity. But, by then, we could translate enough of the hieroglyphics to understand the power of the amulet and start to put it to our own uses. Although, it hardly needs any help or guidance from humans; as you may find out - it seems to have a mind of its own. Two urges seem to drive it. First, the desire to protect its owner - it will use its immense power to ensure that no harm comes to the one holding it. And second, the desire to be reunited with its sisters, the other amulets. We live in dread of the time when one single person is given the power of all three amulets reunited," he said with a far-away look in his eye, before suddenly snapping out of his day-dream.

"Anyway, let's see what you've brought me," Young said, creating some space in front of him by sweeping three piles of paper into one on the heavy wooden desk. Millie produced the tube from within her skirts and placed it on the desk.

"Well. This is... familiar. Seems to date from the reign of Ptolemy the Fifth, as stated here."

"In his letter, Mr Beddoes of Dowry Square, Bristol explains why he thinks the key to the amulets' destruction is hidden somewhere within this tube," Isambard said, handing Young the letter.

"Wonderful – no doubt this is just what we need," Mr Young said, placing the letter on the worktop between the tube and a pot of ink and turning to the table behind him.

"But I was showing you this, wasn't I - it really is quite interesting. Very basic of course, but the principle has merit. It's called a solar concentrator for reasons which will become clear. The reflective parabolic dish focuses the sun's light onto a single point. I'm using it to keep my coffee pot warm which diffuses the beam, but here, let me demonstrate." Mr Young used a mirror to redirect Isambard's beam toward the silver parabolic dish. He then hastily put the coffee pot to one side and grabbed a piece of paper from the worktop.

"Here, you see the bright point of light on the paper where the reflected sunlight from the whole dish focuses? Consider the amplification of energy as proportional to the ratio of the dish and the point. One hundred, two hundred times the sun's normal energy density, depending on how steady my hand is," Young said, concentrating on keeping his hand still and the point of light as small as possible. The point in the page began to turn black and smoke began to rise.

"Mr Young!" Millie called out in alarm.

"Yes it is very exciting isn't it! Of course the principle is no different from an ordinary convex lens but you can imagine how much cheaper and easier such a simple structure would be to produce on a large scale," Mr Young continued, oblivious to Millie's concern. Smoke turned to flame and the piece of paper began to burn.

"Mr Young, the letter!" Millie called, pointing wildly at the burning piece of paper and Beddoes handwriting on its back. Young stammered briefly before realising his mistake. He waved the paper gently at arm's length as smoke filled the still air. All three of them looked on helplessly as the flames consumed the paper and turned it to ash. Young puffed a few futile breaths on the corner that remained, sending wisps of glowing fibre into the air which floated there like as many black feathers.

All three of them stared in stunned silence at the place where the letter used to be. Young gave an apologetic smile and raised his eyebrows.

"Well, that was exciting. Always a good stimulant to the brain, a bit of unintended conflagration. Now, what about this tube?"

"Oh, what a mess," Millie said, seeing that the pot of ink had been knocked over, forming a puddle under the tube.

"Stop!" Young said pointing at the ink-stained tube. "Look."

Isambard and Millie looked on as Young rolled the engraved tube across the papers on the desk, leaving a printed message as it went.

"Wait there," Young said, leaping across the room for a fresh piece of paper.

"What is it?" Millie whispered.

"Steganography – the message is hidden in plain sight," Isambard muttered. Millie peered in closer.

"Some of the carvings leave a mark and others don't," Millie said.

"They must be at slightly different heights."

"Here," Young said, placing the fresh sheet of paper on the worktop and covering the engraved tube with ink.

"One full revolution should do it. Ha. Well, bless my soul."

"What does it say?"

Thomas Young squinted at it through his wire-frame specs.

"Difficult to see. There, the notation for the Achilles' heel and here, the symbol for the amulets of Ra."

"The Achilles heel of the amulets – that's it – the key to destroying them. What else does it say?"

"Just one more thing. A symbol for the catfish 'electrophorus electricus'".

Chapter 38

Cato dismissed the captain and crew and made sure they were well away from the frigate before descending into the hold. Although he had hand-picked them for their loyalty to Napoleon, Cato knew that he had to keep them as far away from their precious cargo as possible. Forcing himself to ignore the stench that seemed to pervade all ships below-decks, he satisfied himself that there were no stragglers on-board before making his way to the fancifully named "guest quarters".

Cato stopped at the door and took a deep breath, ignoring as best he could the coarse shouts and noises that surrounded him in the docks outside. He knocked – and waited.

"Who's there?"

"Robespierre."

There was a long pause.

"Come in, Robespierre," came the reply at last. "Come in my dear friend."

Cato opened the door and stepped in. In front of him sat Napoleon, planted in a chair like a stuffed sack, his clothes grubby, his skin grey, his hair thin.

"Robespierre," Napoleon growled, making an effort to smile.

"Your Excellency,"

Napoleon shuffled in his seat, straightening slightly. "You are shocked by what I have become. This is what five years of mistreatment at the hands of my English captors has done to me."

"We will be avenged, sire," Robespierre said, bowing his head.

"You have the amulets?"

Cato looked Napoleon in the eye and nodded. "Here," he said, pulling a large purse from around his neck and handing it to the Emperor, who received it with both hands. Napoleon reverentially poured the contents out of the velvet sack – a gold cylinder made up of three interlocking discs. Although not glowing, it seemed to cast a beneficial light, an aura. Cato watched as some colour returned to Napoleon's skin, his hair suddenly showed some lustre, his collapsed frame became straightened and upright. Even his clothes seemed to lose their dusty sheen.

"Yes, Robespierre, you have done well," Napoleon said, holding the amulets in the air in front of him. "With this power we will destroy all the foolish leaders and nations that have stood in our way. We will finally create a unified Empire from Louisiana to Moscow. And you," Napoleon said, standing and looking at Cato, "you, my loyal lieutenant, you will be my general on the Champ de Mars, our victorious battlefield," Napoleon said, beginning to look every bit as imposing as he had at the height of his powers.

"I have begun calling up your most loyal armies," Cato said. "They are proving unstoppable. With the amulets in my hand, I have only to imagine it, and so it becomes reality."

"Then let us imagine victory," Napoleon said. Cato closed his eyes and a moment later the frigate began to groan around them. Blue sparks flashed across its wooden ribs and it began to surge and sway.

"To the Champ de Mars."

"And victory."

Chapter 39

"Sir, The Atrium has deciphered the message from Agent Catskill," a young Captain said, presenting himself at the door of War Office's private room, where the six senior members of the War Council sat around a large desk.

"Very well. Come in. Be quick."

The Captain delivered the message on a silver tray and departed smartly.

"As I was about to say, we are currently investigating multiple reported sightings of Napoleonic soldiers rising from the dead in various locations across what was once Napoleon's empire and congregating on the Champ de Mars in Paris."

"Napoleon's soldiers rising from the dead? This really has gone too far," Foreign Office despaired.

"I agree, my Lord," War Office responded. "This has gone too far, which is why we have called this extraordinary meeting."

"Unfortunately, it seems that, on this occasion, even your usual stiff letter to the Prime Minister will not be sufficient to resolve the issue, my Lord," Admiralty said, with a knowing smile.

"There have also been sightings of Napoleon himself, who you will remember recently escaped from exile on St Helena, making his way through the French countryside in a phantom brig named Inconstant, garnering popular support as he goes."

"Across land in a ship. It's not natural!"

"Do we have any idea what all of this means?" The War Council asked eventually, a note of frustration in his voice.

"Our best guess," the Irregular Committee began, slowly, "is as follows. Robespierre, known to our colleagues from His Majesty's Special Intelligence Directorate as 'Cato', survived his apparent execution of 1794 and..."

"My Lords..." the Chair said, attempting to silence the outbursts from around the table. "Gentlemen... Order!" The Chair cried, thumping the table and shocking all into silence.

Foreign Affairs spoke quietly.

"It may be helpful if I bring to mind the words of my dear departed grandmother who used to say: 'to understand an unexpected present, it may be necessary to accept an unexpected past.'"

"I think we should all bear in mind Grandmother's wise words as we allow the honourable gentleman to continue?" the Chair said, smiling purposefully at each in turn. The Irregular Committee smiled graciously and was about to continue when there came another interruption.

"If. I. May, Chair?" His Majesty's Special Intelligence Directorate asked tentatively. The Chair stared at him haughtily, but allowed the interruption.

"It is perhaps pertinent at this point to table some intelligence that has just arrived from our agent in Paris, if I may," he said, waving the message recently received from Catskill. "In an attempt to learn more about claims that Cato is a living piece in this puzzle, our agent infiltrated the household of Joseph Fouché to recover documents from the time of Cato's execution. These papers led to an interview with Cato's doctor who claims to have orchestrated Cato's escape and replacement at the guillotine by a convicted criminal. The doctor claims that the significant facial injuries that Cato sustained at his arrest made the exchange plausible. The doctor also claims that the exchange was effected at the behest of one Napoleon Bonaparte. The historians amongst you may remember that Cato and his brother were strong supporters of Napoleon's early career, which could explain such an intervention as a kind of quid pro quo. A subsequent review of archive material has uncovered a number of unsubstantiated sightings suggesting that Cato may have escaped to America. In summary, our analysis to date suggests that there is a reasonable possibility that Cato is alive today."

A thoughtful silence filled the room, the crackle of a burning cigar the only sound.

"Thank you for that timely clarification," the Irregular Committee said with a nod to His Majesty's Special Intelligence Directorate. "As I was saying, working on the hypothesis that Cato survived his apparent execution of 1794, we believe that Cato propagated the recent Cato Street Conspiracy as a means of flushing out the British Amulet. Correctly informed that the Prime Minister was in the habit of hiding the amulet in extreme matters of national security, we believe that the conspiracy was Cato's way of manufacturing one such incident, thereby giving him the opportunity to take possession. However, whatever your view, and regardless of what may have happened, a man matching Cato's description took possession of the British Amulet from the Prime Minister, and a very similar looking man was seen leaving the scene of a rather grisly incident involving a now very dead antiquities dealer in Antwerp. We have no information regarding the remaining amulet, despite the fact that we have been looking for it for more than ten years."

"So, whether you believe it is Cato, Robespierre or Merlin the Magician, it appears that someone has collected two, possibly three of the amulets and the atmosphere of what can only be described as magical chaos is at an all-time high," the Chair summarised. "How quickly can you get the land-army over to Paris?"

There was silence as all eyes turned to Wellington, who was playing a game of Solitaire with a miniature deck of cards.

"What? Sorry," he said, realising that all eyes had come to rest on him. "An army, in Paris? I can have 15-hundred men there by this time tomorrow and another two-thousand the day after."

"Well then, there is only one thing for it," the Navy said. "We must tell the Prime Minister to prepare for war."

Chapter 40

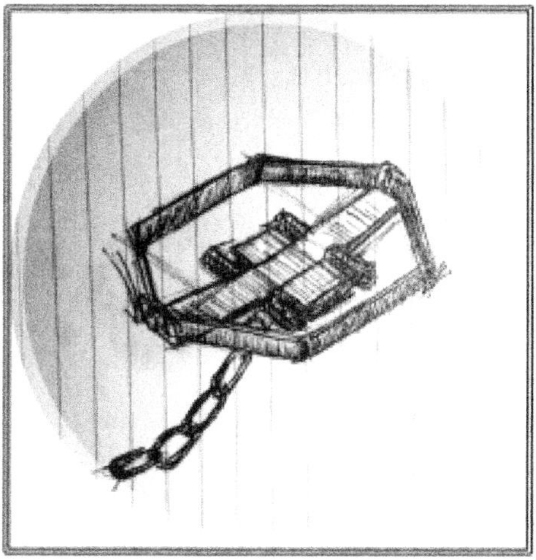

"I DON'T LIKE IT. THE boy should go home. It ain't safe here," Ruthven whispered harshly as he peered out across the field. Agent Catskill lowered her telescope and turned.

"My dear Ruthven, I would like to think he is safer by your side than he would be wandering around with these fellows keeping him company," the agent replied. The 'fellows' that she was referring to were the shambling wrecks of Napoleon's undead army who had collected in their hundreds, perhaps thousands, on Champ de Mars in front of them. Although their uniforms were shabby and threadbare, they assembled into neat rows and, once in position, stood perfectly still, so the overall effect was one of a well-disciplined body of men.

And it was growing; from all directions more of the undead soldiers arrived, hobbling and dragging their damaged bodies, wordlessly joining the formation with no acknowledgement of each other. Watching one of them individually, there was something pitiable about their determination despite their decomposing bodies. They had survived all kinds of attack along the way, from angry mobs to firing squads; nothing seemed to touch, impede or slow them. They were as intangible as air, with no connection to this earthly world either physical or sensory. They walked on the earth but did not seem to inhabit it. The fear that bystanders initially felt often turned to anger, but realising the futility of attack, usually ended in fascination. Even now there were knots of people dotted around the Champ de Mars, watching and pointing from what they judged to be a safe distance.

"I can't believe these crazy Frenchies are out there watching like it's some kind of music hall show. Look, them over there have even got a bottle of wine to wash it down," Ruthven said.

"Very civilised, I'd say. And they will certainly have something to watch when Wellington's men arrive. Ah, speak of the devil," Agent Catskill said.

From behind them, a young man in a very smart uniform came bounding up, making a cursory effort to stay low behind the mound that Ruthven had chosen to use as cover.

"Sirs. Captain Nately, if you please, with word from Lord Wellington."

"Splendid, Captain. Very good. Carry on," the agent responded impatiently.

"Sir, Lord Wellington thanks you for your reports to date and respectfully asks that you pull back as the advanced guard will be engaging the enemy very shortly."

"Engaging the enemy, eh? Chance would be a fine thing. Very well! Please let Wellington know that we will retire to a safe distance at the... earliest opportunity," Agent Catskill said before returning her attention to Napoleon's army by way of her telescope.

"Sir, I'm afraid I have strict instructions to ensure your removal to a safe distance, sir," the Captain said, a note of nervousness in his voice.

"Very good captain. Well, feel free to begin with Ruthven. If it's brute force you are going to use, you may as well start with the heaviest burden. No offence meant, old man," the agent said with a wink in Ruthven's direction.

"None taken," Ruthven replied without removing his gaze from the scene that was playing out in front of them.

After pausing to consider his options, the Captain shuffled towards Ruthven nervously, sizing him up for some kind of physical removal. Fortunately for him, the time for such an intervention had run out.

"Too late. Here they come," Ruthven said, looking over his shoulder at the unmistakable prospect of an approaching British battalion with cavalry. It was an impressive sight, rows and rows of infantrymen followed by a regiment of cavalry, all marching steadily toward Napoleon's ranks in unison, filling the air with the sound of buckle on sword, metal on metal.

However, despite the awesome power of the spectacle, Isambard was scanning the landscape nervously, using Catskill's telescope. The skies were growing heavier by the minute, the deepening clouds, black as tar-smoke, formed and swirled menacingly overhead. Isambard's gaze moved from the silent ranks of Napoleon's undead army to the latecomers, straggling and limping towards the centre from all directions. But one figure, at the tree-lined edge of the field, stood out, simply due to its inactivity - with a feeling of ice cold water down his back, Isambard made out the distinctive shape of a tricorn hat.

"Ruthven! Ruthven look," Isambard stammered, pointing towards the figure.

"What is it son?" Ruthven asked, seeing Isambard's appalled face.

"It's him, over there. It's Cato."

"By the seven bells of Leipzig, it surely is," Agent Catskill said, following Isambard's finger for a closer look.

"We must neutralise him this instant, the troops are in danger," Agent Catskill said, scrambling to her feet and making her way towards the figure, building a plan in her mind as she went.

"Captain Nately, you need not join, but if ever you had a wish to distinguish yourself in the field of battle, this is the time. Probably best if we attack on two flanks: if he is with me, Captain Nately, and I from the South, Isambard and Ruthven from the North. We will need to give a wide berth and approach through the trees at the edge of the field."

From behind them, shouts drifted through the damp air as Wellington's commanders ordered the first line of riflemen to open fire. On the command, a crackle of gunfire filled the air and faded, followed by new orders to kneel and reload to allow the second tier of gunners behind them to fire. As Isambard and his party approached Cato and the trees, they turned to watch the cavalry ride through Napoleon's army as if it were made of smoke. Wheeling and manoeuvring amongst the undead, the cavalrymen whipped the air with sabres but to no effect.

Suddenly the front two rows of Napoleon's army detached and filed towards the gunners who had taken up position 50 paces away. Unprepared for this eventuality, the battalion commander opted to stand his ground and fight with bayonets. As expected the first row of the undead passed through the infantrymen. The second row stopped close by and turned their backs.

"They've been surrounded," the agent said.

"Look, Napoleon's soldiers are forming a square around the cavalry too," Isambard said.

Commands and cries from the British troops became increasingly panicked. Guns and swords flashed but no Briton emerged from their supernatural prison.

"They're trapped," Ruthven said.

"Look at Cato. It looks like he is orchestrating this," Isambard said, pointing through the dense vegetation to the place where Cato could be seen. The Frenchman was holding his arms aloft, sweating through his shirt, eyes closed and face deep in concentration.

"We need to get him now whilst he's distracted. Ruthven, take Isambard wide around the back. We will close in and overpower him once you're in position."

"I don't like this Ruthven," Isambard confided once the two of them were on their way. "You've seen how powerful Cato is. I'm not sure even with four of us we can overpower him."

"You may be right son. And we may die trying. But I don't know that we're going to get a better chance," Ruthven replied ruefully, as he picked his way carefully through the ferny undergrowth.

They were about halfway round when suddenly Ruthven fell with a muted scream. Behind them Isambard heard Agent Catskill and Captain Nately, who, believing that their moment had come, started to charge at Cato. But, with only one flank under attack, Cato was able to defend himself swiftly and easily, using his outstretched hands to produce 10 of his undead soldiers from the earth to block Nately and Catskill's charge. Within seconds the two attackers were trapped within a cage of Napoleonic soldiers. Blades and bullets passed through the supernatural infantrymen, but their push was real enough. No matter what they tried, Nately and Catskill could not break free.

Isambard sunk to his knees next to Ruthven in the long grass and cradled the Officer's head.

"It's a deer trap son. It's made a mess of my leg. I'm out of this one. It's up to you now. Get going. Run!"

"I'm not leaving you..." Isambard murmured.

Ruthven looked up to see four of Napoleon's infantrymen approaching through the trees.

"Stay down. Go!" Ruthven hissed, pushing Isambard on his way and crawling off in the other direction. Isambard ran in a crouch as quietly and swiftly as he could deeper into the wood, taking cover behind the carcass of a fallen tree covered in moss.

Breathing fast, shallow breaths, heart pounding in his throat, he peered through the leaves to see Ruthven being carried, despite his flailing and roaring, with apparent ease by four undead soldiers. Isambard rolled onto his back and sunk into the soft fibres of the rotting tree.

Suddenly the earth in front of him began to stir and a bony blue hand emerged, followed by another, and then two elbows. Isambard pressed himself into the tree in a futile attempt to hide, as an undead soldier climbed up through the soil and clambered to a standing position a few paces in front of Isambard. Its uniform was grimy and shredded, in places revealing rotting flesh and exposed sinew. The stench of decay was overwhelming. Isambard cowered against the tree, looking out through the corner of one eye. The soldier drew his sword and lurched towards Isambard who curled up for what he thought might be his last moments on earth.

But the moment passed.

Seconds later, Isambard realised that he could hear the soldier, striding on through the undergrowth towards the centre of the field, probably to join the ranks. Isambard relaxed his rigid body and exhaled.

He closed his eyes and let the brackish scent of fern fill his nostrils once again.

Chapter 41

Isambard listened as Ruthven's cries receded. In the distance he could hear Wellington's men in full, futile battle. For a moment he thought about waiting it out, staying put and doing nothing until it was all over. An image came to him of Mrs Faraday arriving at the Houses of Parliament on the boat, asleep, exhausted in her soaking oil skins, the rasping cough, the cold. The way she roused herself, found strength and the difference she made to the outcome that night.

Isambard rubbed his face and patted his cheeks, calling on some inner reserve. He peered over the top of the tree trunk and saw no movement, so began to move quietly through the woods towards their original destination to the north of Cato. He had no real idea of what he would do once he got there. The only thing he knew was that he needed to get help. This was his opportunity to change the outcome of the entire confrontation.

Isambard advanced slowly towards the clearing, carefully picking through the undergrowth and freezing with every branch that snapped. But the chaos of battle was enough to mask his noises and he was soon in a position to see Cato standing, his coat and tricorn hat on the floor several steps behind him. It had been the hat which had alerted Isambard to Cato's identity, but now it was the coat that made Isambard's heart race.

If it was the same coat that Cato had been wearing in Bristol, then they were the same coat pockets into which Millie had dropped the eyestone all those weeks ago. Is it possible, Isambard asked himself, that the eyestone would still be there, that it would still be live, that he could use it to contact the Candlewicks? Perhaps, but how would he get far enough across the clearing to pick it up without being seen.

Suddenly, from Isambard's right side, two undead soldiers broke through the undergrowth into the clearing. They marched as best as their decomposing bodies would allow them, towards the centre of the field, a course which would take them to within a few paces of the coat.

Isambard had an idea. He didn't give himself time to question it and before he knew it he was marching next to the two undead soldiers, who, as expected, paid him no heed. He could hear Ruthven and the others suddenly striking up a commotion, he thought probably to distract the attention of Cato and the guards. Within moments, Isambard was walking past the coat; he dipped one hand to ground level, picked up the coat and threw it over his shoulders in one fluent movement. Suppressing a grin, Isambard walked on with the two cadaverous infantrymen until he achieved a clump of trees at a safe distance from Cato and was able to break away from his unnatural consorts.

Isambard plunged deep into the trees and laid the coat on the ground, carefully tipping the contents of the pockets out onto the flattened coat. A dry sausage. A coin. And there, a stone.

It didn't look magical. It was black, empty. Suddenly, it began to glow.

Chapter 42

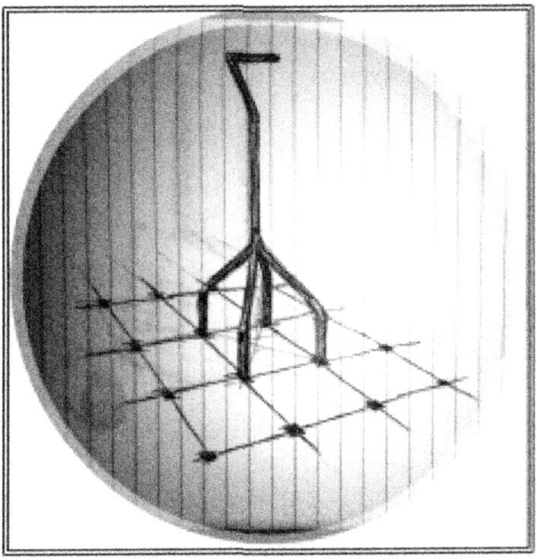

"ESMERELDA, OUR LITTLE band of ragamuffins has turned up in the yard again, even more excited than usual," Madagascar announced as Millie and William bundled in through the back door behind her.

"Ma'am, we've done it, we've found the secret hidden in the tube."

"Hello you two. And how lovely to see you. You'll be having some tea, no doubt?" Esmerelda said, eyes as sparkly as ever.

"Ma'am I'm afraid I don't think we have time to stop for tea," Millie said slightly breathless.

"Oh, come now, we're going to have a natter aren't we? You may as well wet your whistle whilst we waffle, what?" Esmerelda chuckled, firing a smile at William for good measure. Madagascar suddenly loomed over the siblings, proffering a battered copper tea-tray in such a way that they felt they really had no choice but to accept the china cups of tea on offer.

"And isn't there one missing – where is Young Isambard?"

"He went back to discuss the tube message with Lord Wellington. By the time the meeting was over Isambard had orders to join Wellington's army travelling to Paris."

"Oh well. Things are getting exciting, aren't they? But anyway - these hieroglyphics," Esmerelda said. "Did you say you'd had some luck decoding them?"

"There was a secret message," Millie said.

"Hidden in the engraving on the tube."

"Oh wonderful!"

"And what did it say?" Madagascar asked.

"It said that the Achilles' heel of the amulet is Electrophorus Electricus."

"Indeed," Esmerelda said. "And what did Lord Wellington make of that?"

"Well, he basically said that he had no interest in the wisdom of the ancient Egyptians and would prefer to rely on the tried and tested techniques of modern warfare."

"Oh, the arrogance of the Enlightenment...." Madagascar muttered to herself, emerging from the back room flicking through the pages of a large leather-bound book. "It says here that Electrophorus Electricus is commonly known as the electric eel. Actually not an eel at all. More like a catfish. But you get the picture."

"Electric eels are the Achilles' heel. What does that mean?"

"Perhaps electricity is the key," Millie mused.

Esmerelda and Madagascar exchanged a look that Millie found hard to interpret.

"What is it?" she asked.

"Electricity has always been rather... frowned upon by the ParaChemical Society," Esmerelda said, keeping one eye on her sister.

"The enemy of magic." Madagascar whispered.

"So, could electricity be the key?"

"We must show her the letter," Esmerelda said to her sister.

"What letter?"

"A letter we received from Mrs Faraday telling us about some rather funny goings-on around her property."

"What kind of goings-on?"

"Well, it sounds most inconvenient - something about Napoleon's soldiers rising from the dead. Madagascar, bring the letter would you?" Esmerelda said, flapping a hand until the letter arrived.

"Well. What does it say?"

Esmerelda cleared her throat and looked to her sister for permission. Madagascar replied with a look which said, "on your head be it."

"She begins 'My Dear Candlewick Sisters', which I think is rather lovely. 'It was a great pleasure...' dum-de dum '...I was going to send this letter to my Nephew to bring up in Parliament but, as I'm sure he won't read it, let alone do anything about it, I thought you would know better what to do with this information." Esmerelda stopped and put the letter down. "Well, we should know what to do with this kind of information, shouldn't we sister," Esmerelda said hopefully.

"We do like to think so, yes," came Madagascar's rather clipped response.

"She goes on to say more about Napoleon's soldiers – 'it seems that they are rising from their graves - I'm sure you can imagine what ten years in a shallow grave does for a man's complexion.' Ha! Isn't that funny." Esmerelda beamed. Seeing that no-one else in the room was amused, she continued to read. "'I understand they were naval prisoners of war, but they must have been blown dreadfully off course to have ended up in Iffley. The remarkable thing, and the reason I write to you, is that whenever one of these poor unfortunate fellows made contact with my house he seemed to evaporate or spontaneously combust – one minute he was there, in his own undead kind of way, the next, he was a mere wisp of smoke. I've been taking an interest ever since, and it seems that no one else is having any luck dealing with the wretched fellows by conventional means. They seem otherwise pretty indestructible. So I thought I would put it in a letter to you' dum-de-dum.. best wishes etcetera etcetera."

"Napoleonic soldiers rising from the dead. Whatever will they think of next," Madagascar mused.

For a moment there was silence, until William became aware of a muffled rumbling noise.

"What's that noise?" he asked.

They each held their breath and scanned the air with their ears, one or two of them converging on a point above the shiny tiled floor.

"Box 24. Madagascar, if you would," Esmerelda said, bending over an unremarkable patch of tiles in the middle of the shop floor. Madagascar left the room briefly and returned with a large iron prong with four fingers sticking out like a grasping hand. She passed it to Esmerelda who peered at it momentarily before matching the fingers carefully onto four of the small white tiles and pressing down hard. The four tiles sunk, and, with a twist, Esmerelda was able to use the iron prong to remove a plate-sized chunk of floor tiles. The rattling noise got markedly louder. Esmerelda carefully placed the prong to one side and peered into the hole. She very quickly looked up again and fixed her sister with a serious stare.

"The eyestone," she said before delving into the hole and retrieving the motherstone, which wriggled frantically in her hand like a wounded bird.

They all crowded round the stone and peered over Esmerelda's shoulder. The stone became calm and a glowing image began to appear.

"Isambard!" Millie cried.

They watched as the light on Isambard's face changed and his expression leapt to a smile. They could see him crouch amongst overhanging trees with grand buildings in the distance. He was explaining and miming frantically.

"What's he saying?" William asked.

"We can't hear but we can guess. Hat. Tricorn hat."

"Cato!"

"What's he doing?"

"…."

"Meditating?"

"Puppeteering."

"Soldiers."

"Lots of soldiers."

"Rising from the earth. More of Napoleon's cadavers."

"Shouting."

"Afraid."

"Fear."

"Trapped."

"Boot?"

"Wellington!"

"Help. He's mouthing 'help.'"

They fell silent.

"So Cato has trapped Wellington's army using Napoleon's undead soldiers," Millie recapped.

"But what are we supposed to do about it?" William enquired in a rather hopeless voice.

"He said they had orders to march to Paris didn't they?" Millie asked rhetorically.

"Paris. Of course. Oh, whatever was that building in the background? There!" Esmerelda called.

"Is it the Trocadero Palace?" Madagascar hazarded.

"No, no. It's the Military School," Esmerelda said, peering at the stone. "They must be on the Champs de Mars."

"Right. So, now we just have to get to Paris in time to stop Cato destroying Wellington's army and stomping all over Europe," William said. "How are we supposed to do that?"

At that moment there was a sharp knock at the door.

"At last!" Madagascar sighed as she strode towards the shop front door, throwing it open when she got there.

"Madagascar, Esmerelda! My favourite magical sisters! You look ebeautiful today! I get your message. I come as quick as I can. I have the balloon in the buggy – where you wanna go?"

Chapter 43

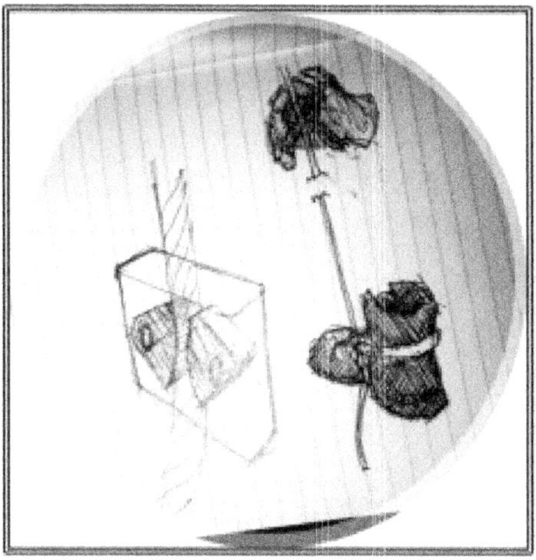

HOURS PASSED. THE CLOUDS had blackened further and now looked like soot smeared across the skies. The air was thick with moisture and smelled of rain. Isambard watched a continuous stream of the undead trudging towards Napoleon's ranks, which now swelled to thousands. His excitement at seeing the eyestone glow into life had passed long ago. There was no way of telling if his message had been received, and, even if it had, he had no idea what anyone would be able to do about it.

Wellington had continued to try various offensive measures, all of them failing. Cannonballs and mortars bounced through the rows of undead soldiers without slowing. Burning tar seemed to stick to their opponents' cadaverous bodies and become part of them, making them even more dangerous. It seemed that nothing Wellington could do would make any kind of impression on this supernatural opponent.

Although most of the onlookers had left, there were still a number of Parisians wandering the fields, mainly adventure seeking youngsters, bewitched by the flash of steel and roar of cannon, skulking around and watching from behind bushes and trees. Seeing these onlookers moving around freely, Isambard realised that he could probably make his way carefully towards Wellington's temporary headquarters, which had been hastily assembled in the Military School at one end of the field.

Despite the chaos on the Champs de Mars, Wellington's men were well trained and were making sure that there was no way in at the front entrance for the uninvited such as Isambard. Changing his approach, Isambard walked purposefully round to the back of the Military School and uncoiled the fine wire from around his belt. From his pocket he pulled out the pen that Fourier had given him, unscrewed the barrel and attached the wire to the exposed eye. He aimed the pen at a meaty piece of timber visible through an upstairs window and pressed on the end of the pen. With a loud bang, the tip of the pen fired, taking with it a thin cord. The pen tip stuck into the timber target above. Isambard used the small ratchets on the instep of his boot and within a modified glove to pull himself up the wire until he was able to climb into the open window.

Grabbing a bucket, Isambard strode through the many corridors and staircases, trying to locate Wellington. He passed a room-full of generals poring over maps. In another room, a crowd of bewigged aristocrats had drawn seats up to the window to get a better view of the most unusual show to come to Paris since Napoleon's last return from exile. In a third room, French soldiers and politicians held several heated conversations, none of which Isambard could understand.

Isambard was just emerging from another doorway when a booming voice from the hallway behind him confirmed that his search was over.

"Boy!" Wellington said, stopping suddenly and causing several of his generals to crash into each other behind him.

Isambard turned and froze in the beam of Wellington's gaze, feeling for a moment even more scared than he had been in Cato's company earlier that afternoon.

"Brunel the Younger, isn't it. Don't tell me your father still hasn't been released from Marshalsea."

"Sir, indeed he is released. Some two days ago."

"Well then, what do I owe you this time?"

"Nothing, sir nothing at all, I just came to share some intelligence that you may find useful, sir," Isambard said, as bravely as his nerves would allow him.

"Well. Go on," Wellington said thoughtfully. An expectant silence filled the corridor as people stopped what they were doing to listen.

"Sir, I have seen Robespierre, the one they call Cato, at the South West edge of the field. I believe he is controlling the undead army and is using them to capture your forces. He has the three amulets. His power is immense. A simple outright attack would be a... mistake... In my humble opinion."

"Thank you master Brunel, but whilst I am sure that your field skills are second to none, you would do well to leave questions of strategy to my Generals," Wellington smiled, to indulgent chuckles from the crowd around him.

"My Lords!" came a shout from the watchman on the balcony, "a ship approaches from the South East!"

Like water down a plug hole, the entire congregation drained into the adjacent room to see for themselves. Isambard was swept along with them and soon found himself squashed between the elbow of a cavalry general and the strongly perfumed biceps of a corpulent Parisian Courtesan. Unable to see anything but the back of a plumed helmet, Isambard's picture of events was formed solely by the words and phrases that passed up and down the excitable crowd.

"It's a brig."

"Sailing across the grass."

"Can you smell the sea?"

"I can smell the sea."

"Look at all those people following in its wake...."

"It's... It looks like Emperor Napoleon."

"Napoleon. On the bridge. Napoleon returning from exile! It is!"

It was too much. Isambard had to see for himself. He bent down and burrowed through the press of people back into the corridor and retraced his steps out of the building.

Outside it was raining steadily and the sky was full of great lumps of black cloud. Within minutes Isambard was back in the training yard, being jostled by regiments of infantrymen and cavalry who hastily criss-crossed the courtyard in an organised chaos of colour, shouts and military hardware.

Isambard emerged at the front of the Military School to see the ship for himself, as it surged across the turf towards the serried ranks of undead soldiers some 1,000 paces away. It appeared to be a perfectly ordinary ship, apart from the moist air around it which crackled and fizzed with a blue glow. In its wake walked hundreds of jubilant supporters waving flags of the Republic. At the helm stood the unmistakable silhouette of Napoleon Bonaparte, exiled Emperor of France.

"This is what the undead army has been waiting for," Isambard muttered to himself. "The return of their glorious Emperor."

Just then an explosion, a fireball and a plume of smoke erupted in the corner of the field where Isambard had last seen Cato.

"And there's Wellington's frontal attack on Cato going horribly wrong. Poor fellows."

Isambard could hear fresh exhortations coming from the balcony, as something even more remarkable was being shared by those that could see. He peered up at the balcony to find an increasing number of people pointing off into the skies to the North. Isambard followed their lead and scanned the horizon, soon finding the object of their fascination: a familiar looking balloon scudding towards them at a significant speed.

"Lunardi!" Isambard grinned, running out into the open and waving his arms. He knew his attempts to be noticed would be futile. But then he remembered the eyestone that he still had in his pocket. They must have got his message, so maybe he should send another.

Grabbing a pencil and piece of paper from his pocket, he sketched a map, showing the Military School, the undead army, the perimeter of the field and Cato's last known location marked with an X. In the ground, under an ornamental orange tree, Isambard carefully placed the map and the stone facing each other, before running across the field towards the site of Cato's exploding fireball.

"FULL SPEED AHEAD MR Lunardi. Not a moment to lose!" Madagascar cried, clinging to the guy ropes as if her life depended on it. She knew that looking down would only heighten her level of terror, but it was difficult to avoid doing so whilst Millie and William shouted increasingly outlandish descriptions of the scenes that were being played out below them.

"There are hundreds of people following behind the ship," Millie cried, leaning over the edge of the basket.

"They seem to be armed with axes and pikes," William added.

Lunardi was more concerned by the worsening weather and scanned the horizon, looking for more lightning. Squally rain filled the air and black clouds writhed across each other like fish dying in a bucket.

"It get very windy, you know? We have to get down soon else the wind do it for us," he said, turning to face Madagascar with a look of concern that none of them had seen before.

"Don't you worry about the balloon, Lunardi. Leave that to Trafalgar. He's got us this far, he'll not let us fall."

"But how do we find Cato in all this?" Millie demanded.

"Anything on the motherstone?" Madagascar asked in reply. Another bolt of lightning ripped through the sky to the East, thunder rocking the dripping basket almost immediately after.

"Yes! Look. One of Isambard's drawings," William cried, seeing Isambard's pencil sketch glow on the motherstone.

"It's a map. Look, that's the palace! There's the army. And look, the X - that must be Cato."

"Over there, Madagascar, by that clearing," William said, pointing across the field.

"Lunardi, Trafalgar. You know what to do," Madagascar said in a commanding voice.

"Yes ma'am," came Trafalgar's monotone response from inside the balloon.

Trafalgar released some gases at a tangent and Lunardi pedalled hard to give them some thrust. But suddenly there was a new kind of explosion. A cannon on Napoleon's brig roared into life and a fireball scorched across the field, smashing into the front face of the Military School, sending flames and debris into the air.

"What was that?" Madagascar cried, eyes wild and face green with nausea.

"Napoleon's firing on the...." William said, faltering.

"...on Wellington's encampment," Millie added. "Look at all the soldiers running like poor little ants."

"We're nearly there. Scoop up those electric eels and be ready to launch on my command," Madagascar shouted through the pelting rain. Another bolt of lightning momentarily cut the sky in two and rocked the basket. Millie and William used jugs to scoop up one fish each and peered over the basket ready to discharge. They were about 20 paces from the ground and it felt like they could reach out and touch Cato.

"Now!" Madagascar yelled. Millie and William emptied their jugs and watched the fish fall towards their target. On contact, Cato seemed to spasm and the blue glow around Napoleon's brig flickered. But the effect was temporary - Cato was clearly shaken but was fast recovering his senses and was reaching out a bony hand as if pulling Napoleon's brig closer.

"He's going to bring the ship over here," William called.

"No. Worse," Millie countered, "it's the cannon!" She added, as the tremendous noise hit them and they watched a fireball emerge from the side of the brig, rapidly growing closer and bigger.

"Evasive action, Trafalgar!" Madagascar called.

"Very good ma'am," came the reply as the balloon lurched high into the air and the fireball flew past, inches below the basket.

"Fire on board!" William yelled, using a jug of water to douse the embers that the fireball had left behind as it passed.

"Well it definitely had the desired effect on Cato, did you see? But we'll need a bigger dose of electricity," Millie said.

"Quite," Madagascar agreed, her face suddenly set in grim determination. "We'll have to go around again."

RUNNING TOWARDS CATO'S clearing, Isambard had seen how close that fireball had come to destroying the balloon and all his friends in it. He knew he would have to distract Cato if they were to have any chance of getting close enough for a second pass. Less than a hundred yards away, Isambard could see Cato standing motionless, concentrating, arms raised and face twisted with the mental effort of orchestrating an assault by mind power alone. For a moment Isambard could only stare in awe, watching as Cato's face flickered with each seismic event in the field of battle. Isambard suddenly noticed the smell of the sea that had arrived with Napoleon's phantom brig and he was able to snap his gaze away from Cato's mesmerising performance playing out in front of him. He looked up at the balloon as he put a hand in his pocket and touched the French Franc that his father had given him before all this had started.

"I'm sorry father," he said, before calling out as loudly as he could, "Robespierre! You're plan will not work. You cannot use this magic for your evil purpose. You will not succeed!"

Cato turned to face Isambard. His eyes opened wide and glowed a fiery orange. He brought an arm forward and pointed a bony hand in Isambard's direction. Isambard prepared himself for a mortal injury, but saw and felt no damage. Instead, the earth at his feet erupted and a putrid hand emerged, snatching at his ankles like a snake. Isambard jumped and danced to avoid the grasping hand, but he found that the earth around him was suddenly alive with the writhing limbs, all hunting for his feet. He ran, but the hands emerged all around him, tearing through the earth at his feet with every step. Cato followed Isambard's meandering path effortlessly with languid motions of his finger, and a deep laugh began to emerge from within his chest, as the game of cornering Isambard became more and more enjoyable.

Isambard was now running through a swamp of flailing limbs, all clamouring and grasping at his feet. He felt something grip his heel, he tripped and fell headlong into the grass. A hundred rancid hands clawed at him and clamped him tightly to the ground.

Trafalgar, meanwhile, had managed to rotate the balloon while Lunardi was pedalling the propeller to ensure they headed back towards Cato.

"How many eels do we have left?"

"Catfish," William corrected.

"Eight," Millie said, counting whilst scowling at her pedantic brother.

"Right. This is what we shall do," Madagascar said, fixing them with a cold hard stare. "I will be lowered down with the fish in those buckets and dump the whole lot onto Cato in one go. There is no time for arguments. You can either help me or step aside."

"Ok," Millie said.

"Cannon!" Lunardi cried as another fireball roared past within inches of the balloon.

William and Millie transferred the fish into two buckets as Madagascar tied a rope round her ankle.

"Where is she?" Millie asked, looking round for Madagascar.

"She jump," Lunardi said with a quizzical look.

"Lower down the fish," came Madagascar's distant voice. "As quick as you can!"

They peered over the edge to see Madagascar dangling like a plumb line, her skirts tumbling down over her chest and revealing black knickerbockers and leather boots. Millie and William lowered their buckets down on ropes towards her as she swung upside down, hanging at ten paces above the ground. A short distance away, Cato stood with his back to them, still distracted by Isambard.

Madagascar collected one of the buckets but fumbled the other one, impotently stretching a hand out as it fell to the ground.

"Cannon!" Lunardi shouted just before another fireball ripped through the rigging of the balloon, causing it to lurch and swing. The balloon was just a few paces away from Cato and closing fast but the shockwaves from the impact had ripped the second bucket from Madagascar's wet hand and it too now tumbled to the ground.

Madagascar strained to lift her head to scan the sky and she knew that there was only one thing she could do. They were in the perfect position, practically on top of Cato. Beads of rainwater washed the tears from Madagascar's eyes. She thought of her sister, and of King George the Third, and of Isambard.

Stretching her right arm to its full extent, she was able to grab Cato's elevated hand. At that precise moment, a bolt of lightning connected the balloon to the boiling black clouds in the sky. For a fraction of a second the balloon seemed to be suspended by a jagged, white-hot wire. A net of electricity wreathed the balloon in pure energy. Energy which wished for only one thing - to flow into the ground.

In a flash, the lightning burnt across the basket, down the wet rope, through Madagascar's rain-soaked clothes and into Cato.

Despite the limbs that clawed his body, Isambard was able to watch as Madagascar was cut loose from the balloon by the searing power of the lightning bolt. He screamed as she tumbled to the floor next to Cato. Suddenly the limbs trapping Isambard withered away, and he found he was able to stand. An untapped reserve of energy drove him through exhaustion to sprint over to where Madagascar lay. As he approached her, he was buffeted by a strengthening wind. In the centre of the field he could see that the winds were turning into a cyclone, sweeping up the undead soldiers and whipping them skywards into a swirling black hole in the clouds.

Isambard reached Madagascar just in time to see the cowardly leer on Cato's face as he staggered off into the trees. Isambard looked down at Madagascar's lifeless face and by the time he looked up, Cato was gone.

"Dump, dump," Isambard heard Lunardi shout from the balloon, which hung in the air behind Isambard, followed soon after by the crack of the wicker basket landing heavily in a cluster of low bushes.

"Madagascar!" Isambard said, lurching to his knees and cradling her head.

"Don't touch!" came the concerned words of a familiar voice. Isambard looked up to see Esmerelda approaching from the trees, dressed, as usual, in white from head to toe.

"Esmerelda!" Isambard said.

Lunardi and Millie arrived and stood at Isambard's side as Esmerelda knelt and looked tenderly at her sister lying on the grass. Esmerelda spoke without looking up.

"Ask Trafalgar to lift my sister. I've brought the shop door. It's behind that tree."

Esmerelda knelt and placed a finger gently across Madagascar's lips.

"Oh sister," she whispered. Madagascar's eyelids fluttered but did not open.

Chapter 44

AFTER A SMATTERING of applause, the violinist struck up a tune and Lord Wellington cut the red ribbon that draped across Marc Brunel's first working prototype of the Tunneling Shield. The intrigued but mystified bystanders of Bermondsey began to drift away, disappointed not to see the great machine explode, or indeed make any movement at all. Some of them joined a small crowd of people huddled around Lunardi as he retold the story of how he saved the world with his unique combination of fearlessness, good looks and aeronautical prowess.

Within the area reserved for the Brunels and their guests, Esmerelda and Officer Ruthven helped themselves to lemonade and beer from a table heaving with confectionery, pies, treacle tart and puddings.

"I'm terribly sorry Mister Brunel," Wellington said, "but as I explained, I do have an audience with the Home Secretary, and it wouldn't do to keep him waiting. But allow me to reiterate, the country owes a debt of gratitude to your son and his merry band." Wellington was taking each one of them in with a munificent smile as he spoke. "You should be very proud of your boy. And I shall give the Home Secretary a nod about this very fine tunnelling device of yours. As you may know, Thomas Young himself approves of the scheme and endorsements do not come much more scientific than that," Wellington said, swinging himself into an ornate cabriolet before giving the command to walk on. "I bid you farewell and oh! I quite forgot," Wellington cried, twisting in his seat as the carriage pulled away, "I'm pleased to see you free of that terrible Marshalsea business. We'll be sure to not let that happen again, won't we," Wellington smiled, waving a handkerchief energetically as his carriage disappeared around the corner.

"Such a nice man," Sophia said, grinning and squeezing her husband's arm.

"When he pays his debts!" Marc joked in response, polishing the edge of a brand new top hat with his sleeve.

"So when does tunnelling begin Mr Brunel?" Esmerelda asked, whilst passing him a glass of elderflower champagne.

"Next week. The exercise is principally to understand the potential of the device. How fast can she go? We are hoping to average in excess of 10 inches of tunnelling per day!"

"10 whole inches? And how many inches is it from one side of the Thames to the other?" Millie asked cheekily.

An involuntary laugh made Esmerelda almost choke on her champagne.

"Excuse me," she chuckled, "bubbles... Down the wrong way..."

But Isambard's smile evaporated as his eye fell on Madagascar, seated a few steps back, staring off at a point on the floor. As he watched her, his gaze followed down the stem of the champagne flute to the brown claw that used to be her right hand, and he remembered the endless care that Esmerelda had given, with Millie at her side, in those anxious days after Napoleon's arrest. Isambard's train of thought was interrupted by the sound of Esmerelda and Millie giggling into a vanity mirror and he found himself smiling.

Isambard looked up to find that he and his father were alone.

"So, quite an adventure you had with Mr Cato, doing the exact opposite of what I ordered," Marc began with a serious look on his face.

"Look, father, I..."

"Isambard, I am not a fighting man, you know this. I was in the Navy but I saw no action. I made the boots for Wellington's army but I never wore them. But.... I always cursed myself for fleeing revolutionary France. I ran, not because it was the right thing to do, but because I was scared. Evidently, I have not changed. But you.... who knows? You must have got it from your mother. You are brave. I am proud of you. If you will allow me..." Marc said, but his words seemed to fail him. His eyes turned downwards, and Isambard's naturally followed. Marc held his old, battered top-hat in his hands, and smiled that familiar, persistent smile.

"Here," Marc said, handing the hat to his son. "My old hat, for you. You are ready now."

Isambard gazed back at his father and took the hat.

"And there is this," Marc said, handing his son the case that Hardleygrieve had given him. "I found this in my office."

"Oh that. I... thanks."

"Sam!" William cried, shoving him from behind, almost causing him to drop the hat.

"Ah, William. I hear you got to see your beloved Paris from the air," Marc smiled.

"Yes sir. Not sure I took much of it in, though. Sorry I'm late. How d'it go?"

"Good. Wellington did a little speech. Mentioned your bravery," Isambard said, still looking at his father, thanking him with his eyes.

"My bravery? He mentioned my bravery? Hey Millie, Wellington mentioned me!" William said, stuffing a pie into his mouth.

"No he didn't. Sam's just being nice," she responded looking at Isambard.

William looked horrified but his mouth was too full to respond.

"But he did say that the Special Intelligence Directorate would be looking to buy your sketch of Cato for future investigations, so that might turn out to be your first sold work of art!" Sophia said.

"Here, Will," Isambard said, handing over Hardley-grieve's case. "I don't need this any more – perhaps you can find a use for it."

William took the bag and was about to say thankyou when Esmerelda chimed in. "Ah, here you are at last. Come over here you two." She beckoned them to join her on the bench next to her sister and Millie.

"Now then," she began, once the three of them had settled around her. "It is quite possible that you, like most of the population of Western Europe, have no notion of just how important your victory against Cato was, and how important a part you played in it. Suffice it to say that the three amulets were separated for very good reason. It is unclear if and how Napoleon could ever have been stopped if he had won the battle on the Champs de Mars. Madagascar and I have been trying to think of a way to commemorate your contribution."

Madagascar produced three boxes, ordinary jewellery boxes except for an exquisite trim of luminous stones around the top edge. She handed them out, one to each: green trim to William, red trim to Millie and blue trim to Isambard. They looked at each other, then at the sisters, before all opening the boxes in unison.

"The amulets!" Millie said. "Are they safe?"

"Very," Esmerelda said.

"They are magically inert," Madagascar said bitterly.

"Electricity, we have found out, appears to have a rather terminal effect on static magic," Esmerelda said, looking at her sister and lowering her eyes.

"Can we keep them?" William asked.

"Of course. A memento of your great adventure."

Isambard and Millie watched as William loosened his amulet from its display case and gazed at it in wonder, tracing the intricate design with his fingers. The copper tones were discoloured by sooty black scars, and it hung heavily in William's hand.

Millie looked up to find that Isambard was looking at her.

"Nice hat," she said quietly.

Hardleygrieve looked down at the scene from the rooftops nearby. There was no need to stop the world and speak to Isambard - it was enough to see the amulets dead. Hardleygrieve allowed himself to be troubled briefly once more by Isambard's aura (does it have a shadow, or some kind of echo?) before passing through the doorway back to the Hinterland. There was still so much work to do.

Continue the series!

Get Book 2 FREE

Scan the QR code

or visit

robertguidi.com/isambard2

[1]

1. http://www.robertguidi.com/isambard2

FREE - Extract from Book 2

Continue the series!

Get Book 2 **FREE**

Scan the QR code

or visit

robertguidi.com/isambard2

[1]

EXTRACT FROM BOOK 2 of the Young Isambard series

Chapter 2

Millie's heart was pounding as she approached the back door. She pushed and it opened soundlessly onto a deep, dark void. Stepping cautiously across the threshold, she scanned the familiar walls for signs. She peered at the certificates which hung there, inspecting them in turn. She rested thumb and forefinger on opposing corners, closed her eyes and concentrated. Esmerelda's certificate was dry but Madagascar's required a neutralising quip. That done, she turned

1. http://www.robertguidi.com/isambard2

and made her way down the corridor, inspecting everything, always alert.

Millie peered into the shop, dark apart from the dim glow of moonlight from the front windows. She halted, sensing a disturbance – the black and white floor-tiles looked perfectly ordinary, but something gave her pause. She took a pebble from her pocket and tossed it into the centre of the room. It landed on the tiles, not with a tinkling bounce that she might have expected, but with an oily plop, sending concentric ripples out towards the walls.

The ripples outlined a kind of platform below the tiles – a shallow area like a submerged circular island in the middle of the room. Closing her eyes, she leapt across the water and was relieved to find her foot landed with a small splash on a solid surface just below the surface of the liquid floor.

Taking a deep breath, she looked around and checked the path again with another pebble-drop to confirm that the approach to the front door was solid. She scoured the familiar corners of the shop as she took tentative steps closer to her goal.

Something moved. She froze and stared into a particularly dark corner of the shop window. A pair of eyes stared back at her before disappearing into the midnight-blue liquid of floor-tiles. Millie swallowed hard and flashed a glance up to the front door, the goal of this test, before looking down again and scanning the surface, alert to any movement or disturbance. She began muttering a charm. The level of liquid began to sink, tiles hardening as they began to form the edges of a drained pond. There, between Millie and the shop window, a solid object was breaking through the falling waterline. As Millie sped up her chant and the water level continued to fall, she began to see that the solid object had a reptilian quality; a rough patterned hide. With an explosion of movement and a shower of water, the shape erupted into life and lunged at Millie, enormous jaws opening as it rose from the shallows.

Millie stood stock-still and closed her eyes as the apparition passed straight through her.

Millie clenched her jaw shut and breathed hard through her nose, trembling as she did so. She glanced up again at the door and, concentrating on her goal, took the last few steps towards it. She extended a hand to reach out and touch it.

But she didn't notice the spider. Suspended from the ceiling by a near invisible gossamer thread, a spider hung, spinning slowly. As she stepped forward the spider brushed her nose.

Several gas-lamps came on at once.

"Down came a spider, that sat down beside her.... and frightened poor Millie away," came Madagascar's familiar voice from behind one of the glass counters.

"I'm sorry," Millie said, brushing the spider away and taking a step back. "I'm tired. I..."

"Millie, you did very well. That was a very advanced test," Esmerelda said, emerging from the shadows.

"But you failed," Madagascar added.

Esmerelda flashed Madagascar a disapproving look.

"You are learning fast. You have a very good instinct."

"Instinct is one thing, sister. Control is quite another," Madagascar purred.

"We'll try again tomorrow, Millie," Esmerelda said, ignoring her sister. "We'll need to work on your Apparent Perception but I couldn't fault your Miasmarine Response."

Just then there was a strange noise at the door – an unusual scratching sound. Bastet, the Egyptian cat, leapt from Madagascar's knee and scampered towards the door.

"There must be something out there" Madagascar said, using her cane to stand from her chair.

"But the front door, sister? Most unusual," Esmeralda said moving cautiously. She established a Wall of Protection before edging the door open. All four of them stared into the space behind the door. Nothing.

It was Bastet who recognised the visitor first – after all, it was one of his own. The two cats greeted each other.

"Ooh look. It's Arthur, Meg's cat," Esmerelda cooed, bending down.

"He doesn't look very well," Millie said.

"No. I'm sure he's not. But we'll give him the antidote. He has been trained to come here when Meg gives him a certain kind of poison. He knows that he will find the antidote here. Rather harsh on the cat perhaps but he'll feel good-as-new in a few moments."

Esmerelda picked the cat up and gave him a cuddle before laying her down on the glass counter. They crowded around, peering at the exhausted cat. Bastet leapt up and joined them on the counter, equally curious.

"Look Esmerelda, the locket," Madagascar said, touching the cat's neck.

Esmeralda froze.

"Meg must be in grave danger," she said. "Millie. You must go to her."

"You can't send the girl," Madagascar objected, crossing the floor to a cabinet stacked with glass vials. "She hasn't completed her proof."

"Oh come now, Madagascar," Esmerelda retorted. "It's just a trip across town. I'm sure she knows better that to use any of her half-cooked charms on the outside, don't you dear?" Esmerelda asked Millie.

"Of course," Millie smiled.

"There. Now, Meg is an old friend of ours from the Para-Chemical Society. She is very gifted mindformer."

"What's a mindformer?" Millie asked.

"She can control people minds," Madagascar said. "Outsiders call her a hypnotist but she is so much more than that. Of course she fell on hard times when she..."

"Tsss," Madagascar hissed as she poured out a green liquid for Arthur to drink.

"Quite, we won't go into that. Suffice it to say, she has since been forced to find employment at the Battersea Circus. I imagine she'll have just finished her evening show. Why don't you cut along there and see if you can't find out what the matter is. But be careful – if Meg's in danger, you could be too."

"You can tell her that Arthur will be as right as rain in no time," Esmerelda said as the cat started to show signs of life.

"And remember. No ParaChemistry!" Madagascar added for good measure as Millie left the room.

2. http://www.robertguidi.com/isambard2

About the Author

Robert Guidi is a curious mix: half engineer, half storyteller. He studied Engineering (Mechanical, of course) at Manchester University where he wrote and staged 2 plays. On graduating he helped design a robotic vacuum cleaner at Dyson, tried writing for a couple of London magazines and failed to organise a charity cabaret. He then spent 6 years installing engine production lines for a car company before going solo as an engineering consultant and, latterly, landing a grown-up job in Mergers & Acquisitions.

In his idle moments, Robert enjoys creating musical and visual doodles that, until now, have never seen the light of day.

Say hi **@RobJGuidi** or email **me@robertguidi.com**

Read more at www.robertguidi.com.

Printed in Great Britain
by Amazon

46810631R00199